Launch the Ready!

"DNA AMERICAN PATRIOT"

A Proud Life in the U.S. Coast Guard
(One Big Adrenalin Rush)

By Fred Tanner
Master Chief U.S. Coast Guard
(Retired)

Order this book online at www.trafford.com
or email orders@trafford.com

Most Trafford titles are also available at major online book retailers.

Printed in Victoria, BC, Canada.

ISBN: 978-1-4269-3238-0 (sc)

ISBN: 978-1-4269-3239-7 (sc)

Library of Congress Control Number: 2010907069

*Our mission is to efficiently provide the world's finest, most comprehensive book publishing
service, enabling every author to experience success. To find out how to publish your book, your
way, and have it available worldwide, visit us online at www.trafford.com*

Trafford rev. 5/17/2010

 www.trafford.com

North America & international
toll-free: 1 888 232 4444 (USA & Canada)
phone: 250 383 6864 ♦ fax: 812 355 4082

Editing by:

Special Friend

"Hobie"

Technical assistance provided by:

Jean Lewis Beacham
John McMahon
Mike McCleary

Semper Paratus

About the Author

Fred was born just a year before the Japanese forced the United States into World War Two. He was born into the typical poor Appalachian mountain family. The early death of his mother forced the decision on his desperate family to let his sister and him grow up in an orphanage or home for children. At the orphanage Fred survived the many hardships other children suffered of family separation from entering at such an early age. His life at the home would be nurtured and guided by some of the nation's best and devoted caregivers. There were many trying times in his growing years as he was a very spirited lad. Fred was slightly smaller than many of the boys his age but there was no smallness in his heart. Competition was a matter of survival during all of his youthful years. With much forgiveness, devoted staff members helped set his style in life. He learned from the adults everything they were willing to teach him. (Being all boy, sometimes not always in his studies though.) He learned to work hard early in his youth, and that hard work ethic would be noticed by all that knew him in his lifelong career in the United States Coast Guard. Fred's learning experiences in his youth of making things better would be carried with him into his career. He feels that these experiences actually saved his life and that of his fellow crewmembers on many occasions. Fred loved his orphan home and wished every child could have a year with the experiences he lived and with having over four hundred brothers and sisters to learn to live with.

This will be Fred's second published book. His first was (Tanner "Boy Orphan".)

Preface

This is a story of my journey through a career in the United States Coast Guard. Also, it is a brief glimpse of my family's contribution to America from its very beginning and of those that influenced me in my dedicated life to my beloved America. My birthplace was near the town of Hayesville, North Carolina, on the edge of the Nantahala National Forest. My family members are descendents of the original pioneers that settled the land and also fought for our American independence. Their pioneering spirit and bravery would make me want to be a part of something as great as serving my country in the US Armed Forces. At age one, I lost my mother and soon was sent to an orphanage along with my sister, Charlena, to live the rest of my youth. My orphan home, The Methodist Children's Home in Winston-Salem, North Carolina, became a place I would cherish the rest of my life. Life wasn't always easy, and the chores were demanding; but that life made me the person I would become. The adult caregivers had a lot of patience with us boys. Several caregivers had served in the military during WWII, and they knew we would be there in the near future protecting our country as they did. They did all they could to prepare us for service to our country, whether we would choose a military or civilian career. Many of the children entered the adult world and became business leaders, medical and educational professionals; and many served in the armed forces. The hard work that I learned and the determination to do things right would be my trademark for the rest of my life. Along with the hard work, they taught us how to play hard. There has to be a little laughter to keep one healthy. My career in the military would span thirty-four years. My career was not without controversy; I took personal risks to protect my fellow Coast Guardsmen and to protect the dignity of our Coast Guard and my country. My pride in being a part of the United States Coast Guard was so strong that if my Coast Guard would allow me at my senior age, I would volunteer again. Being a part of this great organization and sharing in an often risky and dangerous profession with many of my fellow Coasties was well worth serving until I reached my senior years.

Chapter One

My life began in the Appalachian Mountains of North Carolina near the town of Hayesville on the edge of the Nantahala National Forest. I am a descendent of the original pioneer settlers of the area. My ancestors served our great country all the way back to the Continental Army in the war for America's independence. Through their pioneering spirit, the wild woods of the Appalachian Mountains became the home of my family. My family members have served in nearly every conflict since the war for independence. Blood of my ancestors was spilled in the sands of many of our states and in the soils of many foreign lands for the freedoms we enjoy today. So many of our countrymen take these freedoms for granted or disrespect our country. That saddens me!

Absalom Hooper, my great grandfather (times seven), fought during the Revolutionary War. He was wounded in two different battles and imprisoned by the British as a POW, but continued to fight for our independence.

Absalom was born around 1764 on the Main Broad River, near the mouth of the Green River in S.C. Absalom left his mother, who was an adherent of the Tories, to join the Continental Army of the American territory during the Revolution.

He enlisted in the Continental Army in 1776 with Captain Richard Dogged in Charleston, South Carolina. Absalom was only twelve years of age at the time he volunteered to fight for our American freedom. He served in the South Carolina regiment under Colonel William Henderson, Commandant; Major Brown; Captain Richard Dogged and Lieutenant Jesse Baker. He was to receive a bounty of $30.00 in Continental money. He was to receive $5.00 per month pay and a bounty of 640 acres of land at the end of the war, considering our revolution succeeded. According to his declaration in 1833, he never received his pension after the US Government took over the pensions of the disabled American Revolutionary War Veterans from the State of South Carolina in 1832. After nearly giving up his life in several battles and being imprisoned as a prisoner of war, he had to petition our federal government for what was promised him.

Absalom was on Sullivan's Island, South Carolina under command of General Howe when the island came under attack by British forces led by Sir Henry Clinton. From Charleston, South Carolina, he marched under command of General Howe into Florida against the British post on Little St. Mary's River. The British evacuated the post on arrival of the Continental Army. The army returned to Charleston about the time the British took Savannah, Georgia. At this time, General Lincoln took command and Absalom marched under General Lincoln to Purrysburgh, South Carolina above Savannah. After Nashe's defeat at

Briar Creek, Absalom marched up to Augusta, Georgia, and crossed the river into Augusta.

About that time, the enemy crossed Savannah River at Jubley's Ferry and marched in the direction of Charleston. Absalom was marched down the river and crossed at a place called the Three Sisters. After crossing the river his regiment pursued the enemy. When the Americans arrived at Bacon's Bridge on the Edisto River, they found that the British had built and fortified Stono Fort. Absalom was in the attack on that fort under Colonel Henderson in a regiment called the New Infantry. From Stono Fort, the British retired onto Beaufort Island. The Americans marched to Seldon Bulls opposite the Beaufort Island where they remained for some time. From there the Continental Army marched by way of Purrysburgh, crossed at Jubley's Ferry and on to the siege at Savannah. At the time, the French General D'Estaing and units of the Continental forces besieged Savannah. In the battle, Absalom was wounded in the right arm by a musket shot.

After that battle the Continental Army returned to Charleston where they remained until the town was attacked by Sir Henry Clinton and Lord Cornwallis. In this battle, a musket ball in the left thigh again wounded Absalom. He was taken prisoner and kept under close confinement in the hospital for five months. As soon as he felt sufficiently recovered and opportunity offered, he escaped, leaving his company prisoners of war with the British in Charleston. Absalom fled to the frontier of Georgia to an uncle. Here, he was taken by the Tories and confined for five days. Wounded, and after trial by court martial, he was released by the Tories.

Shortly after this he heard of Colonel Clark and his regiment of Georgia Militia marching towards Augusta. He found this regiment and was enrolled in Captain Daniel Gunnal's company. They took Brown and Greyson's Forts and their garrisons. From that place he marched with Colonel Clark's Regiment to Freeman's Station on the frontier of Georgia. After remaining there a short time,

Absalom and his regiment marched to Big Brier Creek to dislodge a party of Tories.

After performing that service, the regiment returned to Freeman's Station. Not long after, the regiment moved into South Carolina and joined troops under command of General Pickens Under Pickens' command the united forces of General Pickens and Colonel Clark attacked a party of the enemy composed of British and Tories under command of Lord Rowden on Little River, South Carolina. There was a skirmish between the advance parties of the two armies, and the British retreated to Ninety-Six District. Absalom returned to Freeman's Station with Colonel Clark's regiment.

Not long after, he and his regiment marched to the last siege of Savannah where General Wayne commanded the Continental troops. After the British left that coast, Absalom marched back with Colonel Clark's regiment to Freeman's Station.

Shortly after, he and his regiment went on an expedition against the Cherokee. Being defeated in a battle at the Long Swamp on the Hightowa River in the Cherokee Nation, the regiment again returned to Freeman's Station. Not long after this, peace was declared.

Absalom finally was able to settle down and get married. He married Sara Salers on Pistol Creek in Elbert County, Georgia, with Rev. Mackey performing the service. He settled in Caney Fork, present-day Jackson County, while it was still Cherokee Territory. They then moved to Table Rock, South Carolina, then back to Haywood County (now Jackson County) North Carolina. Absalom and his family lived among the Cherokee. The Cherokee liked him and called him "Steke Santons" (meaning "Little Keg") because he was little in stature. They raised a family of twelve near present-day East La Porte on the banks of the Tuckasegee River in the shadow of some of the steepest mountains in North Carolina. In 1832 congress passed a law that the Federal government would take over all state-paid pensions from duty during the Revolutionary War. It took eight years before the federal government would pay my great grandmother her deceased husband's duly earned rewards. The bounty was paid, only after her grandchildren provided proof of my great grandfather's heroic efforts during the Revolutionary War.

Great Grandfather (Times Seven) Absalom Hooper's petition for promised entitlements from our government. (cir. 1833)

My great grandfather's (times 7) petition reads as follows:

> To the Honorable The Senate & House of
> Representatives of the State of So, Car.
> The Petition of Absolom Hooper, I herewith,
>
> That your petition is a Revolutionary
> soldier, old, infirm, & wounded, having
> spent the best days of his youth in the
> arduous struggle for independence, now
> comes before your Honorable body to
> (remuneration)
> ask a small remunisation, to render com-
> fortable the few remaining years of his life.
>
> Your petitioner is well aware, that,
> petition upon petitions have been laid before
> you, by persons claiming great rewards for
> unimportant services, as every man suites his
> own suffering, of services at an exaggerated rate,
> but your petitioner will be able to substantu-
> (indisputable)
> ate, with the most indisbitable vouchers,
> (Assertions) or (Aspersions)
> the truth of his Aspirtions, that he is entitled
> to considerable arrears of pay, and bounty
> land, from the State of So. Car.
>
> Your petitioner rests with the most
> Confidence on the Justice & liberality of
> your Honorable body, & is in duty bound for
> his
> Absolom X Hooper
> mark

My earliest known great grandfather on my mother's side
of the family was William Ledford. William was born in
1685 in Lancaster, Northern England. He was born into a
family that farmed land lying next to the Irish Sea near
the Scottish Border. The land was poor so his three sons
and one being my great grandfather (William B. Ledford
Sr.) decided to go to America. Henry was the eldest at age

7

18, William 16 and John 14. They would sail with Sea Captain James Patton on the Ship Walpoole to Virginia in 1738. To pay for their voyage to America, the three brothers would become indentured servants to Captain Patton for a period of seven years. They landed in America at a place called Belhaven located on the Potomac River. They set out with Captain Patton westward overland to what was then Augusta County, Virginia. Augusta County has since been divided into counties in Virginia and West Virginia. By the time the three brothers had worked off their indentured servitude, all three were married. They continued westward and southwestward down the Shenandoah Valley with Captain Patton. They bought land along the West Fork of the Roanoke River near Bradshaw's Creek. Their land was located about ten miles east of the present-day town of Blacksburg in Montgomery County, Virginia.

The Ledford families left Virginia because of Indian uprisings. Great Uncle Henry along with Captain Patton had been killed at the Massacre of Draper's Meadows. The remaining two brothers and their families migrated south on the Carolina Road to Rowan County, North Carolina. They settled on land near each other. Henry's sons Obadiah, Henry and Fredrick settled on Abbott's Creek. As Rowan County was divided into smaller counties, my great grandfather John's land would first be in Guilford and then Randolph County.

My great grandfather, John Ledford, Sr., had seven children, one being my great grandfather John, Jr. John, Jr., would have nine children, one being Fredrick C. Ledford. John, Jr., and many of his children would migrate into western North Carolina and into Kentucky. John, Jr., and his wife, Elizabeth, would be killed while crossing Cumberland Gap, Kentucky. While they were sleeping one night, a tree fell across their wagon.

Great Grandfather Frederick C. Ledford had a son, David, Sr. David Ledford, Sr. had four children, one named David Ledford, Jr. (my great grandfather). When the Civil War broke out Great Grandfather David and his brother

Center joined the 7th Battalion North Carolina Calvary in 1862. They were transferred August 3, 1863 into the 65th Regiment, North Carolina Troops (6th Regiment NC Calvary). They were both missing for roll call, and Center had joined up with another unit. David was apprehended by the Home Guard after accidentally crossing the Tennessee line. The Home Guard was notoriously brutal to southern troops that were separated from their command or were trying to get home to their families. The incident much resembled the story and movie *Cold Mountain.* Some in my family were friends with the Cherokee Indians; and due to this, the Home Guard suspected them to be traitors. Decisions were hastily made; and he was put to death by hanging or firing squad, carried out by the local Home Guard. David's wife Dulcena Hicks Ledford along with her eight-year-old son, David Laranza Ledford, drove an ox and wagon to Tennessee and retrieved David's body to bring home for burial in Clay County, North Carolina. Even after this sad incident, the Hoopers, Tanners, Ledfords and their descendants have always answered the call of duty for our America. Some of the names married into the Hooper family tree include: Salers, Chastain, Cathy, Kimsey, Vandora, Ledbetter, Eller, Ledford, Tanner, Gibson, Maney, Garrett, Arrowood, Barrett, and Sewell. Some family members fought in the war of 1812.

My Great Grandfather (times two) William Hooper enlisted September 27, 1862 in Hiawassee, Georgia, in Fain's Regiment, Georgia Infantry, which subsequently became the 65th Regiment, Georgia Infantry. After being in battle for a while, he received word of his wife Caroline expecting a baby and that he was needed at home because of her difficulty. He left his unit to check on his wife. The Home Guard acquired word of his being home, and they immediately went to his cabin. Caroline's mother Mariah had been staying with her daughter to give her support. When the Home Guard came, Mariah refused to let them into the cabin as William went running out the back door and into the woods. She knew they would shoot or hang her daughter's husband if they caught him. Mariah sustained injuries that she never recovered from when the men burst through the door of the cabin. The last Caroline saw of her William was a glimpse of him as he was running through the woods and the Home Guard in hot pursuit. Caroline and the children never heard from him again and considered the worst had happened to him. William, however, didn't die at the hands of the Home Guard, but he did meet with an awful fate. He made it back to his unit to fight another day. On September 2, 1864, General Sherman's Army at the Battle of Jonesboro, Georgia, captured his unit after he was wounded. He became a prisoner of war. He and the other prisoners of war were marched and sent by rail to Illinois and confined in the filthy Camp Douglas Prison in Chicago, Illinois. Without his family knowing where he was, he died helplessly on February 6, 1865. He was buried in the Chicago City Cemetery, block 2, grave number 684. It is said that a Union leader designed the prison specifically for punishment of southern soldiers, allowing southern soldiers wounded in battle and sickened by the filthy conditions in the prison to die of malnutrition, bitter cold weather and lack of medical attention.

William and Caroline had five daughters before he died a prisoner of war, and four of them married men with the name of "Jim." One daughter was named Sara Florida, and she married my great grandfather named James (Big Jim) Tanner. Because the girls married Jims, some kinfolks in the mountains still rattle off a rhyme that goes like this:

"Big Jim Arrowood
Little Jim Garrett
Big Jim Tanner and
Little Jim Barrett."

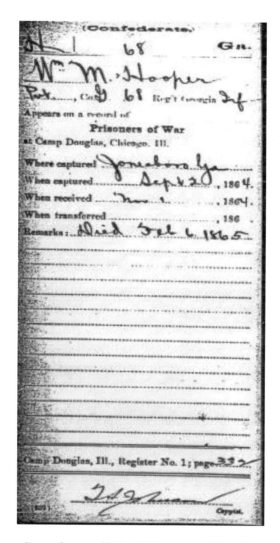

Copy from official Prisoner of War files

My Uncle Roy Hooper died fighting the Japanese during WWII on Leyte Island in the Philippines on November 9, 1944. Two of his brothers, Olen and Guy, were fighting the Nazis in the European theatre at the same time.

Families from our part of the mountains were peace-loving people but people that would protect their family and country if threatened. Most could shoot a fly from a fence post from a good distance and knew their way in the wilderness. Georgia, North and South Carolina, Virginia and other loyal southern states have always provided volunteers in great numbers to all of America's conflicts. In many American families, most of our ancestors had to fight for survival for hundreds of years before their families came to America.

My grandmother, Nannie Gibson Tanner, was a proud American mountain mother and patriot. She had the gumption to fight for her country; but being she could not, she was always loyal in her support for those that gave their lives and risked all, including her very own. She wore one of her son's army insignias on her lapel as a sign of pride and support for her son and our American troops. She was preciously sweet to my sister and me, but I could always see it in her face that she meant no one was allowed to tread on her family or intend harm to her country.

Grandma Nannie Gibson Tanner with Army insignia on lapel.

One of Grandma's sons, Aude, served in the US Army, just as many of my family had done for past generations. Grandma had a special love for Aude.

Uncle Aude William Tanner on furlough.

Uncle Aude on right with fellow troops in
Germany during WWII.

Chapter Two

I was born just over a year before the Japanese bombed Pearl Harbor and the United States was forced into World War II. Six months after the war started, my mother passed away; and our family was thrown into another crisis. The Appalachian mountain people were hard-working people, and making a living was difficult in those years. Luckily, Dr. Killian was our neighbor and a friend of the family. Dr. Killian brought my sister and me into this world in our tiny cabin and attended my mother when she became ill. He also provided some work for my dad and my uncle Roy. He did the best he could to try to help our family. Dad was really having a difficult time nursing my mother and trying to raise my sister and me.

Knowing what he did about comforting my mother as she was dying and the wishes she had for her children, Doc Killian was able to find us a safe place to grow and get a decent education. With a great deal of suffering, my dad finally let Doc Killian send us to The Methodist Children's Home in Winston-Salem. "Pop Woosley," the superintendent, drove the three hundred or more crooked, mountainous miles to our home and carried us in his big Buick to our new home at the orphanage. My way of life would be sent in a different direction. I was so young that remembering feeling the loss of my family was short lived, but I always felt a strange need for something. Not so, though, for my sister. It was much more difficult for her as she was old enough to experience and remember our family tragedy of our mother dying and now separation from our dad and mostly from her baby brother. Even though we were at the same place, we no longer lived together in the same home and only saw each other on Sundays or on special occasions.

Our life now was structured to care for many children that were in our same situation. Love had to be shared among so many. Discipline had to be taught and administered equally. My new home life was a beginning. Even though there were sad and lonely days, I would learn to love this children's home. Even though there were sad times, there were lots of times that we were happy playing with each other and sometimes receiving a caring hug from our caregivers. Even a smile from an older person would make the happiness last all day, making me feel as if I were someone special.

I found out that if I smiled at the older girls and Home Mother, they would smile back at me. The older girls that I called the "almost grown up girls" would help us little ones with our every-day needs. So at that moment, I decided to smile at people the rest of my life. When I smiled it seemed that I would feel better, and my worries didn't seem to bother me as much. When I would get in trouble, I would smile at the adult getting ready to give me a spanking; but that didn't help.

As I grew up in the orphanage, I would learn more about this discipline-thing. We would have about thirty boys living in a cottage; and one can imagine, with one Home Mother, how important control of us boys was. Discipline started early, and peer pressure played an important role. No one wanted to be singled out and spanked in front of the others, especially not in front of the girls. If you did something wrong and didn't admit your guilt, then all would take the brunt of your punishment. If you didn't learn to behave while you were young, the punishment became harsher with extra work to fit the infraction, as you grew older.

I crossed paths with many people that would influence my life and give me the pride that I wore on my shoulders throughout my adult life in the military. As we grew older, we began to spend time with our male coaches, teachers and the men that worked us at the different jobs on the farm. These men, most having served in the military, returned to the orphanage after WWII to help guide and support us in a better chance at life. Mr. Gray Todd had served in the Army Air Corps in Europe. He has given his whole life back to the Children's Home he loved. At over the age of eighty, Gray was still at the home offering words of encouragement and sharing his wisdom and experience. Gray left the home he loved on July 27, 2009.

After retiring from my long career in the military, I was asked by Gray's special friend and sister orphan Colleen Hutchens to speak at Gray's memorial service. I was honored to have the privilege to speak.

Gray Todd Army Air Corps WWII (Europe).

I spoke the following words to Gray's friends and especially to our many brothers and sisters.

My Big Brother "Gray Todd"

When I came to the Children's Home Gray Todd had already lived the experiences that many of you and I would follow.

America was at war around the world and many of the Children's Home's boys and girls would volunteer to leave our shores and go fight for their country. Gray, along with many of his brothers, left to defend our homeland from the harmful intent of others to destroy us. Gray made it back from Europe and came back to the home that he was so proud of and a home he felt blessed to have been raised in. To Gray it was all about giving back what he had been taught. Hard work, loyalty and now caring for many children would be partly on his shoulders. Gray's style of work ethics would affect us all, as we grew stronger and able to do heavy tasks required to feed so many children. Gray allowed us to learn to pull our share of the workload. However, I do remember a tap on the noggin from his hoe handle, when I was in need of a learning experience. Never was that tap from his hoe handle more than just to get my attention, as if somehow Gray never forgot he too once stood in the shoes, now resoled, and handed down to another young child. Even though we were not old enough to get a license Gray trusted other young boys and myself with driving heavy truckloads of grain and hay from our outlying farms.

Gray served his country bravely and he was a proud man to come back to face the many years of toiling in the farm fields. Gray not only mentored me while I grew into manhood, he became my lifelong friend. Every "Children's Home boy or girl" that I knew liked Gray. He was strong from his laboring years and tanned from hot days in the sun, something far from going unnoticed by many young women. He remained true to his conviction of helping those in need and doing so until his aged body would no longer allow him to accomplish such demanding tasks. Until his last breath, his special friend Colleen witnessed his desire to work one more day as if to say "Thank you My Children's Home." Now, that was my big brother "Gray Todd" and he was a brave man.

Now from all of your brothers and sisters we say "thank you Gray for the DEED OF CARING that you unselfishly demonstrated during your lifetime here at The Children's Home.

Gray's ashes will be buried in the pasture next to another orphan girl named Polly Wray.

Mr. Harmon didn't grow up at the orphanage, but he dedicated thirty-three years to the care of children just like me. He had served his country in the army during World War II. He assisted in the planning and took part in the Battle at Normandy. He and his wife Tex raised a daughter, Shelia, while they gave their care to so many other children. Shelia lived at the orphanage with her parents; and later after college, married John Ammons who grew up at the orphanage. They, too, decided to give their adult lives to the care of children. John served as an administrator, and Shelia was a schoolteacher and later principal of the Children's Home's (Kingswood) School.

Mr. Dwight E. Harmon (Sgt. WW II).

Coach Gibson and his brothers and sister were raised at the orphanage.

E.T. (Mike), Hubert Back: Hilda,
Julian Gibson.

Julian with a new friend.

When the war broke out between Japan/Germany and
America, Coach Mike Gibson and brother Julian
volunteered to fight for our country by joining the Navy Air
Corps.

Coach Gibson was a Navy fighter pilot during our WWII battle campaigns in the Pacific. He became an Ace fighter pilot while fighting the Japanese in air combat. He came back to the orphanage where he had grown up to give encouragement to young boys like myself. After risking his life for his country during WWII, he gave all that he could to us children for the remainder of his life. All of these brave men saved our country from one more threat to our freedom and existence.

At the orphanage we were taught determination and winning through working hard on the farm and playing to win in sports. We were taught size didn't matter. Hit a little harder; work a little harder; and you will be a winner.

Ensign E T "Mike" Gibson (left), with fellow pilots at war in the Pacific

Mike Gibson
Orphan pride and determination.

Coach Gibson's fighter squadron was awarded the Air Medal for air combat during a fight at Quadalcanal during WWII.

Copy of one Air Medal citation reads:

Four pilots of Fighting Squadron Twenty Eight, Ensign Kirchberg, Ensign McCutcheon, Ensign Gibson, And Ensign Calhoun, engaged in combat with approximately 15 Zeros on the morning of April 1, 1943, about 15 miles South-east of the Russell Islands. They were at 10,000 feet when they were attacked from above. In the Melee that followed, Ensign Calhoun was seen to go into a spin after being attacked by three Zeros and is missing in action. Ensign McCutcheon, his wingman, continued aggressively to attack the Zeros until his guns stopped firing. He then broke away from the Zeros and went into a cloud to charge his guns. As soon as he had charged all his guns, he went back out and engaged the Zeros again, but his guns failed to fire. Once more he went back into the clouds, charged his guns, came out, jumped on the Zeros, but his guns still failed to fire. During this time his plane was hit repeatedly, one bullet coming through the cockpit and cutting the electrical leads to his gun sight. A third time he broke away safely into the clouds, and returned to the field. Upon his return, it was found that his ammunition had been expended. For this aggressive action in continuing to fight after his ammunition was expended, he has been recommended for the award of the Air Medal.

Ensign Kirchberg and Ensign Gibson noticed below them a pilot going down in a parachute with two Zeros making runs on him. It is now believed that this pilot was Ensign Calhoun as no other Grummans were in that vicinity. They dove down to protect the pilot in the parachute and were immediately attacked by Zeros. Ensign Kirchberg received a 20 mm hit in his engine, which cut an oil line and other hits which damaged his plane so that he crashed on landing at the field. When the oil covered over his cockpit, he broke away from the Zeros and returned to the field. Ensign Gibson continued to fight with the Zeros utilizing cloud concealment and attacking at every opportunity. He remained in the area until the Zeros had withdrawn and then returned to the field. For this aggressive action against the enemy he has been recommended for the award of the Air Medal.

After the war Coach Mike and beautiful wife, Doris, came back to the orphanage to spend the rest of their lives giving children like me a better life. Coach Mike sacrificed time with his own family to encourage us children to make the best of life. He started a Boy Scout troop. He taught us in grammar school. He coached us in sports. Never in the many years I lived in the orphanage did he ever fall short on his commitments to us nor neglect the opportunity to talk with a kid. He taught us to stand up for ourselves and to take responsibility for our actions. He taught us to be free and run like the wind in the woods and pastures. He raised two children while giving so much to us. His daughter Linda and son Stevie played right along with us orphan kids. Linda would become the Chief of Police in Winston-Salem during her outstanding career in law enforcement and public service.

Coach "Mike" and Mrs. Doris loved all of us children.

Julian Gibson
Orphan pride, once you've got it; you can't
hide it.

Coach Gibson's brother, Julian, was also a fighter pilot
during World War II; and after the war, he too, returned to
mentor children. He became principal of Mineral Springs
High School.

Coach Clary was an all-sports coach who demanded
physical conditioning and stamina. Our hard work on the
farm benefited us when he demanded physical
performance from us while competing in sports. He
expected nothing less than 100% effort and participation.

Coach Wilburn Clary

On the farm the men in charge taught us to do every chore the right way or do the job over until you would get it right. This training while young would mold us into our adult attitude about hard work and doing it the right way. From the very simple chores of picking vegetables, Mr. Paul Booze, Mr. Hege and Mr. Johnny Horton wanted us to do it right. "Mr. Johnny" was a black man who worked us in the fields. He saw to it that we would do our work correctly and was always fair to us. They were molding us each day to become trustworthy and not fear a good day's work. As we grew older they taught us to use sharper tools such as axes, swing blades and scythes. They taught us to not hurt each other with our tools while we were working in close proximity of one another. Each Saturday morning we would clear farmland at a distant farm or split firewood with axes and wedges for all the cook stoves in the cottages. There were eight or ten axes being swung by the boys all at one time. Occasionally one of the boys would trip or his axe would glance from where it was aimed and either hurt another boy or cause injury to himself. All of this just happened to be a part of learning. You can get over it and not fear a bruising or a little blood once in a while. Besides, when we went to school, we could show off our stitches. Among us all there would be a lot of blood to flow, a lot of broken bones, bruises and black eyes as we grew up. We would get into disagreements and someone or both boys would have bloody noses and black eyes. That was to be expected in a family as large as mine. I had over four hundred brothers and sisters that competed at something everyday.

We were learning more and more as we grew older. We learned how to can food for the upcoming winter. We hoed corn and other vegetables. We were allowed a break from working in the fields. We could get a drink of water and rest for fifteen minutes.

A lot of the times we boys would continue our challenges even when we were allowed to rest. We would race, climb to the top of a tall tree, or shoot targets with our slingshots. It was all part of the learning experience of what a rest break was intended for. Each year we would be assigned a little harder chore. The more capable we were, the more we learned. When we started working on the farm at age eight or nine, we would be allowed an allowance of twenty-five cents a month. That was a lot of money to us. The orphanage would match that amount to go into a savings account so we would have some spending money when we graduated from high school and left our home the following day.

Coach Edwards taught us our very first football rules and how to play the game. We all were pretty much in shape all the time we were at the orphanage because we didn't have time to gain weight. Our team was legitimate competition for many other larger schools, mainly because we worked hard all year and played even harder.

Coach William Ralph "Bill" Edwards

Coach Gibson continued our competitive sports playing when we reached our next age level. He would prepare us for our next step up to the varsity team. Along with our fierce determination to be good football players, Coach Gibson shared another part of his plan for us. He had started a Boy Scout troop for us. He knew how much we would learn from the Scouting experience and how this experience would help shape our lives.

Coach Gibson would be a great leader for us. He always taught us fairness in our competitive lives. He wanted us to be able to go out into this world and be able to handle anything including success and the struggle to survive. He spent many hours away from his family sharing his military experiences with us and sharing his time if we needed someone to talk with. He showed us his Navy squadron's battle films. I'm sure he did so to let us know what to expect if it were our time to do our duty for our country. Many of our boys became military pilots and performed other military professions. He taught us patriotism and the respect and dignity for our flag. His influence would stay with me the rest of my life.

As we grew a little older, we would begin to learn to stand up for ourselves. This was not by any intentional structure but by the very fact that so many boys lived, worked, played, ate, and occasionally disagreed with each other. There was always a bully; and most times the bully got his dues, as one boy would grow a little larger in time. Most of the times if you learned to stand up to the bully, then the bully stopped his aggressive behavior. As we got older, fewer fights would take place. I guess we found that missing teeth and many stitches were not worth the punishment, and, more importantly, not very popular in our social environment. However, being a little smaller, I never forgot those rougher days. I was always aware that bullies came in many different sizes and positions, even in the world outside the orphanage.

As we took on harder chores, we also learned more responsibility. The many tasks included operation of the dairy farm run by Mr. Eugene "Dad" Shaver. We learned how important care of the milk cows and their calves really was. If a cow weren't properly cared for, from milking the cow to feeding the cow, then the cow would become non-productive and ill. We learned how to grind and mix different kinds of cattle feed in our grinding mill, according to the various needs of our animals.

We worked on the "Big Farm" with Mr. Brady Angel, Mr. Gray Todd, Mr. John McClamrock, and Mr. Red Holland and for a short time, Mr. Raymond Russian. We learned how to raise and harvest corn, wheat, oats and other grains. We learned how to drive large grain trucks and tractors and how to harvest and store hay in the barns and grain in the grain bins. We chopped silage corn with machetes and learned how to store the corn in the silos. We learned how to butcher and preserve hogs. We helped with the construction and repair of farm buildings. We were getting an education outside the school building environment from doing our daily chores. I had a regular job of driving a large 2½-ton truck at age fourteen. That was two years before I could get a driver's license.

In the Boy Scout hut, Coach Gibson and Mr. Eddie Newsome found us some woodworking equipment that we learned to use. We learned to do all kinds of woodcrafts.

"You gotta ball? We'll play ya!"

In our free time on Saturday and Sunday afternoons, we would engage in a tackle football game or play baseball. A lot of days we would play in the woods and pastures. Once in a while the boys from the colored neighborhood would come over to our woods, and we would play battle. We had slingshots, slings, mud-clods, bow and arrows and dried reed spears. They had BB guns. We never got into fistfights, as we knew them and their families. We had some fierce battles on a young boys' level. We all took some abuse before the battle was called off due to lack of ammunition or the cry of someone really hurt. We were deadly shots with a slingshot and we had a lot of experience in the trajectory of where our creek pebbles needed to land. It didn't take long after one of the colored boys had to reload his BB gun until a few well placed pebbles from our sling shot usually ended the battle. Before the gun would run out of ammo though, we all were peppered on the face each time we tried to look out from our hiding place. This kind of dangerous play would somehow benefit us later as we entered our military careers. Most orphan boys would do well in jungle warfare because we had played hard at making weapons from what was available in the woods.

Some Saturdays we would work in the yards for the wealthy people that lived just outside our orphanage in the area known as Buena Vista. We could make a dollar and sometimes more for an afternoon of work.

At times one of the boys would bring back a 22-caliber rifle from their summer vacation. We all wanted to shoot the gun, so we would buy bullets with our monthly allowance. We all seemed to be very accurate with the rifle, maybe from shooting our primitive weapons for so many years. Some of us became good enough with the rifle that we began challenging each other while hunting for squirrels.

If we were caught with having a rifle, we would surely be punished. There were so many chances of someone being hurt since we were learning without the advice of an adult who knew the dangers.

One Saturday morning Coach Gibson took me rabbit hunting with him and his family. He gave me a big shotgun and told me to watch ahead of where the dogs were running. I really thought that was a big deal to be carrying a shotgun with a group of grown men. The dogs were yelping and running through the briar bushes. All of a sudden, a rabbit came running out; and I wasn't sure it was my turn to shoot. Coach gave me the go ahead, and I got my first rabbit with a shotgun. Always before, a half dozen of us boys would chase down the rabbits on hunting day. We were in such good shape we could run nearly all day. Varmints were always cautious when we orphans were out playing in the woods and pastures. Their lives depended on whether an orphan was going to shoot them with a slingshot or whether the orphan was going to make the varmint a pet. Either way they were at the mercy of the boys.

Before we knew it, our life at the orphanage would be complete; and we would go out into the real world to seek our futures. The caregivers that wanted us to make it in this big world influenced many of the boys and girls.

Many of the boys and some of the girls would volunteer to serve our country by joining the different military services. There was a great admiration of Coach Gibson and Gray Todd that led many boys to serve their country, serving most of their adult lives in the military. Just to name a few.

Larry McCarn was four years older than I as we grew up at the orphanage. He served in the Air Force and is seen as Chief Master Sergeant Air Traffic Controller. Larry served around the world in Korea, Japan, Spain, Thailand, Philippines and many bases within the States.

Chief Master Sergeant Larry McCarn

Captain Beverly "Bev" Witherspoon, U. S. Navy, boasts of the influence Coach Gibson made on his life while growing up at the Methodist Children's Home. His decision to give his life to his country was made all because of the character and bravery demonstrated by Coach Gibson. Bev became a pilot and served his country in many valuable capacities in the Navy. He put his life on the line by volunteering to be an aircraft test pilot.

Test Pilot Beverly Witherspoon
Captain US Navy (Orphan Pride)

Another orphan big brother named Perry Lefeaver played hooky from school one day and ran away to join the Navy. He found the recruiting office in Winston-Salem and just told a little story about his age. The Navy sent Perry to Raleigh to be sworn into the US Navy Reserve. Perry almost finished Boot Camp before his underage of 15 caught up with him. He was sent home. He was able to finish school at RJ Reynolds High School. He played sports for the school and received a scholarship to Catawba College. Perry again volunteered to serve his country and again signed up for the Navy. After WWII, Perry participated in the Pacific nuclear testing while on carrier duty in the Pacific and extreme cold weather testing of helicopters and cold weather equipment in the North Atlantic. He was recalled to duty during the Korean War. The very places he sailed, Kwajalein and Eniwetok in the Pacific and Baffin Island in the North Atlantic would be in the same areas twenty years later where I would serve my duty. I have much pride from having so many patriotic brothers and sisters, even though we were not blood kin.

Lieutenant Perry LeFeaver at right with fellow officer. Small with big "orphan pride" heart.

USS *Rendova,* one of Perry's assigned ships.

Orphan brother, Arnold Bell, made a career of serving his country in the U. S. Air Force. He was a pilot and served in many campaigns. His younger brother Ron served as an Army engineer. Their older brothers didn't grow up at the orphanage but served during WWII and Korea. One brother paid the ultimate sacrifice of giving his life for our country in the Korean War, and one brother was a POW in Germany. Arnold and Ron Bell were others influenced by Coach Gibson and other orphanage staff to serve their country bravely and with pride.

Lt. Charles Arnold Bell (Orphan Pride)

Headquarters
United States Military Assistance
Command
Vietnam

By direction of the President

The Distinguished Flying Cross

Is presented to
Major Charles Arnold Bell
United States Air Force

For extraordinary achievement while participating in aerial flight: Major BELL distinguished himself by extraordinary achievement on 18 February 1968 while operating alone, unarmed, extremely vulnerable experimental aircraft over Can Tho, Republic of Vietnam where sections of that city and an airfield had come under heavy hostile mortar and recoilless rifle fire. Enemy 50 caliber air defense weapons were also strategically placed around the city. Totally disregarding the hazard of enemy fire from the air defense weapons and incoming friendly artillery rounds, Major BELL repeatedly circled over and around Can Tho while directing and controlling a withering fire from four United States Army helicopter gunships, one Air Force fixed winged and two Navy river Patrol boats. He remained on station approximately two hours and departed only when the enemy was compelled to break off the attack and withdraw. He was then informed by radio that his home base was under heavy mortar and ground attack. Assessing his available fuel and closest suitable alternate airfield, he elected to fly to Vung Tau. About 30 minutes from this alternate he was advised that the wind at Vung Tau had increased to above the safety limits for his aircraft. Unable to obtain contact with search radar and with no reliable navigational aids, he proceeded under marginal weather conditions to safe landing at Bien Hoa with a minimum quantity of fuel remaining. Major BELL's extraordinary achievement reflects great credit upon him and the military service.

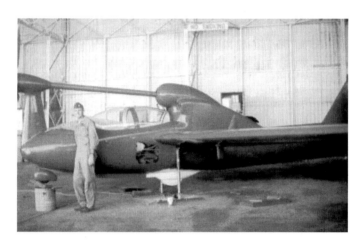

Maj. Charles Arnold Bell, Forward Arial Combat Control, experimental aircraft, Viet Nam.

My Brother-in-Law, Sam, served in the U. S. Air Force doing some duty in Europe during the Cold War.

Sam, "Air Force Sharp"

While Sam was serving in Europe, he lived in this WWII Quonset hut.

Sam's European home away from home.

His older brothers served during WWII and the Korean War. Sam's younger brother Jerry served as a Naval officer. Jerry served part of his duty on the U.S. Navy aircraft carrier Shangri La during the cold war, performing national security in the Mediterranean and North and South America.

Jerry Murdock
"Always Dedicated"

Sam's twin brothers, Gilmer and Graham, served in the U.S. Marines during Viet Nam and the Cold War. Gilmer made a career of the Marine Corps, serving in Viet Nam as a helicopter gunner. He also was a member of the Marine Corps Rifle Team. Graham served aboard the aircraft carrier USS Forrestal. Among his missions were several European and Mediterranean cruises during the Cold War. Growing up with these twins in the orphanage, I can assure you that our enemies would not fair so well if the enemy were to engaged these two brothers. Slingshots, slings or spears were our weapons of choice while we were young, and I can only imagine what these two could do with Uncle Sam's toys. A bunch of orphan guts and Uncle Sam's toys and boy ole boy look out!

US Marines Graham and Gilmer Murdock
"Semper Fi"

My sister's friends, Voncille and her brother Clarence "Kissel" Russell both served proudly in the Air Force during the Cold War.

Voncille Russell
My older orphan sister

Another orphan sister, Marian Barnett, served in the Marines during the late fifties.

Marian Barnett
United States Marine

These were just a few of the Children's Home's boys and girls that served their country with pride.

When I graduated from high school, I faced a lot of challenges. There was another boy waiting to take my bed, so we had to leave the orphanage the morning after graduation. I would leave the only home that I had ever known and join a world that I knew little about. I would have to learn how to live outside of the orphanage environment. I found living on my own came with a lot of learning experiences.

Fred (18 and Apprehensive)

The morning after I graduated from high school one of the other boys told me he was going to the YMCA to get a room, so I decided to go there also. My stay at the "Y" would be short after learning the hard way about thievery and grown men wanting to put their hands on me in the shower. This quickly turned me against living where I was and forced me into getting away from those that attempted to abuse me. I found a boarding house with help from my orphan brother, Roy.

I had found a job with Western Electric Company as an illustrator/draftsman working on defense projects. After graduation from high school and after company sponsored schooling for the rest of the year, I began working in what I thought was the beginning of my life-long career. Fate would intervene and change the direction of that notion as I would have the most challenging, exciting and memorable adult years of experiences anyone could hope for.

Jack Hartness 1945
May I serve my country?
(17 and ready)

Jack, serving in the Pacific.

Jack Hartness, a friend to several Children's Home boys
and a friend of mine that I met at work, told me about how

he had served his country as a Navy Frogman. I couldn't imagine being underwater in the middle of the ocean. Jack knew some of the older orphan boys from when he played high school sports. He encouraged me to continue playing sports with the company team, and this activity helped me stay in great physical condition. I couldn't find a nicer bunch of people to be working for. We all were working on defense projects at Western Electric Company. Even though I was never good at basketball, I practiced and supported their team. On occasion I did enjoy playing softball with the team but never played as well as these men. They, and especially Jack, seemed to take an interest in my welfare. I felt I wanted to experience what made these men so proud of their country. They were really good role models just as the men and women that raised me at the orphanage were.

1959 Western Electric Champs

The same influence of these men that had served their country during WWII and Korea was strongly evident, just as it was with Coach Gibson and the support staff at the orphanage. These were mostly family men who demonstrated their maturity and devotion to country even in their civilian life after serving their military duty.

Jack taught me a bit about living on my own and also about surviving walking the streets of Winston-Salem at night. There was always a threat from a couple of toughies in a neighborhood gang wanting to strut their toughness or just some bad person wanting what I had in my pocket. I just walked with determination as I had been taught as an orphan. I think most of the night people knew that they were going to get every bit of my one hundred and forty-five pound body if they wanted to do me harm. (Scary thought!)

A military draft system was occurring in the early sixties in which every eligible man would be called to serve his country in the armed forces for a certain length of time. Several of the men where I worked were serving their military duty time in the Army Reserve after their active duty hitch. Many had served in WWII and Korea, and it gave me a sense of honor to be working with such brave men and women. There was something special about being in the company of men and women that had served or were serving their country. I always had an admirable affection for their sacrifice and knew that I wanted to serve as well. I always thought that I wanted to be a paratrooper. I liked excitement in my life.

My cousins, Virlin, Charles and Harold Sewell, had served in the Army. Troy, Noel, Rex and Harold Ledford had served in the Navy, and that extra influence sealed my decision.

Virlin Breedlove, US Army

Troy Sewell, US Navy
1951-1959

I decided to join the U.S. Army, and before long I was on my way to Fort Jackson, South Carolina. I was there for quite some time before we were issued uniforms, as uniforms were in short supply at the base at that time. The only parts of my clothing worth saving were my belt and shoes after marching in one set of civilian clothes for a week. Everyone was issued a box to send his clothing items home or some other place. Wow! I was in the real United States Army and finally had a real Army uniform to play army in. I couldn't wait to get my gun so I could shoot some tin cans or maybe even a squirrel or two.

A sergeant walked up to me, and I gave him a big smile. That sergeant looked at me and shouted as loud as he could, "Give me twenty push-ups, Smiley." I had been smiling all my life, and now the good sergeant didn't want me to smile anymore. It wouldn't be the last time I was on the ground for smiling as that habit was hard to break.

In our company every troop had to look alike and do exactly the same things. If the sergeant called, "smoke break," "everybody that's got-um, light-um up." Everyone had to light up. When he called "Put-um out," everyone had to put their smoke out, field strip their cigarette butt and bury their pieces so that the sergeant couldn't find a scrap of their smoke. On occasion the sergeant would find a soldier who didn't think it necessary to strip their smoke; and boy, did he get angry! That sergeant would make that man put his butt in his pocket and keep it until we had finished training for the day. At the end of the day the sergeant would make the soldier dig a hole in the sand for hours, until he thought the hole was deep enough to bury that butt. The tool they had to use was their mess kit spoon. Then he would tell them to spoon the sand back into the hole. Some were there long after dark. Army training! I was getting good at it. I spent time spooning sand out of a hole and then spooning sand back into the hole, but only once.

We had two squad sergeants while in training at the base. The first one had developed a hustle of asking nearly every trooper to borrow money until payday. Soon we found out that he had no intention of paying the money back so we let the company First Sergeant know of his scheme. That Sergeant who was hustling us was removed from our command and given orders overseas. Our next squad sergeant would be Sergeant Bolware. He was a tall black man with a very southern drawl. We all liked him as he treated us with as much dignity as allowed in this training environment.

I was staying in shape doing all the exercises that the sergeant wanted me to do. We were up long before daylight every morning to begin our training with a vigorous exercise workout. We then performed a double-time march for miles, all the way to "Tank" hill and back to our Company near the back gate. Our commanding officer, Captain Floyd Hummiston, loved to run in front of his company as he was in perfect physical shape.

If one person fell out for muster in the morning without an item that was required for the day, the sergeant made everyone remove that article of clothing. One time of forgetting that item and peer pressure wrath from the company would come down on you like a ton of bricks.

The sounding of reveille in the morning and being greeted by the sergeant were really treats. He would come into the barracks and scream at the top of his voice, "I want every one of you soldiers running out of this barracks like a bunch of wild Indians looking for a place to crap." Our bunks had to be made up to Army specifications, and the sergeant would inspect them all. Not an article of clothing or any other item had better be out of place, or a piece of trash in sight. He would test the tightness of our bedrolls to see if a coin would bounce from our blankets as he flipped the coin into the air.

After our long march in double-time, we would have to do pull-ups on the handlebars and do sit-ups on the inverted sit-up board. There were a lot of big boys in our company and those exercises took their toll on them. The big boys just couldn't lift 200 to 250 pounds of their body weight. We were required to work our way up to a certain number of repetitions in each exercise. After finishing the exercises, we were allowed to enter the chow hall and eat breakfast. The sergeant was there to make sure we wouldn't waste any time in the chow hall. At times he allowed us four minutes from the time we sat down to eat our breakfast. There was no talking or that time was taken up by completing the amount of push-ups the sergeant would like for us to do. Sergeant Bolware wanted our platoon to get good scores. Sergeant House was an Army Ranger from the old school and wanted his company to outscore every company on the base. They both had served in WWII and Korea. Captain Hummiston was as sharp as a West Point graduate. They all demonstrated how proud they were to be wearing the uniform of an American soldier.

We were getting into the groove of things marching to training sites with our backpacks and canteen and mess gear hanging on our ammo belts. We were getting into great shape with more and more of the men being able to complete the full number of exercises.

Soon we were issued an M-1 rifle and off to some serious training. I asked the sergeant, "When will I get to shoot my gun?" That sergeant turned to me and screamed, "That is your rifle and not a gun." He then said, "Get down and give me thirty and don't let that rifle touch the ground." So I laid the rifle across the backs of my hands and gave the nice sergeant his thirty pushups. The rifle could also be called a "piece" or "weapon."

We learned to clean our weapons and take them apart and put them back together. We learned to care for other more modern weapons, but they were in short supply at that time. We would march to the woods and training grounds to learn combat maneuvers and how to fire weapons. This was a treat for me as my childhood playing had made everything easy for me. The ammo that was given to us for training seemed only half charged with gunpowder; once in a while I would see the bullet exit the old rifle. I knew there could be very little rifling effect in the barrel because the rifling was worn completely out of mine. The exit end of the barrel was egg shaped from the wear of all the bullets that had gone through in training. When the sergeant said to adjust my rifle sights for distance, I faked it because I knew just how weak the bullets were and could see how short of range the projectiles had. I easily passed all the range firing qualifications.

We went to the grenade range where we were taught the proper way to deliver a grenade to the enemy. We were taught how to use the grenade launcher that would be mounted to the exit end of our M1 rifles. We would fasten a grenade to the devise, and then we would load a blank cartridge in the rifle. When we were ready to fire, we placed the butt of our rifles on the ground and aimed and fired. The butt of the weapon on the ground absorbed the shock.

When it was our turn to throw live grenades, we took turns climbing into a foxhole with an instructor sergeant. We had previously tossed dummy grenades with smoke charges, but this was the real thing. I thought it was cool--just like when we were boys at the orphanage throwing mud clods. One boy, however, was so frightened that when he pulled the pin he just dropped the grenade into the bottom of the foxhole. The instructor pushed the boy out of the way and grabbed the grenade in time to roll it over the rim of the foxhole as it exploded. That instructor sergeant saved his and the troop's lives with his bravery and experience. This was for real.

One day as we were marching to another training site, my bunkmate Tim marching in line next to me just happened to catch out of the corner of his eye the soldier behind me having his rifle raised and bringing the butt of the rifle down toward the base of my spine. Tim turned as hard as he could and knocked the soldier down with his weapon. Evidently that soldier was angry about something and was going to take it out on someone the first opportunity he had. The captain caught sight of what had happened and was going to see that justice would be dealt with. The last man in the company had to carry two sets of boxing gloves on his pack. The captain would make use of these gloves anytime anyone got into a scuffle or disagreement. At break time, he would have the troops make a circle and the ones that had a confrontation would box each other until they were exhausted. To him, this was a way to save the paper work of putting someone on report and to break down hostilities within the company. After all, he was the captain of the company. This would be my first real boxing match. I had boxed with toy gloves when I was small. I watched boxing on the Gillette Cavalcade of Sports when we got our first television set. I was a youngster when I boxed, but it's a lot different when someone is out for blood. I was lucky that day and finished him off pretty quickly as he had a shorter reach than I. I sure am glad one of the big boys didn't have a beef with me. To this day I have never forgotten my army friend, Tim Stafford from Biloxi, Mississippi. I have tried locating him several times but never have found him.

A few weeks before the end of training those who had done well with all of their requirements were given a three-day pass. Well, that three-day pass was the shortest three days that I have ever experienced. We were allowed to depart at 1200HRS (noon) on Saturday and report in at 1700 (5PM) on Sunday. I caught a bus to Winston-Salem, spent the night, and then I caught a bus back to the fort the very next morning--a short three days!

Finally, we had completed all of our basic training. Now it was time for our company's big parade on the parade field. We had an awards ceremony in the theatre, and I was quite surprised. The first sergeant, Sergeant House, called me to front and center. The captain then handed me a trophy for being the best rifleman in the company. One other trooper and I attained the highest scores. Then he announced the top ten trainees in the company. He called my name as the fifth best. What a good feeling to be in that group of the best out of over two hundred men. I still have my trophy today; and once in a while, I read the inscription: "High Firer" "D-10-5"

After completing our training, we were issued orders to our next post. We were given several days leave en-route. I was offered a ride as far as the bus station in Charlotte, North Carolina, with Rodney Hutchinson and his parents. Rodney worked for the telephone company before he entered the Army. I spent several days with my friends in Winston-Salem before it was time to report to Fort Bragg for duty. Fort Bragg was a slightly cleaner and more modern place than Fort Jackson. There were big brick barracks on part of the base. There was a paratrooper training division (the 82nd Airborne), the 7th Special Forces and other combat divisions.

There was an overhaul group that overhauled tanks and other weapons. Civil service workers, Mr. Grady Weaver and Mr. Coats, were in charge of the shop. I worked with Sgt. Douglas of the Army National Guard and a civilian lady with red hair. I learned to overhaul, repair and calibrate combat weapons. I calibrated binoculars and other aiming devices attached to the weapons. After overhaul the weapons were driven to the firing range and tested for accuracy and reliability. There were some old tanks and artillery pieces that came through our shop. The M-42 Tank, with no top, was designed to drop from a plane behind enemy lines. The old M-48 Tank was big and cumbersome, but the tank did have a lot of heavy metal protection. The big 8" Howitzer was scary just to think of the damage one of its projectiles would cause.

When I think of Fort Bragg, I remember the long pay lines when it could take from morning till evening to receive our monthly pay. The lines were long; and if your name were in the later part of the alphabet, you would be standing for a long time. Our pay was pitiful in those days. I was drawing $64.00 a month after my savings bond was taken out. Now, I am not saying there was influence in wanting to take out a savings bond; but it seems if you did take out a bond, then when liberty came you were allowed to go. Also KP (Kitchen Police) duty didn't seem to come as often. For some of the troops, a few times having the pots and pans duty and peeling twenty bags of potatoes until 2200 (10PM) really made them want to buy a savings bond. In those days, we peeled the potatoes with a small knife. Also, at muster, the sergeant somehow found a way to let all of the other troops know that you had not had the opportunity to take out a savings bond. If we had 100% participation the captain was happy. If 100% was not achieved, there needed to be much more training and latrine holes dug.

Sometimes when liberty was granted on the weekend, we would go to the Cape Fear River or one of its tributaries and fish. The river was not clean, but it gave us a place to relax. One of the men I had lived with at the orphanage, Charles White, was assigned to my barracks. He and his friend, Lonnie Rolf, had been injured in an 82nd Airborne practice jump and were receiving treatment. We all used to go fishing and once in a while drive in their convertible down Bragg Boulevard to Fayetteville while on our way to the river. One day we planned to stop at a carhop hamburger joint with a disk jockey booth on top of the restaurant. We had picked up a little beer at the base and had planned to go fishing until sunset after we ate. We stopped at the traffic light just before entering the burger joint.

All of a sudden another convertible with four black soldiers pulled up along side of us. They looked us over, and one of them flipped out a 45 caliber automatic pistol. One of them shouted, "Alright, honkies, I'm going to blow your brains out." Fayetteville at that time was famous for violence, mostly coming from the soldiers at nearby Fort Bragg. We knew we were no match for any kind of conflict with those men. Charles and Lonnie, both with injured backs, and I wouldn't be of much protection against four angry black men that seemed to have spent some time consuming much alcohol. Charles shouted, "Go through the red light!" At that time Lonnie stomped on the gas pedal and flew down the street. As we looked back, the other car was closing in behind us. We made it out of town back to Bragg Boulevard, but it looked as though we were going to die really soon as they would get closer to our car. Charles said, "Give me one of those beers." I handed Charles a beer from the back seat where I was riding. As the other car tried to get closer, Charles tossed the beer like a grenade and the beer splattered in front of their car. The car slowed down as the driver was trying to miss the beer grenade in front of his car. We drove a little further down the road, but we could see the other car was not giving up. Before we knew it we were on our way towards Sanford, Siler City and then Greensboro. Our only hope was to be stopped by the highway patrol or the other car running out of gas. As long as we had a beer to throw, we could keep them at a distance. Eventually we lost sight of the following car. What a relief.

In those years Fort Bragg soldiers knew that if they stopped in downtown Fayetteville at any of the many bars that lined the street, they would at least have to prove themselves in a fight. There were a lot of soldiers there that had to prove how tough they were; and after they consumed a few beers, it didn't matter whom they picked for a fight to prove their newly acquired toughness. We stayed clear of the bars.

On Saturday morning if there were no special duties for us to perform and we passed "a strict" personnel inspection, we were allowed to go on a weekend pass. On one of my weekend passes to Winston-Salem, I had purchased a 52 Chrysler coup. Some of the time I would let my friend James keep my car as his was broken down during that time. I would hitchhike to Winston-Salem, spend some time with my orphan brothers and friends and then hitchhike back to Fort Bragg on Sunday. This practice of hitchhiking had long been a military tradition since military men in those years didn't make much money. This way of travel gave many soldiers a chance to go home. Most travelers would give a G.I. a lift as far as they could in those years. Some would even buy the G.I. a cup of coffee. We traveled in the rain, in the cold and heat and on dangerous roads.

In the sixties all military men were required to wear their uniforms to travel. That was a good idea for us as most people showed respect for military men and women.

When we were required a physical, we would go to the old wooden Womack Army Hospital on base and go through all of the different tests. The medics would draw our blood, upgrade our necessary vaccinations, give us a chest x-ray, eye exam, check our blood pressure and line us up for the doctor to give us his exam. There were forty or fifty men at a time lined up in a row. We would be standing at parade rest. As the orders were given to take up different positions, we would assume those positions. As the doctor passed down the line of troops, he would check our mouths with a tongue blade and look into our eyes with a flashlight. The sergeant would give the order to drop your trousers for short-arm inspection, usually reserved for those soldiers returning from liberty and that had engaged in private adult activities with the opposite sex. Then the doctor would go back down the line and check every soldier for a hernia, telling each to cough as he poked. Then the order was given to bend over as the doctor passed. With all the different medical staff transiting the long hall, we were standing there bent over with our bottoms poked out when our turn came to spread our cheeks for the doctor to check our bottom ends. This was the army way in those years. We were not hurt, maybe a little embarrassed; but it was a time saving, efficient way of getting several hundred troops through their physicals. Hundreds were there every day to get their turn.

From time to time our unit would be ordered to report to Pope Air Force Base. There would be several hundred of us. We would help load many aircraft for operations about which we didn't have the need to know. The large numbers of us made the effort quick and easy.

When my active duty time was complete, I returned to Winston-Salem and assumed my job at Western Electric working on government contracts. It was a good feeling to get back to a job that I liked, but I would still miss some of the military life that I had grown accustomed to. I still wanted to be a paratrooper, but the training required for my army profession did not require me to be a paratrooper. Now I would be required to finish my six-year obligation to my country by attending monthly and summer training while standing by to be called to active duty again. The Vietnam War was building up and beginning to require more troops. Our company was standing by to be called; however, it was another company in our unit that the pentagon called. They were needed as a combat medical unit. Two of my orphan brothers, Roy Byrd and Arthur Spaugh, were in that company. Dr. Underdau volunteered as our football doctor at the orphanage and was the commanding officer of that medical unit. He had cared for a few of my injuries as I was growing up and playing hard and injured often. Dr. Underdau was an orthopedic surgeon at the Baptist

Hospital in Winston-Salem. Their medical company would serve for a year in Viet Nam as a MASH unit.

Arthur caring for an unfortunate little girl, a casualty of war in Viet Nam. Arthur always cared about people.

Roy and his pleasant personality always kept the morale high with his constant joking and trickery.

I thought that I would try to further my education, so I drove to High Point after work to attend classes at High Point College. I was enjoying being a college man and realized the fear I had of college was really not warranted. I even thought of asking the orphanage to help me get a work scholarship to attend college full time during the day. I could work my way through college washing dishes or doing maintenance on campus. I was always a little embarrassed being around anyone smarter than I and anxious about giving an incorrect answer to a given question. I also thought of the horror of going to a strange place to attend college with not a red penny in my pocket. One of the biggest errors in my life is not following through with my intuition of finishing college. By not taking my education seriously, my life's ambitions would be limited to occupations I would be allowed to pursue in the military. I always thought that I could be anything that I wanted to be with hard work, but delaying my education would haunt me for the rest of my career. I found out that I was blessed with a positive attitude and the ability to perform hard work. At that period in my life, a lot of us young working people were having the time of our lives dating, partying and driving to Myrtle Beach, South Carolina, for the weekend or Polo Grill in Winston-Salem on Thursday and Saturday nights. We would carry our dates there or dance with girls already there. Many Wake Forest students hung out there on weekends. Pretty soon it seemed that that life style was becoming the norm for so many of us that work seemed to be second in importance. I crashed my car so I dropped out of college night school. Our Army unit was getting boring with not being called on to help in Viet Nam. Other boys were coming back from Viet Nam or not returning at all, and all I seemed to be doing was letting life slip away, one party after another. There was too much in my upbringing at the orphanage to continue the path of life that I had fallen into. I was too proud and patriotic, and I wanted to do better with my life and serve my country. What influence the orphanage had left on me was still ever present in my mind. I wanted to make my only home (The Children's Home), my big sister and the boys and girls that I grew up with proud of me.

Chapter Three

Several times I had noticed on television an advertisement of needing men to serve in the U.S. Coast Guard. I thought that part of the job of the U.S. Coast Guard men were lifeguards at the beach! There was a large sailing ship shown on the television advertisement; and the advertisement asked, "Wouldn't you like to serve in the U.S. Coast Guard?" I thought at that moment that I could see myself high up among the sails in the crow's nest of that ship. I thought my job would be shouting "Land Ahoy," just like in the movie of Robinson Crusoe. On days that I wouldn't be sailing, I would be on the beach protecting pretty girls from the dangers of the deep blue. It seemed that every time I found myself feeling useless and wasting time, this commercial would come on the television screen.

US Coast Guard training barque *Eagle*

Well, I decided to check into this new vision of my future. I looked around Winston-Salem and could find no Coast Guard recruiter. I asked one of the Army recruiters where a Coast Guard recruiter could be found. He said the closest recruiter was in Greensboro. I had such an interest in getting on that ship that I drove to Greensboro. There I met a big, tall Coast Guardsman who seemed to speak a language that sounded like something between Irish and Old English. He told me he was a "High Tider" from the Outer Banks of North Carolina. He said that he came from the village of Kitty Hawk. I thought he was, for sure, from a foreign country. I still could hardly understand him or knew little about this place he was talking about except that Orville and Wilbur Wright flew their invention there. As fortune would have it, I would get to know this man's family, serving with several of his brothers, and end up friends with the family for the rest of my life. The man's name was Hope Beacham. He was a boatswain's mate and worked in the recruiting office.

Terry being sworn into the Coast Guard by
older brother Hope Beacham.

His brothers, Terry and Conley, and I would serve in Coast
Guard air rescue together. Over my career I would become
friends with many of the "High Tiders" (Outer Bankers).

Hope and Terry, last two on right
Janette Yoerg, left, a member of the Wright
family, welcomed attendees to the second day of
the celebration [First Flight Centennial]. She is
standing next to the descendants of Kill Devil
Hills Life Saving Station workers who helped the
Wright brothers with their experiments.
(The Daily Advance)

Hope and Terry's grandfather, William Thomas Beacham, had served at the Coast Guard Life Saving Station on the Outer Banks and assisted the Wright brothers with their flight experiments.

Young boy holding father's hand is Hope and Terry's father, John Leland Beacham. Their grandfather is William Thomas Beacham and their dog was named Bounce.

I told Hope about the advertisement I had seen on television. He seemed to understand what I was interested in doing in the Coast Guard, or at least I thought he understood. He did let me know that "life guarding" on the beach is not what the Coast Guard duties are. I took the entrance exam; and he told me that with the scores that I had made on the exam, I could pick any type job in the Coast Guard. I knew nothing about what the different rating symbols meant but later would read a little about each. I still had in mind that I wanted to be in the crow's nest of that beautiful sailing ship. Hope told me that if I signed up in the Coast Guard that I would go through a short indoctrination at the training center at Cape May, New Jersey, and then he could get me into one of the Coast Guard schools after about two weeks. Well, what I was told sounded reasonable with me, so I signed the papers.

I went back to Winston-Salem and began preparing for my departure to my new life. There wasn't much to prepare for, as I had no family or valuables. The uncertainty of not seeing my friends for an unknown time and not knowing where it was that I was going gave me some concern. It was a lonesome time in my life with much uncertainty, but it was a time in my life when I wanted to be a part of something good and a time to head my life in a positive direction. Time passed quickly, and now it was time to meet Hope in Greensboro to begin my long journey being a member of the United States Coast Guard.

The day August 5, 1964 happened to be one day after Coast Guard Day. Hope instructed me on how my trip plans would be carried out in order to reach my destination in New Jersey. He told me that I would be traveling to Norfolk, Virginia, by bus. There I would meet up with another recruiter for further instructions. I said my goodbye; and with a handshake, I was on my way to Norfolk.

When I arrived at the bus station in Norfolk, I called the number that I was given and a driver picked me up. He drove me to the Coast Guard office where I was sworn in again along with numerous other men. The office recruiter checked over our papers to be sure we were ready to leave the next morning for New Jersey. Here I met a man that came from Virginia Beach named Vaughn D. Williams. He said his family owned an Esso gas station. He and I would become acquaintances for our journey to New Jersey. After all paperwork was in order, the recruiter took us to the Navy YMCA. Here we were to spend the night and the recruiter would pick us up the next morning. As we were nearing the "Y," I glanced over and saw a sign in the post office front yard. The sign read: "Sailors and Dogs keep off the grass." I thought, "What have I gotten myself into?" As we were registering to get a room, Navy Shore Patrols were dragging sailors from some of the rooms. In one room, the occupants were suspected of having homosexual activity. The Shore Patrol picked up another man for drunkenness and fighting in another room. I thought, "Wow! This is just like in the old Saturday movies when the sailors made back to shore for some entertainment after a long voyage at sea." Once I got to my assigned room, I closed and locked the door. I didn't open my door until the next morning. I had lived in a "Y" for a short time after I had left the orphanage. That was not a pleasant experience. I didn't want to go to the Navy brig for breaking someone's face, especially on my first day in the Coast Guard.

The next day the recruiter drove us to the train station where we boarded a train to Philadelphia, Pennsylvania. Vaughn and I had a chance to talk some more, and he told me he served in the Virginia National Guard. We were pretty much in the same situation. We arrived at the train station in Philadelphia and boarded a bus to Cape May, New Jersey. After we got off the bus at Cape May, we waited for the Coast Guard bus to come and pick us up for the ride to the training center. When the bus did arrive, it was just like boot camp all over again. The seaman in charge started shouting for everyone to grab a seat, and he didn't want to hear a word out of any of us "pogues." "No talking on my bus," he shouted again. I wondered what the word "pogue" meant.

When we arrived at the base, the seaman in charge began reading us the rules and regulations he expected us to follow. He had everyone empty all of his pockets of everything in them. All of our possessions were spread out on a table and Seaman Glenn Reed would determine what items we were allowed to have while at the base. You should have seen the amount of different kinds of knives that piled out on the table. Boys from the big cities had switchblades. There were carving knives, sheath knives, and a strait razor. Country boys had their whittling knives, and some had small hunting knives. All of those items were confiscated as they were supposed to have been told by their recruiters that certain kinds of knives were not allowed. All of us received a stern warning that if anything illegal were found on us during training, that person would face brig time. He then asked if there were any barbers in the group. Maybe one person said he had some experience. Then he walked around the room and started picking people out. He said, "You, and you, and you, and you look like good barbers. Now all of you barbers grab a set of clippers out of the box." He told a recruit to sit down and then began to demonstrate how everyone's hair would be cut. He then said, "All of you pogues line up and get a hair cut." All hair had to come off. Some recruits were sweating losing their long wavy locks of hair. Seaman Reed overheard one recruit asking what a pogue was. Seaman Reed let everyone know that a pogue was a critter living on the bottom of the ocean, one layer below whale droppings. At that time, we knew just how high we were on the respect ladder.

Seaman Reed then made a roll call of all the prior service troops and directed them to another area of the barracks. They would be called Victor Company. They would go through a Coast Guard indoctrination program instead of the full boot camp training. This is the group to which I would be assigned. The next day after the officer in charge (OIC) of forming company, Boatswains Mate 1st class McKeithan, had reviewed everyone's record, he asked me if I would be willing to work in forming company preparing troops for their beginning of training. Being knowledgeable of my army training, I knew it wise for me to agree with whatever my seniors asked of me. I said I would be glad to do what he wanted me to do.

I began assisting Seaman Reed in his around-the-clock care of the new recruits. Some recruits had a very difficult time being away from home and absorbing the instructions of a new life. Our job didn't make it any easier for them. It was mentally challenging to many. Some would be screened out of training for other medical reasons before they would be assigned a company. Those that were screened out were sent home. It may seem harsh, but this time in a Coast Guardsman's career was the best time to challenge a young man's adaptability to the stresses he would face in his career. Mental stresses were a part of the training, much more so than I remembered in the army.

I began to understand the importance of a young man being able to withstand the mental challenges brought about in Coast Guard training. A young seaman apprentice just finishing his training could be sent to any location in the world and be on isolated duty for a year. I didn't realize just how many places in the world the Coast Guard operated. There were stations with a few men located in the far north of Alaska, in the Mediterranean, on islands in the Atlantic and the Pacific all the way to Southeast Asia. Our operations covered all of North and South America and the Polar Regions. During the Cold War, Coast Guard ships were stationed across the Pacific and the Atlantic as part of the American defense shield. A strong ability to withstand stress was necessary for men sent into those environments. The company commanders wanted only those that were healthy and able to complete their training requirements without interruption.

Preparing young troops to join their training companies was a trying job; and every opportunity I had for liberty, I would leave the base and go into Cape May. There were some real nice bars and restaurants in town. Most all the people I met were nice to me. One evening I ran into a crew from a fishing boat. They introduced themselves, as I did. They asked where I was from, and I said, "North Carolina." We hit it off since they fished out of somewhere in the Carolinas. They asked me if I would like to have dinner with them, and I accepted the offer. They took me to what they called an oyster bar or raw bar. I wasn't sure where they were taking me, as I really didn't want to get in the raw; and I also didn't want to eat any raw food! I had never eaten oysters before. After we arrived at the bar and sat down at the table next to other people, I took down my guard. The men ask me if I liked steamed crabs. I told them that I had never eaten them before, but added, "I'll be glad to try them." The leader of the group told the waitress to bring us a bushel of steamed crabs. After she placed the order, she came back to the table with hot sauce, other condiments and napkins. She also brought everyone a miniature baseball bat. I thought that was very strange. For sure, what she was going to bring for us to eat was not alive. I didn't say anything, but I had a lot of thoughts run through my head as to why I would need to kill what I was going to eat. She brought the crabs and dumped them up and down the middle of the table. The crabs were stacked so high that I could barely see the fishermen on the other side of the table. They bought me a cold beer, and I began to see what they were doing and learned how to eat those varmints. Boy, they were ugly. The fishermen would take those little ball bats and wallop the crabs' claws, crushing the claws to get to the meat. I thought I was "somebody" learning how to eat crabs like the salty fishermen. The crabs were good, and the fishermen were awfully good to me to buy my dinner. I couldn't wait to get back to the base and tell the others how salty I had become and how to eat at the raw bar.

They talked a bit about their experiences on their boat while they had been at sea. In past fishing ventures, the captain and one of his mates had been rescued by the Coast Guard after a storm had disabled their vessel. The captain stated that he was mighty grateful and indebted to the Coast Guard crews that they depend on to protect them while they try to make a living on the open sea. What the captain said made me feel good since I would become a part of this Coast Guard that would save people at sea. At that time just how important a job I would have began to sink in. Well, they all had enough to eat and left me at the table to finish the remaining crabs. I said how much I appreciated their kindness. I stayed there and continued beating those crabs and splashing red juice all over the table. When I had finally gotten enough meat out of those crabs to satisfy my hunger, I started wiping my face and hands. When I looked down, the splatter of red juice had completely covered the front of my white uniform. Boy, was I in trouble with a messed up uniform. My plan to have a good evening was ruined, as I had to hurry back to the base. I thought it all worth it to get to eat with a crew from a real ocean fishing boat. I would go on liberty plenty more times and get to enjoy myself. Cape

May was a tourist town, and the fall of the year was a good time to get to enjoy the people. Maybe I would be lucky and find a nice girl to spend the evening with.

Weeks passed by and I hadn't heard anything about going to school. I decided to drop Hope a line in Greensboro and find out when I would be going to school. Being many weeks more than the two that I thought I would be there at the base had passed, I mentioned that I would have a conversation with him if I ever were able to come home on leave. I dropped the letter in the mail and within a few weeks, an officer came to me and started asking me questions. I was in hot water and really didn't understand why. Someone at the recruiting office must have read my letter and determined that my letter was disrespectful to a senior. Shucks all I wanted was to get into school as Hope had promised. I explained what I meant in the letter and that I had no intent of disrespect. Boatswains Mate McKeithan vouched for my dedication to the Coast Guard. Nothing happened, but that sure was a scare as I could have been charged and received Non Judicial Punishment or even received a court martial and given brig time. I would work there for a few more weeks with CWO Grady Fulcher in Public Works. We hit it off real well as he was from the island of Ocracoke on the coast of North Carolina. Within a few weeks I had my orders to another base in Charleston, South Carolina.

Chapter Four

Charleston is where I really began to be involved in the
real Coast Guard mission.   Boatswain's Mate Jimmy
Davis, Chief Ward and Chief Hayes were mostly running
the show there at Charleston. We had a clean barracks to
sleep in, even though there were four or five to a room. I
was assigned to the boat crew of Boatswain's Mate Darvin
Ramage. Most of the time, Ramage, Seaman Davis and I
crewed our boat. We had two wooden-hull thirty-foot
boats, several steel-hull forty-foot boats and a reserve
thirty-two-foot boat to take care of. The buoy tender
Papaw operated from the pier. One eighty-two footer and
one other boat were also tied up there. Darvin and I hit it
off right away. He invited me to his family's home in
Millen, Georgia, when we were authorized liberty on
weekends. He taught me all he could about operating the

different types of boats. Right away, he put me at the helm showing me how to navigate the Charleston harbor and how to give right-of-way to the Navy and other large commercial ships. He told me how to line up with the day markers and warned me about going aground on the mud flats or especially on the rock jetties. We would go out on rescue calls, and he would show me how to secure the line properly while towing a boat. I spent days with his teaching me how to use the charts for navigation. In those days, the compass was the mainstay of navigational instruments so figuring wind and current would take some experience before mastering that calculation. In those days, we also could deliver fuel to boats in need and give the crews a tow back to safe harbor. Today, many troubled boaters are referred to commercial towing companies unless lives are in danger.

Our forty-foot boats had twin engines with a steel hull; and, to me, they were more fun to operate, especially when docking the boat. You could steer the boat with the throttles and put it in the exact position you desired when docking.

40' Patrol/Rescue Boat

Our thirty-foot boats had only one engine and a wooden hull. This boat seemed to ride smoother, probably because of its hull design. We would take turns with the different boats as we had many tasks to perform each day. Even though the thirty-foot boats were smaller, the boats and their crews still answered the calls to go off shore when there was a boat or life in distress.

Wooden hull 30' Patrol/Rescue boat

We performed two harbor patrols a day. One patrol would last two to three hours and sometimes longer. We would provide assistance if a mariner was in trouble. If there were a navigation light out somewhere in the harbor or in the channel coming into the harbor, we would repair the light as quickly as possible. Sometimes there was a suspicious small boat or dingy departing or heading towards a foreign vessel. We would monitor those vessels to ensure a legitimate operation was taking place. We also monitored vessels operating near the Navy piers as we patrolled up river. We would repeat the patrol at night.

Sometimes we would go out on a rescue call, and the fog would be settled over the harbor on our return to base. We would have to use our compass going from buoy to buoy to find our way through the inlet channel. All the time we posted a watch on the bow to listen for moving ships in our path. On one mission as we were returning, our compass became unreliable. We were in the channel in a very vulnerable position since the fog was so thick. If we could find the nearest buoy without running aground or being crushed by a large ship, we planned to tie up to the buoy and wait for the fog to clear. We finally found a buoy, tied up, and notified the base of our predicament, our intentions and where we were by the number on the buoy. We left about a ten-foot length on the line so the buoy would have room to sway without damaging our boat. We kept an ear out for passing vessels because ships are known to bump buoys in bad weather. We heard a ship coming as the splash of the water became more noticeable. The pilot ships, Navy, and commercial ships had the luxury of radar for use in navigation. The one ship passed by, and we couldn't see it. Then shortly after, we heard the splashing of another ship and heard its foghorn blowing ever so often. We kept looking for the ship since we could hear the splashing getting louder and the foghorn sounding like it was almost on top of us. All of a sudden everyone looked up, and the bow of the ship appeared out of the fog and directly overhead! Everyone scrambled to the stern of the boat to get as far away from the impact as possible. All of a sudden the ship struck the buoy that we were tied to and slammed it into the bow of our boat. The impact knocked us to our knees as we held on to whatever we could grab. My heart was pounding out of my chest from the fright of that big monster ship sending us to Davy Jones' locker (the bottom of the sea)! My adrenaline was pumping overtime. The first ship passing must have been the pilot ship and the next a large freighter. We were a very lucky crew that day.

I learned more and more of the harbor's navigation, sometimes not always without near misses. Several times at night and in bad weather, I thought I was headed in the right direction only to have the keen eye and experience of Darvin direct me to the right heading just in time as to not go ashore where I shouldn't be. I could see how important and serious a job the Coast Guard would be. As I studied more and read more about the responsibilities of the Coast Guard, I learned more about the different missions and why these missions were needed. This was quite a change from the old cement-mixing box that we used to float on in the tadpole pond back at the orphanage.

As a seaman I had many different chores to perform from assisting in the galley to keeping the barracks clean. I didn't spend much time in the galley because I was needed on the boat crew. On occasion, however, I did help clean the barracks. General daily cleaning was the norm: cleaning and shining the scuttlebutt (drinking fountain), the head (bathroom), and bunkrooms and swabbing the passageways.

Once the barracks Master-at Arms asked me to clean the head so I started cleaning the toilets and sinks. I had helped clean bathrooms since I was a young boy and then latrines in the Army and heads in the Coast Guard. As the Master–at-Arms stopped by to see how I was doing, he noticed the deck in the head was stained somewhat. He left and then came back with a gallon of something called (HydracloXXXXXXXXXXXX). I told him I would scrub the deck super clean. He told me to just splash a little around on the floor and scrub. Well, I splashed the liquid all over the floor at full strength. I began scrubbing the tile floor as hard as I could. Shortly after I started scrubbing, smoke started coming from the tile. The fumes were so strong that I could hardly breathe. I glanced down at the tile floor, and bubbles were coming from between the tiles where the grout was lifting out as I scrubbed. I was getting dizzy so I left the head. I found the Master-at-Arms and asked him, "Just how clean do you want me to get that deck?" He said, "I want the head to pass Captain's inspection." I told him that he didn't have to worry about the stains because the stains came out with the grout. I told him that the fumes were so bad that no one could go into the head. I took him to the head and showed him what I was talking about and he shouted, "Get the water hose." I ran for a water hose and flushed the entire head. As I was flushing, the deck pieces of grout were washing up. He seemed to have great concern as the barracks were fairly new, and he had screwed up the head already. The chemical was banned shortly after our incident as other incidents happened Coast Guard wide. The chemical was deemed highly toxic for human use.

Sometimes we would have to stand Gate Guard Security as one of our duties. We would check identification cards of all that wanted to enter the base. There were civilians that worked in the buoy repair shop next to the pier. We had to know our military courtesies so we knew how and whom to salute.

Coast Guard buoy tender, dangerous
hard work.

Once, a sister ship to the buoy tender *Papaw* sailed in from Galveston, Texas. The ship tied up along side the *Papaw*. This was cause for celebration by the two crews. The *Papaw*'s crew invited the other crew to a night on the town (a seafaring tradition in those years). That was one long night and a night to remember in Coast Guard history. The crews were enjoying being ashore in Charleston for the entire night. Things were not politically correct in those years. It was a bit more colorful and entertaining just as life on the sea was portrayed in the WWII and early seagoing movies. I am glad I served at least part of my career during some of those colorful years and experienced the sometimes-naughty behavior of seamen letting it all hang out.

Our base was located at the end of the Charleston Battery on Trad Street. The crews walked together down the Battery and all the way to the old Slave Market. There was a bar there that was a regular meeting place for the Coasties. After many seafaring stories from the crews, many headed downtown to sample the bar life where many of the Navy sailors found entertainment. As the night dragged on and the bars began to close, they began to return to the base in much worse shape than when I had seen them in the early evening. Working on a buoy tender was dangerous and very physically demanding. These sailors were hardened by the tasks they performed. I only could imagine exactly what happened, but several of them were bloody and their uniforms were in need of repair. They were headed back out to sea the next day, and it was a very quiet ship when they departed the pier and headed out to sea.

Soon I would leave this base and be assigned for a time to the lighthouse across the Cooper River from Charleston on Sullivan's Island, not knowing at the time that my great grandfather (times seven) had fought the British on this very island. He had spilled blood here on the island and in Charleston. He was wounded in the shoulder in one battle and lived to fight another battle before being wounded in the thigh and becoming a POW in a Charleston prison. I wish I had known something of my heritage at this time.

At the lighthouse, there were a chief, a cook, a civilian, and two crews of two each for standing the watch on the lighthouse and standing by with two small boats for rescue duty. The duty rotation was port and starboard. That meant that every day you would begin your turn at duty at noontime and be off duty at noontime the next day.

Sullivan's Island Lighthouse

Being stationed at Sullivan's Island Lighthouse was an interesting job as I learned how a lighthouse operated. I wasn't crazy about the smaller boats at the unit. I had rowed a boat at Hanging Rock State Park between Walnut Cove and Danbury, North Carolina, before; and I had been in a powerboat like these with friends of mine in Winston-Salem. Herbie and Shelvia Johnson used to take me to High Rock Lake to ride in their small-boat. Herbie was a Sergeant in the Army unit I was assigned to in Winston-Salem. When I first saw the small boats, I was a little apprehensive of their size, thinking that I might be going into the ocean on a mayday call. I would find out that the main purpose for the smaller boats was to allow access to the shallower water on the bayside. Only in a dire emergency would we use them in the ocean waters. We took on water on one of them at the launching ramp as we were attempting to launch the boat on a rescue call. We launched the other boat to complete the mission.

The care of the lighthouse itself was really an enjoyable job. The lighthouse was made of metal and was flexible. We would ride an elevator to the top of all but the last two floors. There, we would climb a ladder through a hole to the light floor. We would go up every day and clean the entire area. The glass had to be cleaned of all the salt spray and left spotless. The lighthouse and its supporting buildings required constant care.

The civilian who worked at the lighthouse looked after the electronics and control of the light. He had a hobby of treasure hunting with a metal detector, finding cannon balls and all kinds of artifacts. I couldn't wait until I could afford a metal detector.

One of the Coasties was the cook that provided us with a breakfast and lunch. For supper he would take our order, go to the local market on the island, and have our supper in the refrigerator ready to cook; but we would cook for ourselves at suppertime.

At night we continued to stand by for rescue, but we also had other important jobs to perform. We would provide fire-watch during the night, and every hour we would monitor the beacon signals from the Georgetown and the Tybee Lighthouses. If there was bad weather or an out of sight range of the light from a ship, the ship could pick up a radio signal beacon from the lighthouse and use that signal for navigation. Each job we did seemed to be of importance to those that relied on our station. It was also important for us to monitor the lighthouse beacon signal to the north and to the south. This guaranteed good beacon signals up and down the entire coast of our country. An inoperable signal beacon from either lighthouse could very easily put a ship's crew in peril during bad weather.

I liked going to the top of the lighthouse and climbing out on the catwalk. Since we cleaned the outside of the glass, one could see forever and get a great view of the sunrises and sunsets. As the wind would blow, the lighthouse would sway. The swaying was like being in the top of a windblown tree at the orphanage where we had seventy-five to one hundred feet trees, and we climbed them often. Only this light structure was 163 feet to its top. That's equivalent to a sixteen-story building.

After a period standing duty at Sullivan's Island Lighthouse, I was transferred back to the base in Charleston. I went right back to doing what I did before-- working on and crewing the rescue boats. I liked that part of my duty. When we were not out on a mission, I would scrub the lacing on the rails of the boats to make them nice and white and touch up any paint that had chipped. One day I was cleaning the paint from the brass bell so that I could polish the bell to make it shine like it was supposed to shine. As I was working on the bell, I heard someone walking on the pier behind me. I turned around and there stood the commanding officer of the base, Captain J.J. Shingler. I immediately assumed the position of attention and saluted. The captain shouted, "At ease, sailor." The captain asked what I was doing, so I told him that the boat had a brass bell, and I thought that the bell was supposed to be shining instead of being coated with ten coats of black paint. He asked for my name. He then said, "It's been years since I've seen a man make an effort to polish those bells." The captain asked me a few more questions about where I was from. I told him that I was from The Children's Home in Winston-Salem and born in the mountains near Hayesville, North Carolina. He engaged me in general conversation. He said keep up the good work, then turned and walked away.

Some of the other seamen said, "Why do you want to take the paint from the bells and have to polish them every week?" I said, "I want the boat that I operate to look good as well as run good. Wait and see when I finish; then see how much better it looks."

Every week we engaged in some form of athletic activities. Some of the gigantic men liked to see how big of a cement buoy anchor weight they could lift. One seaman who weighed around three hundred pounds and stood six foot six inches tall could lift a very large cement anchor. Some of the anchors weighed five hundred pounds and some as much as a thousand pounds or more. One day we all were playing volleyball. This seaman who was able to lift such a heavy weight was playing opposite me. We were deep into the game and engaged in a lot of across-the-net spiking of the ball. On one jump for the ball, the big seaman reached over the net and spiked my head instead of the ball. The ball was two feet away from my head. We always played jokes on each other. He almost knocked me out. I went down so fast that I couldn't get my feet flat on the ground. I landed on the top part of my foot. I was in such serious pain that I felt like my ankle was broken. I sat there for a while, got up from the ground, and the sharp pain subsided somewhat. We went on back to work. That evening it was my crew's turn to patrol the harbor. I took my duty even though I was in pain. We came in from patrol around 2200hours (10PM), and I had difficulty untying my shoestring. My foot had swollen over the top of my boot. I showed the OOD (Officer of the Day) my foot, and he immediately piped for the duty driver to carry me to the Charleston Navy Hospital.

The Navy corpsmen at the emergency room x-rayed my foot and told me I had a bad sprain. They then instructed me to stay off of my foot and to put ice soaks on my ankle. The captain came in, took one look at the injury and instructed the corpsmen to re-x-ray my foot at a different angle. Sure enough my bone was split. The Navy corpsmen put a cast on my leg from my foot to the top of my thigh. They gave me a pair of crutches and helped me try to walk. On the bottom of the cast was a rubber knob for support and to help keep my cast dry.

I was put on light duty by the Navy captain and instructed on the care of my injury. I returned to my base and found myself helpless in the support of the rest of the crew. I could no longer be a member of our patrol/rescue boat crew, and I couldn't help with the rest of the duties.

Seaman Tanner ready to serve.

Captain Shingler called me to his office. He said that I would not be able to perform my duties for quite some time. He said that I would not be able to take the pounding of the surf on my foot even after my cast was taken off. Then he asked me if I would like to go to school. I said yes. Then he asked me where I would like to go to school. I remembered at times when the helicopters from the air station in Savanna, Georgia, would bring in rescued mariners and land on our pier. I thought that was an awesome job, being able to fly over the water and help people in trouble. Months earlier I had completed a flight physical when I applied for aviation school. I told him that I would like to go into air rescue. He said, "Let me see what I can do."

Chapter Five

Within a few days, I was told to report to admin where the yeoman handed me a set of orders. He instructed me to travel to Jacksonville, Florida, where I would be attending Aviation Electricians Mate School. I packed my sea bag and a suitcase. I checked out with all of my supervisors and said goodbye to those I had served with. They all wished me good luck, and off to the bus station I went with the duty driver.

The duty driver helped me with getting my baggage to the check-in desk. I hobbled on my crutches to make my way to board the bus. Jacksonville, Florida, was not that far of a ride. After arrival I recovered my baggage. I was on my own with two bags to carry and trying to walk on crutches. It was a bit of a challenge carrying a sea bag in one hand

and carrying a suitcase in the other. I had to take very short steps since when I tried to step too far the swing of the sea bag and suitcase nearly threw me down. I was in a predicament. I boarded a local city bus that would take me to the Jacksonville Navy Air Station. I boarded the bus to what I thought would be my final destination at the training center.

The bus arrived at the Jacksonville Naval Air Station main gate and pulled up to the offloading point located outside the main gate. I asked the driver if he was going to drive onto the base, and the driver said, "This is as far as I go."

I retrieved my baggage and found myself in a predicament again, only this time I was in the middle of a rainstorm. I stowed my sea bag and suitcase under a bush and went to a phone mounted on the main gate wall. I thought I would call the school office and tell them what my situation was. I didn't think it wise of me to try to walk to the school in the condition I was in. I talked to the person on the other end of the line and tried to explain my problem. I told him that I had just broken my leg and that while walking on crutches I was trying to carry my sea bag in one hand and my suitcase in the other. I also told him that the water was several inches deep in places on the sidewalk and the rain was still coming down heavily.

The man on the other end of the line said, "You are a (XXXX) student, and we don't give students rides! You walk like everybody else." I thought, "What have I gotten myself into this time. It sounds like this place is another boot camp."

The rain looked as though it was going to continue to pour so I decided to make a move towards the school before I caught pneumonia. I grabbed my sea bag and suitcase from under the bush and began walking down the sidewalk. My cast was getting wet and sloshing with every step that I took. I had to walk slowly because of the bags and crutches in my hands. I had to stop, once in a while, to get the circulation back into my hands and take another grasp. As my cast became more soaked the gauze began to unravel. Soon the rubber-walking pad on the bottom of the cast began to drag behind me. I continued my struggle to make it to the school. I was concentrating on getting there so much that I passed the building where I was supposed to report in and found myself in front of the Headquarters Building. I did the normal thing that any good sailor was supposed to do and dragged my bags into the building. I removed my cover and stood, with my crutches, at attention in the threshold of the commanding officer's office. I shouted, "Seaman Tanner reporting for duty, sir." The captain looked up from his desk, looked me up and down and saw how drenched I was. He saw my Coast Guard shield on my sleeve and saw the knobby from my cast dragging behind me several feet. He stood up with some astonishment and said, "What in the (XXXX) are you, and don't you know it's raining out there? At ease, sailor." The captain asked me how I got into this situation; I explained and told him the events that took place from the main gate. I told him that the person at the school didn't give students rides. The captain became furious and dialed the phone. In what seemed like less than a minute, two chiefs were there standing at attention. I thought, "Now I'm in for it for creating a problem with the chiefs." The Captain shouted at the chiefs and told one to get me to the hospital and one to carry my baggage to my quarters and dry every item in those bags. He shouted, "Now get moving; I expect a follow-up report on this man's condition. Dismissed." The chiefs knew they were catching the abuse, all from a young duty seaman that happened to be on watch that day. I was glad I wasn't in that seaman's shoes on that evening. The chiefs took good care of me. One stayed with me during the entire exam at the Navy clinic on base. The corpsmen x-rayed my ankle and said there was no break in the bone. Oh, no! I hoped that I would be able to explain to them where the break was, but to no avail. I asked them to call the Charleston Naval Hospital and talk to the captain there. They tried but couldn't make contact. The doctor decided to put a walking cast on my foot. They put a short cast up to the knee with another rubber pad underneath. I would still be on crutches for a while longer, but I would be able to start school with my normal class.

The next morning all of our class was called to muster. We would be given an indoctrination of the school. Being that I was the most senior in the class, the chief made me the class leader. My job was to oversee the class in cleanliness of the barracks, ensure every student was in class on time and be the liaison between the instructors and students. One other job that was my responsibility was marching the students around the school and to and from the barracks. It was the morning school was to begin, and I had all of the students in their proper uniform. I called attention, right face and forward-march; and the students did as the commands directed them. I was on crutches and could only move at a very slow pace. My students just marched off and left me! When I finally did make it to school, I told the Chief that my being class leader just wasn't going to work, so he assigned the next person with the most seniority to the task.

School was just not that easy. This school required more studying than in any school I had been to before. There was a lot to learn, such as mathematical formulas for electricity, current flow in AC and DC circuits and flight instrument operation.

Sometimes after a week of studying, we would go to Jacksonville Beach on Saturday or Sunday while on liberty. There was a boardwalk with booths set up like the ones at the fair. One of the booths was a shooting gallery that used twenty-two caliber rifles. As a reward the winner would receive a nice big teddy bear. Shooting came natural to me, so I decided to take a chance. The targets were wooden safety matches standing up or red dots on paper. Several of the men tried their luck, and one of them won a teddy bear. When it was my turn, I began shooting at the matches. I started striking the matches, it seemed. Every time I would shoot until I won enough bears for all the men with me. The men said they would take them home to their girl friends. The manager became quite concerned at the loss of his teddy bears. He was hoping that I would have a run of bad luck, but that just didn't happen. He banned us from his shooting booth. Some of the boys never made it back to the barracks with their bears as the local girls were able to separate them from the bears in short order. One sweet smile from a pretty girl, and it didn't take long for them to have a memory lapse of their previous intention.

One evening the men that I hung around with took me to a bar in downtown Jacksonville. We were having a good conversation among the ones in our group. The lights were very dim in this place; and as my eyes were becoming more adjusted, I began seeing paintings on the wall. As the paintings become clear to me, they began to resemble that of the male anatomy. I thought, "This is a strange place, and I'm glad I don't have a girlfriend with me to be embarrassed." One of the men in our group asked if he could write his name on my cast. I said, "Sure," as I had had many casts before while I was growing up. When he finished writing his name on my cast, another man was standing there and, very politely, asked how I broke my leg and would I mind if he signed his name on my cast. My friend gave him the pen and the man signed my cast. When that man finished, he dragged his hand to my crotch. I nearly fell off of the stool. I grabbed my crutch and started swinging. I was mad as a hornet, and somebody was going to answer for that invasion of my privacy. Well, all of the men in our group knew what was going to happen. They had set me up, and now they had to stop me from killing someone. They all rushed me, grabbed me, and calmed me down. The bartender ran us all out of the place and told us never to come back. What had happened was typical of military humor of pulling pranks on each other, but this prank wasn't at all funny to me. It was the first time I had been to a homosexual bar. They called it a queer bar. I have no problem with people and the private lives they live, but don't force their intentions on me nor should they force themselves on others. Only then will I learn not to hate the ones that have tried their sickening intentions on me.

I would spend my next liberty day in a way that I knew to relax. Harvey Harris, a Navy friend from Valdosta, Georgia, and I rented a small boat from the base recreation locker. We gathered up some fishing gear and put the boat in on the St. Johns River. We carried a picnic dinner and a little beer. We motored back and forth across the river trying to catch a fish. We caught a few fish and decided to ride for a while. We rode until we thought it was time to return to the base. We turned towards the base and rode for a distance and all of a sudden the motor sputtered and quit running before we reached the base. We pulled and pulled on the rope starter to no avail. We paddled for a while until we were beginning to get blisters. So I thought I would look inside the gas tank and see if there was any gas at all in the bottom. Sure enough there was a little gas that had not been sucked into the motor. I thought, "What if I poured a little beer into the tank and maybe the beer will lay on the bottom and lift the fuel to the top. Maybe then the suction will grab what fuel is left and get us the remaining distance to the base." I poured in a can of beer and began pulling on the starter rope. Sure enough, the miracle that I was hoping for happened. The motor sputtered long enough for the boat to get close to the dock, and we landed safely on shore. I won't say the brand of beer that we used, but I'll bet it would have made a good commercial.

I felt a little more confident in my schoolwork and what I was supposed to be learning. Sometimes, though, there was so much to learn that parts of the material became mush. Adding electronic components to various types of circuits became very challenging in computing current usages across each component.

I was surely glad when the training was over and I could look forward to going to a Coast Guard base. When graduation came I found out that I was able to go to my first choice of duty assignments. I really looked forward to getting to fly on a Coast Guard aircraft even though I did have a hidden fear of flying. I loved to see the ground from up above but really felt safer while I was on the ground.

Chapter Six

I had a couple of weeks' leave time. I went back to the orphanage and visited with a few of my old coaches and teachers. I visited with friends and then left for the airport in Greensboro. At the airport I saw the pretty girl Bo with whom I had had my first real date where you sit down and talk about stuff.   She was my first girlfriend that I received my first kiss from who was wearing real lipstick. She was saying goodbye to her husband on another flight and probably didn't even recognize this handsome sailor. I climbed aboard my Piedmont plane, and I was on my way to my first air rescue duty station in Elizabeth City, North Carolina. I arrived at the terminal in a Piedmont Airlines F-27 that landed right on the Coast Guard base.

Coast Guard Air Station Elizabeth City, North Carolina, patch with mascot "Rescue Rabbit."

I would be stationed at the Air Station where all of the rescue aircraft were ramped. I checked in with the duty yeoman and was sent to the barracks for my bunk assignment. There was no privacy living in the barracks in those years. What an exciting place to be working though. There was always activity happening on the aircraft-parking ramp with plane engines roaring and planes departing for takeoff on the runway. After some planes took off, other planes returned after their missions were completed. They were fueled and the discrepancies repaired. After a post flight/pre flight inspection, they were ready for the next flight. All kinds of planes that I would eventually be maintaining were on the aircraft-parking ramp. There were Grumman HU-16E Albatross seaplanes. There were HO4S helicopters with reciprocating engines that sounded much like the seaplane when the engines were cranked, backfiring and popping. We had a half dozen C-130 aircraft and a C-54/R5D. A control tower was mounted on top of our hangar #55. Our maintenance control and the various shops were located around the hangar. We had our own weathermen and radiomen. Our line control office was located on the corner of the hangar with large circular glass facing the ramp and the river. The glass was there so the line Chief could monitor the parking ramp during flight operations and monitor the seaplane ramp during water operations.

Fred
(I'll take the flight!)

Right off the bat, I thought I would enjoy my new Coast Guard career. Most of us lived in the barracks in those years. Not a very pleasant way to spend a couple of years of your life. Our bunks were lined two feet apart in a large open barracks. We had steam heat in the winter but no air conditioning in the summer. We each had one small locker to stow all of our belongings. Windows had to be opened to rid the smell generated by that many men sleeping so closely and to provide cooler air at night for

93

sleeping. The barracks had a galley, a television room reserved for the different ranks, and a recreation room with pool and table tennis tables. The Chiefs had their own quarters.

Often we would leave the barracks in our time off to seek some sort of entertainment. There were several service clubs on the base for use by the different ranks. I would go to the Enlisted Men's Club to find relaxation playing pool or listening to the jukebox. We had no women in the Coast Guard in those years. Some girls that everyone knew came from town, and they would dance or shoot pool with the Coasties. A few Navy personnel were stationed there operating a Ground Control Radar System on base. I met Don Ornsby from the Navy crew and his girlfriend Dot. Don explained to me what his team used the ground control radar for. He told me about his crew being able to guide landing aircraft safely onto the runway during inclement weather by use of the radar.

Anyhow, I met a few of the men with whom I would be working. They introduced themselves, and I felt welcomed by their friendliness. I liked the way they called each other by their nicknames. "Buda" Randolph was the first to introduce himself to me and offered to buy me a beer. He told me where he grew up nearby in Perquimans County, and I told him that I was born in the mountains and grew up in the orphanage in Winston-Salem. Another man was standing nearby, and Buda said, "Let me introduce you to my friend, 'Cotton John'." Cotton John Moss was from Texas. We talked for a while and Buda told Cotton John that I was from the mountains of North Carolina. Cotton John was all excited and wanted to know where they made good corn liquor. I told him some of my family used to make a little recipe and sell a little to make ends meet. Anyhow, they wanted to check me out to see if I was a real mountain man or a city slicker; so they bought me a few beers and decided to put me to the real test. They invited me to the parking lot, so we walked outside to a nice shiny thirty-nine Ford coupe. Cotton John opened the trunk to his car and brought out a ceramic jug and said, "Here, I want you to sample this."

He passed the jug to me, and I slung it over my shoulder in an act of confidence and took a swig. I passed it back to Cotton John, and he passed it over to Buda, and Buda took a swig. Then Cotton John took a swig. This continued for a while until the jug was getting light. We all were feeling the effects of the recipe and beginning to stammer. Out of the blue, Buda reached out with his hand and said, "My name is Buda. Pleased to know you." Cotton John reached out with his hand and said, "My name is Cotton John. That goes for me too. Now let's put this away before it's all gone." I guess they found me to be acceptable to their liking. We became friends from that day.

That experience was the beginning of many friendships I would make. Soon I met "Dooky" Dorn, "Barney" Knox "Brownie" Brown, "Piney" Ledden, "Hoss" Whitehurst, "Shaky" Helms, "Lippy" Lipscomb, "Lips" Menne, "Mac" McConnell and "Mac" McNary, "Butch" Purcell and "Butch" Hampton, and some names that weren't spoken to the person's face like "Alligator" Collins. "Pig Pen" Alexander grew up in the same neighborhood as Buda.

In those years most of the entertainment was found at the service club or in town at a carhop drive-in hamburger joint called Beefy's. Mary, Jeanie and Butterbean were the attractive, girl waitresses working for the owner, Mrs. Effie. The men liked talking to the girls. There were lots of other places that attracted the many service men: the Circle Restaurant, Tucks, the Moonlight Room, Jewel's, and P and J's Boat Club. Some of the boys wouldn't want their mothers to know they had been to some of the places; but as tradition goes for a service man away from home, many for the first time, the men just went along to have fun and follow the group.

When I started work at the hangar, I worked on the line crew learning how the flight line operated. We learned how to give directions to departing and returning aircraft. Each of the taxi signals was important so the pilots would not taxi their aircrafts into another. We learned how to fuel the different aircraft and how important putting the right fuel into the right aircraft was. Each operation was critical because we were working with a flying tank of gasoline. We also learned how to operate the firefighting truck or crash truck. We had two of the very old Oshkosh crash trucks. Everything was manually operated; even the fire suppressant foam came in five gallon buckets. In an emergency, the foam had to be siphoned from the cans into the water stream. Everyday our responsibilities became more important. Each job was intertwined with the fact that if you failed at your assignment, someone died. We were young with little experience, but we were put in situations to test our manhood. Training would be mandatory every week to assure proficiency in our tasks.

Every third day was our 24-hour duty day, but we worked the weekdays in between. We were allowed two days liberty on weekends if our duty day didn't fall on those days. We were on standby during some liberty days off. We were on alert to carry out the duty assignment that we were given by our Watch Captain. I could operate the rescue boat, so every other duty day I would be on alert for a rescue call using the forty-foot rescue boat.

Oshkosh crash and rescue vehicle.

Another duty day, I might be the duty crash truck operator or crew. While we were waiting for a rescue call, we would perform maintenance on the aircraft.

Soon I found myself working on the aircraft. At first, being hesitant to touch anything that I wasn't familiar with seemed to be the smart approach. Switches and handles were everywhere. They seemed to make something happen, so I paid careful attention to my experienced seniors. While in school, I had trained working on different aircraft that didn't function in any way. We learned how to apply external power to the different aircraft, but mainly we were learning to work on the HU-16 Albatross seaplane. We called it the "Goat." My friend Mac and I, in our learning environment, would ask the older men if we could learn to start the engines. It was a more challenging task than we expected. You could do great harm to the aircraft while just trying to crank the engine. There had to be a fire watch on the ground with a fire extinguisher. If you set the mixture improperly, then you could blow an exhaust stack or a jug (piston housing) as you went through the meticulous priorities in starting the engine. I practiced starting the engines with close supervision from my seniors. I tried over and over to start the engines without getting a backfire; and, finally, I became proficient enough to crank the engines on my own. Eventually we learned to prepare our plane for flight. We learned the different items to inspect and how to check for their proper operation. When we completed our preflight, all locking pins and ground safety devices were removed.

HU-16E Albatross "Goat"
(Courtesy of ADC Butch Purcell, retired)

All that was needed was a crew. The Coast Guard always worked on a limited budget. Our support equipment was very old, and not enough money was in the budget to allow flight or hazardous duty pay to all of the flight crewmen. If we wanted to learn to be rescue flight crewmen, we would have to volunteer to fly without hazardous duty flight pay. We all volunteered, as we wanted to be air crewmen. Once in a while we would get a half amount of monthly flight pay, and that was a big deal.

When we began training, I was a little apprehensive about the plane staying in the air. We did a lot of bouncing on the runway as the pilots practiced improving their landing skills. A lot of times the pilots would shut down one engine and practice flying with only the other engine. It sounded as if the old seaplane was just barely able to stay in the air. Thankfully, the plane had enough power to stay airborne, as the airspeed was high enough before the pilot shut down one engine.

Grumman HU-16E Albatross on takeoff.

On one actual engine shutdown emergency, we were several hours off the Carolina coast. We were in bad weather, and the pilots were having a difficult time controlling the plane with just one engine operating. As we started in towards the coast, our propeller low oil warning light on the only operating engine came on. We used the replenishing oil from the engine to re-service the propeller. Here we were just hoping the good engine would get us home, and this other emergency had to happen on the only good engine! We constantly pushed the replenishment button each time the propeller needed oil. Thankfully, we were able to use enough oil from the engine reservoir before our only good engine quit. Three hours later we were on the ground. Thank God for all of the training hours. Each emergency would eventually seem routine as we practiced them often. However, some emergencies would not be in the flight manual; and our crew would rely on quick thinking, ingenuity, and a blessing from above. We would practice landing in the water, rescuing seamen, and tying up to buoys. We also practiced jet-assisted takeoffs. Rocket bottles were strapped to the side of the aircraft, and these were used to give us extra power when we were in a critical takeoff situation. I loved my duty even with the long and many times hard-working hours. After operating in the water, the aircraft had to be washed to help prevent corrosion caused by the high salt concentrations.

Sometimes I would operate the boat at night laying out the sea-lane lights for the seaplane to practice making night landings. The work was always dangerous for the boat crew and especially the flight crew, but constant training made the task safer.

Some nights a helicopter would make night hoists from our boat. We always asked for a volunteer to be the practice victim; and if we didn't get one, we volunteered the lowest ranking man to be the person hoisted up into the helicopter. The seaman on the boat had to know how to handle the basket or harness being lowered to the boat. Carroll Hill was the rescue seaman on my boat crew, and I was glad to have him. He helped operate the boat, knew how to navigate and especially knew how to help with night operations. The helicopter's rotor blades would build up a huge amount of static electricity. Sometimes there was enough electricity to knock a man to his knees while he was retrieving the rescue basket.

I went out on many calls in the boat when fishermen or recreational boaters did not return home when they were expected. One rescue call came when four teens had stopped at the local Causeway Marina and asked the owner, Floyd Owens, how to start their dad's boat. Floyd called the Coast Guard Base and told me that the teens, two boys and two girls, wanted to tour the Albemarle Sound. Every local mariner knows how dangerous the Albemarle Sound can become since many professional mariners and others sailing pleasure craft have lost their lives to its treachery. Floyd said that he advised them not to go into the sound, but they had their minds made up. Floyd showed them how to start their dad's boat motor. He gave us a description of the boat, as they had not returned at nightfall. Right away I knew it was an urgent matter. The teens were in an open skiff and out there somewhere in the dark of night with the cold weather turning for the worse. We launched the forty-foot rescue boat at about 2000 hours and headed towards the sound. We zigg-zagged from one side of the river to the other on our way out towards the mouth of the river. We used our searchlight to comb the shoreline. Carroll shouted on the bullhorn when we stopped the engines in hopes of getting a reply or signal from the teens. The weather was worsening, and the search became more difficult. We searched and searched and didn't see any boat on the water. Cdr. J. V. A. Thompson was the OIC (officer in charge) that night, and we were relaying our position and results back to him. Finally, he gave us orders to return to the base. As we turned to head towards the base, Carroll caught a glimpse of light coming from the Camden Point shoreline on the other side of the river near the Albemarle Sound. At the time, land was being cleared in that area and there were several piles of stumps burning. As I looked in that direction, I could see what Carroll had found. The light was there for a minute or two, and then the light would go out. I called in to the base and gave my intentions to take the boat closer to shore. The night air was turning colder for the victims, and we would be going into an area heavily laden with stumps several hundred feet offshore. I maneuvered the boat as close as I could to try to identify the light. I recommended support from one of our helicopters to identify the target before we continued in towards shore for the rescue. The Commander thought that with the marginal risk of launching a helicopter in the prevailing weather conditions and the target being unidentifiable, we should wait for first light that was only a few hours from then. If the target was for sure the teens, then it looked as though they were in the swamp. At least they were ashore and not in the deeper water. We returned to base after marking their suspected position on the navigation chart. We tried getting the sheriff to go by land and check out the target, but the area was inaccessible by land. At first light, the rescue aircrew launched our helicopter and found the teens in the exact location we thought.

After all of them, nearing hypothermia, were air lifted to safety and transported to the Albemarle Hospital, they gave the details of their traumatic adventure and swore never to do such a stupid thing again as they had nearly lost their lives. The light we saw was the teens trying to send a signal by pouring gas onto a seat cushion and setting it on fire. They had gas but couldn't start their boat motor. By an unfortunate coincidence, the burning stumps from the land clearing resulted in the teens not being rescued until morning.

These teens were lucky not to have made it to the sound. I can attest to the violence of the Albemarle Sound when its waters are in their furry. Boats twenty to thirty feet have met their fate on the sound. Our forty-foot boat had been tested in the rages of the sound. The crew clothing we wore in those years was not nearly the protective clothing personnel wear today to protect themselves from hypothermia. Mostly regular work clothing was worn with a foul weather jacket.

On another night, Carroll and the rest of the crew had to seek shelter inside the cabin and hold on because of the fierce waters caused by the strong nor'easter winds. At one position the keel of the boat was impacting the bottom, and the choppy waves were coming over the bow as I eased my boat back into deeper water before I damaged the boat's screw and rudder. I got a big adrenalin rush that night, and it wouldn't be my last.

At different times we found mariners in the swamp, in deep water, walking the shore in an isolated area, hanging to the bottom of their boats, or hanging on to buoys. My fellow Coasties found one sitting at a bar while we had searched for him all day. It was never a good feeling not to find a mariner or pilot or to find one that didn't make it.

Floyd, the owner of Causeway Marina had sold me a twelve foot mahogany Barber Skipper boat. The boat had a twenty-five horsepower Johnson engine and was fast on the water. When the throttle was pushed fast towards full throttle, the bow of the boat would go up into the air and the boat would nearly be riding on its propeller. Once in a while I would take the boat out at chow time just to run it for a while. Once Captain Brinkmeyer wanted to know who that person was in the boat that was doing all of those reckless stunts. Someone told him that it was Tanner, his rescue boat coxswain, just giving his boat a workout on his chow break.

One morning after a bad storm, I found my boat had sunk during the night. I asked for some help from the rest of the boat dock crew, and we pulled my boat out of the water. We took the engine off and pulled the spark plug. We blew compressed air in the engine and on the electrical components. We reinstalled the plug and cranked the motor right up. What luck! I did not have to buy a new motor. I have found boat motors to be pretty rugged pieces of equipment if properly cared for.

I finally found an automobile to drive, as I had not brought one with me when I reported to the base. My friend Mac sold me a station wagon that had been driven in Salem, Massachusetts, for some years by another Coastie. The car ran great but had some metal termite damage caused by the salty roads in the North Country. I liked the way it drove, so I decided to fix the car up. Mac said that he would help me get the car in tip-top shape. First, we had to find a way to keep my feet from dragging the road as I drove. Mac said, "Look over there at that plywood." Many sheets of plywood were leaning against a wall where he was pointing in the shop where we had backed the car. I thought, "Now, that will work for a floor in the wagon." The plywood was three quarters of an inch thick. We grabbed a sheet of the plywood and started cutting a piece to fit over the large hole that was rusted out of my floorboard. I placed the wood in the floorboard and used screws to secure it to the floor. I did the same to the other side. Worked great. I found a pair of black leather bucket seats for the front of the car. Things were really coming together in the rebuilding of my new transportation, so I decided I would ride to town to show off my "new", old, green station wagon. I drove to Beefy's, where a lot of my friends were. I ordered a hamburger and hoped the girls would rave about my new wheels and the black leather bucket seats. The seats were not bolted down to the floor yet, but the seats would sit in the upright position so no one would know the difference. The girls never noticed my new wheels. I looked around and saw that my wheels were the oldest in the parking lot. Old station wagons were really not a hot car to impress someone. So much for trying to impress someone-- anyone! I thought, as I left the parking lot, that I would put my foot on the gas pedal a little hard to maybe impress someone. As I squealed the wheels with only my fingers steering the car, my seat rolled over backwards and no one was driving my car. The car didn't stop! It was heading towards the Pepsi-Cola building across the street. I scrambled to get to the brake just in time to avoid hitting the building. Wow, I needed to bolt my seats to the floorboard. I drove back to the base and told Mac about my nearly crashing the station wagon. Mac called my wagon the "Buckboard." From that time on, everyone called it Buckboard. Mac was a real friend to me and would remain my friend for life. He was a friend to a lot of people. Mac would become a big volunteer in the Shriners and worked many years helping hospitalized children around the country.

When I had finished my duty and had more time off, I would drive Buckboard all the way to Boone and Winston-Salem. My orphan brothers had introduced me to Nancy, a very pretty girl from Charlotte, North Carolina, who attended Appalachian State University. I began driving there every opportunity that I had. With duty every third day and getting more qualified on the aircraft, it seemed that my time became more limited. We were only allowed to travel so far from the base without a special pass at that time. Often I would break the rules to go and visit with Nancy. As I tried to make my trips, I found myself pushing the limits, driving in all kinds of weather with less and less time off to make my trips. She had the opportunity of a college career; I had my military commitment. I didn't make enough money to have a family, so I finally gave up and stayed near the base on my time off. Regrettably, I gave up a very good friend that I cared about. Lack of money and seventy to eighty hours of duty a week finally took its toll on another relationship. I stopped traveling out of bounds to visit with my friend Nancy.

The more we became qualified on the aircraft, the more we were expected to fly. We would fly on training flights several times a week, and many times rescue flights occurred during the night or other times.

I liked flying in the old slow-flying Goat. The views from low altitude over the land and the ocean were unbelievable. If we were looking for a downed pilot or a mariner in the water, the seaplane seemed to go slowly enough to really get a good look. The plane was very noisy, and you needed to wear earplugs along with your headset to be comfortable. In the wintertime we would wear as many clothes under our flight suit as would fit. The heater often became inoperative, and the temperature would drop rapidly below freezing, especially in the wintertime. We were used to trouble shooting the heater problems when the plane would return from its flight. While in flight we would take any measure possible to get that heater back in operation. We took all precautions before we rigged the wiring system to fool the heater into ignition. The heater operated off the gasoline from the main tanks so there was always a chance of an explosion on ignition. We would place a jumper wire between pins G and H in the ignition circuit and energize the start circuit. We then would stand by for a "Boom." If the "Boom" weren't too loud and there were no signs of fire outside the heater, then we knew we were going to have heat for the rest of our flight or until the heater decided to give up again. I learned a lot from many older Coasties about flight operations in the seaplane.

Some days we would do our training while landing in the water. The pilots practiced their skills of landing and takeoffs. We would practice our rescue procedures and practice tying the seaplane to a buoy. We would open the forward hatch and use a boat hook to grab the tie up point on the buoy. On special air show days we would place Jet Assist Bottles on our crew doors. We would demonstrate to the crowd of visitors how the Jet Assisted Take Off system (JATO) helped propel the plane from the water on takeoff. Instead of landing on the runway, we would taxi the plane from the water up a ramp to the parking ramp.

One day Charlie "Piney" Ledden and I were installing a new Auxiliary Power Unit into the only HU-16 Albatross remaining on the ramp. We heard the rescue alarm go off and the message announced, "Launch the ready HU-16. Navy pilot down." We had just taken out the old APU and set the new APU in the holding frame. The crew came running out to the plane and said, "We have to take off immediately!" We told the pilot that he could crank the engines using the battery instead of the APU. The plane was started, and we were able to install a couple of bolts to secure the APU during take off. We strapped in for take off; and when the after takeoff safety checks were complete, we then continued with the installation in flight. The crew searched for a while looking in the swamp for the downed pilot. We were busy making all of the connections and getting the APU ready to fire off. All of a sudden Charlie looked through a small porthole in the APU compartment and said, "Isn't that a person I see in the swamp?" I looked; and, sure enough, there stood the Navy pilot waving his hand to us. Charlie called on the headset and let the pilot know what direction to fly. Within minutes after our pilot notified the helicopter, we watched the pilot being lifted from the swamp in a rescue harness and brought aboard the rescue helicopter. We continued working; and before we landed, we had that new APU running and on the line for landing. Continuing repair work while performing an in-flight rescue was not a normal operating procedure, but in the Coast Guard we just made things happen.

Always humor was around our crews. On special occasions our air station would invite the community out to look at the aircraft on display and give a flight demonstration of our ability to rescue people from the water. People were climbing into the old seaplane, sitting in the pilots' seats, and asking questions about different parts of the airplane. This one lady wanted to know what was behind that cabin door located in the rear of the plane. The crewman said that that was a head and also where some of our electronic equipment was located. The crewman opened the hatch and let the lady look inside. He explained that a head is a Coast Guard and Navy term used for a restroom. A honey bucket was in there, and a urinal tube was mounted on the wall. The lady wasn't satisfied with all the answers, so she continued to question the crewman. The lady asked if she could go inside the head; and the crewman said, "Sure." The lady lifted the lid to the honey bucket and then asked the crewman, "What is this thing hanging on the wall?" The crewman had a little mischievous humor; and he said, "You blow into it and talk through it, like on a ship, and you can talk to the pilot in the front of the plane." Well, the lady grabbed the urinal tube from the bulkhead and began talking to the pilot. Before the crewman could tell her he was only kidding, the lady was already trying to talk to the pilot. She was saying "Hello, pilot. Hello pilot. This is Lilly speaking." She then said, "Damn, this thing stinks." The crewman didn't have the nerve to tell the woman what she had been talking into and had a rough time holding in the laughter.

When we were not flying, we were learning how to put together propellers and test their operation. We learned more and more how to keep the engines running properly. We were taught how to troubleshoot and repair the aircraft after each flight. We were taught how to deep cycle and overhaul nickel cadmium batteries. We were taught how to analyze and repair electronic circuit boards. We would crawl inside the wing fuel tanks on the C130 aircraft to repair the fuel pumps and the fuel quantity indication circuitry.

In those years when our crew worked inside the wing fuel tanks, not much effort was put into personal health safety. We repaired/replaced fuel pumps and rewired the insides of the fuel tanks. The metal smiths were busy repairing any fuel leaks from inside the tanks. We drained the tank of fuel, all but what puddles were left in the low areas after we POGOed the drains. POGO drains were located on the bottom of the wings to take fuel samples to check for water contamination. We had a blower sitting on the hangar deck pushing air up into the tank through a large flexible duct. We took turns being the safetyman, sitting just outside of the tank's hatch. When one man crawled into the wing tank and worked for a period of time, he would come out of the tank and have to lie down on the wing. The safetyman would see that he didn't fall off. It would take some time for the man to sober up from the effects of the JP4 jet fuel. We never wore a breathing mask in those days. The fuel contained Benzene, a carcinogen. Lying in the fuel residue reddened our crotches and armpits many times. We paid a price for shortcuts in safety in an effort to hurry and get the planes back in the air.

The oil that we used in the turbine engines was also dangerous for human contact. The C-130 air conditioning and pressurization system used air from the engine's compressor for its operation. The engine compressor seals would wear, and the seals would leak the oil fumes into the air conditioning system for all crew and passengers to breathe. That oil use was finally outlawed by all services when environmental concerns became more important to military flyers.

Thank God, in later years we had a better sense of personal safety and required each man to wear safety equipment. But those in my generation were not so lucky.

Nearly all men in my rate that worked in our environment would end up with cancer. Too late for us, but not for the men and women today if they are smart enough to pay attention to our misfortune. Unsafe environmental operations have put many a serviceman in an early grave; but the impact on their lives would save future generations, aware of their misfortune, but only if they dared to care about their own health.

Chapter Seven

Eventually we would become qualified to fly on the C-130B model aircraft. We began flying longer and longer missions. We would fly to Europe, Africa, South America, Alaska, Southeast Asia and above the Arctic Circle. We would regularly fly to Bermuda in support of the U.S.C.G. Air Detachment located on the US Air Force or Navy Air Station. We would routinely be called to search the ocean for downed pilots or mariners in distress. Sometimes we would fly missions in support of fisheries, environmental or national security. Sometimes we wouldn't know how long our mission would last.

Our experiences in what we learned at home in the care of our aircraft, being able to repair the plane and getting it back into the air, would greatly improve the chances of a victim being able to survive if caught at sea in nature's furry. Sometimes we operated our aircraft in other than comfortable or normal conditions. In Honduras, we only could get aviation gasoline instead of jet fuel. The gasoline still powered the engines; but it was more hazardous to use, especially while fueling over the wing, on starting the engines and when take off power was applied. Any leaks could easily become a bomb at the slightest static spark or hot surface. The aircraft engine's fuel control system allowed for the use of the aviation gasoline.

The Coast Guard decided to decommission several of our air stations around the world. Argentia Air Station in Newfoundland would be one of the first to be closed. Later, over time, Naples Air Station in Italy, Sangley Point Air station in the Philippines, Annette Island Air Station in Alaska and Bermuda Air Station would phase out operations and combine planes and crews with other air stations. The host countries would take over their own operations or with U.S. Coast Guard support. Our mission in Elizabeth City would widen to cover some additional responsibilities. We would take over the International Ice Patrol in Newfoundland. We would cover the Bermuda area of search and rescue. We would provide support to the Mediterranean Coast Guard LORAN Stations and other missions in that area.

Most of the Argentia, Newfoundland, Air Station crews and aircraft came to our station in Elizabeth City in 1966. We began making thirty-day patrols during iceberg season. We would fly to Argentia and operate from the Navy field. Our job was to locate icebergs nearing or entering the North American shipping lanes and then to notify all maritime vessels of the iceberg location. A lot of the time we worked on icy ramps and runways.

HU-16E Albatross helping out in the southern fringes of "Ice Berg Alley."

On our pre-season patrol, we would fly to the far north to Goose Bay, Labrador; to Keflavik, Iceland; to Sonderstrom and Thule, Greenland and beyond the Arctic Circle in an effort to estimate how much ice may be coming our way when the glaciers calve their large bergs. The temperature could be anywhere from minus 40 to minus 60 degrees. Working in that cold could quickly become deadly to a person not fully aware of the dangers. Aircraft operations would become more difficult and more dangerous.

After the Coast Guard closed the Argentia Air Detachment in 1966, my friend Mac was on the first crew to begin ice patrol operations from Elizabeth City, North Carolina. Chief Horner had been stationed in Argentia, Newfoundland, so he led the crew on the first operation. Mac had just gotten there when he had a family emergency.

Orvil "Mac" McNary
"Shriner"
"American Patriot"
"Friend"

Chief Stickney called me and said "Pack your bags for thirty days for cold weather operations. You will be relieving Mac on ice patrol." Another C-130 from our station flew me to Argentia to carry parts and relieve Mac of his duty so he could come home. It would be my first look at icebergs. Many were the size of several city blocks and hundreds of feet in the air. That was only one eighth of the true size of the berg as that is how much sticks out of the water. We could have landed our big C-130 on the tops of the bergs.

When we were finished with our duties for the day, we would walk to the ship's refueling pier and fish for cod from the pier. In the sixties the cod were plentiful, and we would have a lot of fun catching them. Stew, our Chief, thought we should take the fish to the civilian and military galleys. We caught enough fish to feed the entire base. We were carrying fish to the galleys in banana boxes. It was my first time eating codfish, and I found them very tasty.

The Navy had a nice woodworking hobby shop that they offered to us to use. We would be there for thirty days, and we were not allowed to leave the base for a trip to St. Johns or to other places in the area. We would visit the Navy club for entertainment, and a lot of times we were invited to join the U.S. Marines at their club called the Blue Room. I really don't think that I would want to be stationed there in Argentia for any length of time and not allowed to leave the base. It was cold, and the wind blew hard all night long. While trying to sleep at night, you could hear the shrill of the wind as the cold Arctic wind leaked through the windows and doors.

At night the fire watch would make his rounds through the barracks. Each round he would shine his flashlight at our racks to see that we were not on fire. We lived in a big open, fireproof dormitory. Did you know that before we left, that fire watch slipped on a piece of ice while shining that light into someone's face at 0400 in the morning? The next fire watch never switched his flashlight on while in the barracks.

The ramps outside the hangar were so icy that we started our inboard engines inside the hangar and taxied the aircraft out of the hangar. A tow tractor (mule) would slide on the ice, and that made it more hazardous while trying to pull the plane out of the hangar. The B-Model C-130 empty of fuel weighed around 75 thousand pounds, and we were able to carry a little over 40,000 lbs of fuel in its wing tanks. On one operation there, the pilot applied too much power while leaving the hangar; and the sprinkler system was energized from the heat of the engine turbine exhaust. Everything was soaked. Our friendship with the Navy men working in the hangar was tested to the limits.

Flying in and out of this base also tested the pilots' skills as the approach was over the top of a mountain, always in limited weather conditions. Flying this approach was extremely unforgivable. Weather often was a factor in keeping our plane grounded.

Typical iceberg several hundred feet out
of water; 7/8 total size hidden under water.

When our deployment time of chasing icebergs was over,
another plane and crew came in to relieve us. This
continued until mid summer or until the threat of large
icebergs in the shipping lanes became less dangerous.
The Coast Guard along with our Canadian friends has
protected the shipping lanes in the North Atlantic since
the Titanic sank from iceberg damage in 1913. Not a
single ship has been lost due to collision of an iceberg
because of our joint efforts.

At times within a few days after returning to home base,
one might find himself on his way to the tropical zone.
You may end up in Panama, Guantanamo Bay, Cuba, or
in the Bahamas. It was exciting to me. I felt honored to
get to help people, rescue people, stop terrorist and illegal
aliens and protect our country from drug smuggling.

Sometimes after duty I would find myself in the company
of young ladies from the surrounding area. Many people
from town would join the celebration being held on base
on New Year's Eve. We did not have a U.S.O. site in our
town, so the chances of ever meeting a girl were limited to
church, bumping into on the street or what activities were
available on base. I finally met a girl; and once in a while

we would go to a dance or drive to Norfolk, Virginia, and have dinner at one of the military bases.

Flight experiences were becoming more interesting and fun as we were called on for different missions. Our long hours of flying on security and rescue patrols brought out not only our loyalty to duty but humor from some of the crew. That humor helped keep up our morale. Some of the humor, since men made up all the crew, was for men's ears only. Other times the humor was funny and should have been put in the comics. We made fun of each other and called each other whatever name fit at the time. Different nationalities were given different names, as were different physical characteristics. That was part of our humor. That nicknaming had been part of military tradition for as long as there had been an American military. It's also a part of most societies.

Occasionally, I would fly with Lt. Barker in the Albatross. Everyone liked him because he treated us with friendliness and a smile when we flew with him. Even with his friendliness, he adhered to strict flight safety operations and looked after his flight crew. He was also my Officer in Charge of the rescue boat operations when I ran the forty-foot patrol/rescue boat. Humorous stories were told about Lt. Barker throughout his career and are still being told today by a few of us airmen that remember those days of flying. R5D/C54 Plane captain Hoss Whitehurst told one story of Lt. Barker that happened while they were on a LORAN Calibration flight from Elizabeth City, North Carolina, to islands in the Pacific Ocean. Lt. Barker was an ensign just out of flight school when he was called upon to join the flight crew for this distant flight. The flight crew departed Hawaii on their way to Midway Island. Unfamiliar with the effects of draft on the aircraft while in flight, Lt. Barker opened the copilot's cockpit window. "Swoosh", out the window went all of his flight notes and papers. His Radio/Electronics mentor, Charlie Hardison, helped reestablish a backup flight plan information packet. Lt. Barker said Charlie looked after and guided him in his first days of aviation.

Humor continued as flight crews told their stories of flying with Lt. Barker.

Later photo of now Captain Barker

On one flight Lt. Barker was forced to perform an emergency shutdown of an engine for a mechanical failure. As he stuck his head out the window to visualize the engine, off flew his headset. The crew became hysterical as he pulled his head back inside. He initially seemed surprised and then, with his gentle way, grinned from ear to ear and laughed along with the crew. Lt. Barker flew many different aircraft while in the Coast Guard. He flew the C54/R5D, HH-52, HU-16 and was a training instructor with the Navy during the Vietnam War. Lt. Barker touched a lot of lives with his easy-going demeanor. He would again be assigned to the Elizabeth City Air Station as commanding officer before his career ended in retirement. He was also heavily involved with volunteering in the local community and influenced me.

A lot of great pilots were at our station. One pilot was Master Chief John Greathouse who had flown as an enlisted man during World War II. He was one of the last APs (enlisted rating of Aviation Pilot) still flying. All of the younger pilots respected his knowledge and most learned how to fly the Albatross under his direction. He was like a father or grandfather to them. He always liked his cigar between his teeth when he was flying. All aviators in the Coast Guard knew of this man, and many had been taught to fly the seaplane under his guidance. During the war, Master Chief Greathouse had been assigned to transfer a helicopter from a Philadelphia Navy base. The parachute rigger at the base told him and the other pilot that it was Navy rules that they would have to carry parachutes on their flight. Master Chief said that he didn't want a parachute as they could auto-rotate to the ground if they had a mechanical problem. The Navy Base told Master Chief Greathouse that he would not be flying if he did not put the parachutes on the aircraft. He finally agreed to carry the parachutes and took off on their flight. A very short time after take-off and after reaching their desired altitude, his helicopter had a major malfunction; and they could not control the craft. They were forced to bail out! The first time he had ever carried parachutes on a helicopter and had been forced to do so then, the parachutes saved him and his crew's lives.

A few crews were trained and always ready to go on specialized missions. We had one remaining C-54/R5D that was used for the LORAN Calibration Flights. We had a few aircrews remaining that were qualified to fly and operate the equipment on the #9147 plane. Hoss Whitehurst was the head flight mechanic and his assistant was Cotton John Moss.

These two individuals created humor whether they were flying or on the hangar deck preparing their aircraft for flight. They were as country as country gets.

Hoss was always saying, "Let me bum a smoke 'til payday." Even in the presence of ladies of questionable character, he would ask to bum a favor until payday. He knew everything about the old airplane. He would say to us young Coasties, "I'm an R-5D plane captain, want to buy me a beer?" Sometimes he would say, "Let me bum five 'til payday. I got something going with Mary Lou." Just for humor, every time Mary Lou walked into the club, Hoss would put two bar stools together for her to sit on. Hoss would say, "Come on, Mary Lou, you can sit beside me." Mary Lou was quite a large-sized female. She didn't mind the attention and always took it in stride, sometimes with an "Aw, Hoss, you crazy nut;" but always she enjoyed getting to sit near her friend at the bar. Hoss and Cotton John were known in the Coast Guard aviation circle for their humor and distinct southern character.

Another special crew flew the #339, #1340 or #1345 C-130 as the Commandant's Crew. Commander Bates, Lieutenant Commanders David "Boz" Bosomworth and "Hammering Hank" Wilson were the pilots. Later Lt. Steve Carrier would join the pilots' duties as he had flown as navigator on other missions. Chief T.V Linkous was the first and then Chief Grable (Willie) Sutton was the head flight engineer/plane captain. Pete Jones and Bill Raynor were on the crew. Don Parks and Roger Schmidt were the radio operators. Eventually James Matthews, "Hoot" Gibson, Dick Wells, Fred Honeycutt, Bill Provost and Odell Moore would take over the crew duties. When the Coast Guard bought the commandant a special aircraft, the mission to transport him was moved to Headquarters in Arlington, Virginia.

A day or so before each flight, a dozen of us would hand polish the aircraft to make it VIP presentable. We slid a special VIP pod into the aircraft from the cargo ramp and door at the rear of the aircraft. The inside of the aircraft was detailed to look as good as possible. Supplies were loaded depending on the length of the planned trip. The crewmembers would prepare for their trip by ensuring their uniforms were immaculate and that they packed their nicest clothing. They would fly the commandant around the world to meet with dignitaries. The Coast Guard had many outlying navigation stations located in countries throughout the world. Maintaining a good diplomatic relationship with foreign countries was important to the success of our worldwide navigation system. Many treaties enforced by the US Coast Guard were of great interest to the United States.

One day we prepared C-130 #1345 aircraft to leave for Viet Nam. Along with the Navy, we already had a large presence of watercraft in the harbors and along the coast and gunboats patrolling the deltas and up the rivers. Bill Pittsenbarger, Ray Morrow, Dick Trevele, John Moe, Rick Savage, Lt. Tom Brougham, Lcdr. Mat Ahearn, Ltjg. Clark McKean and Chief Pete Davis made up the flight crew.

Elizabeth City flight crew; 42 Missions flown in Viet Nam.

The crew had orders to assist in support operations for several months. When other military services found out that the plane would be available, they asked the crew to assist in all kinds of missions. They would carry heavy equipment to inland sites and deliver supplies where they were needed. Our planes are bright in color, so there wasn't much camouflage to hide from the enemy. At that time the C-130 was white with international orange stripes. The crew did its job well, and all returned safely to home base. Before they left for home, they had completed forty-two missions inside Viet Nam.

The C-130 aircraft #1345 had made a previous run into Viet Nam in July of 1965 carrying Admiral Edwin J. Roland, Commandant, and Mr. Craig C. Reed, Assistant Secretary of Treasury. Their mission was to evaluate firsthand the Coast Guard operations in Viet Nam and welcome the first of the Coast Guard coastal defense cutters to Viet Nam. The Coast Guard's Squadron One would operate eight of its WPB cutters out of Da Nang. They would continue to work in support of coastal defense with the U.S. Navy throughout the rest of the war. Some Coast Guard operations were in team with the Navy in its river patrol operations. My friend Roger Schmidt was the radioman on this flight; and, thankfully, he saved his flight log and notes on this mission for all of these years.

Many Coast Guard C-130 flights to Viet Nam would continue throughout the war. Nearly all-future flights to Viet Nam were launched from our Barber's Point Air Station in Hawaii.

One early morning just after midnight, our alarm went off. The operations center told everyone to quickly go to the galley and get something to eat. They were expecting us to be gone for a very long day to look for a troubled boat that was assumed to be a long way out to sea. Extra crews were called in from home. We all had something to eat while the cooks prepared flight lunches. Lots of coffee was put aboard the aircraft as the fuel tanks were topped off. Three aircraft were launched long before dawn. One after the other took off into the darkness over the river, across the sound and outer banks. Within minutes the three planes were over the ocean on their way towards the middle of the Atlantic. After a couple of hours, the radioman received a message that said, "All aircraft return to base." We thought that maybe the mariners whom we were going to try and help had been found. So our radioman called the rescue center and asked why we were returning to base. The Officer in Charge, back at the base asked the radioman if anyone on the plane was sick or felt nauseated. The radioman asked each of us how we felt, and we all replied that we felt fine. The Officer in Charge then told the radioman that all of the crewmen who ate eggs that morning had had their eggs cooked in metal polish. When we heard of what had happened, there seemed to be some apprehension among some of us. The Officer in Charge said that there was a possibility that we all could have a serious case of diarrhea in the very near future. After the medical officer was notified, he ordered all crews to return to the base for immediate medical attention. In a hurry to get breakfast for the flight crews, the cook had picked up a gallon can of metal polish instead of cooking oil. The cans were identical because most liquids in the military came in the standard issue, silver gallon can. After that incident, our cook was given a nickname "Ptomaine" to fit the occasion. From making that one mistake, he has never shed the nickname. For anything they could relate to you, the crew gave you a nickname. It really didn't matter if you liked the name. We all survived the ordeal with little consequences. As we returned to base other crews launched and finished the mission.

My first nickname was "Country." When I worked on the line crew, one of our responsibilities was to clean the hangar deck to prepare for inspections. Only two of us were available one afternoon to scrub the hangar deck. Chief Grable "Willie" Sutton and Chief Howard "Spanky" Sawyer were in charge of the hangar. They both were there to let us know how clean they expected the hangar deck to be when we finished scrubbing it.

The other man said, "You mean that you want the two of us to scrub this entire hangar deck by ourselves?" Chief Sutton looked the man in the eye and said, "Well, (pause) yes."

I turned to the other man and said, "Come on, this hangar ain't no bigger than our cow barn!" referring to the big cow barns I helped clean at the orphanage where I grew up. The chiefs thought what I had said to the other boy was humorous, and they started laughing. So we quickly moved everything out of the hangar and swept the deck really good. We found several cans of scouring powder and some scrub brushes. We brought the aircraft wash hose, an old fire hose, into the hangar and blasted the deck to wash free any loose debris. We then spread the scouring powder all over and started scrubbing. Mainly we concentrated on the oily spots that were left from the aircraft engines leaking. We scrubbed that deck until it looked almost new. We rinsed the soap from the deck and used our squeegees to push the excess water to the drains. It didn't take long before the deck was dry enough to walk on. I would imagine the other man was amazed at what two people could do. After that hangar cleaning, Chief Sutton and Chief Sawyer started calling me Country.

Before my career would be over, there would be many more nicknames that the crew decided to call me. Some names would be in retaliation for demanding that they do a good enough job to keep themselves, their rescued victims, and me alive. But as long as we were alive, I could live with the harassment even though some of them didn't earn the honor to harass me; and I would often feel like giving them a hand-full of knuckles in the ole kisser.

When I was flying as crewman on the C-130, Buda Randolph was the flight engineer in my duty section. We would get called out in the middle of the night and sent to places all over the country and beyond. For three duty nights in a row we were sent out of the country. One morning after finishing our search, we landed in Panama. The next duty night we landed in Halifax, Nova Scotia. The next duty night we landed in Guantanamo Bay "Gitmo," Cuba. Our duty rotation was every third day, and during the week we worked those days between our duty days. Some duty days we had just landed the day before from a search that started the previous duty day. In my early years in the Coast Guard, we averaged anywhere from seventy to eighty hours a week of work and flying. We were tired at times; but when we accomplished a mission, something about it made us feel proud. One night we landed at Ramey Air Force Base, Puerto Rico, an active B-52 bomber base. We had been flying all day on a search and rescue mission and had just landed before midnight, New Year's Eve. We were sweaty and in our dirty flight suits, but we were also hungry so we stopped by the NCO Club to grab a bite to eat. We ordered a sandwich with a cool one, and we were looking forward to falling into a bunk somewhere to get some rest. Some of the Air Force men asked us where we came from and what our mission was about. We told them, "North Carolina," and that we had been searching points south for a sinking boat. Before we could leave to get some rest, the word had gotten to the ballroom of our being there and what we were doing. The Air Force base was having a New Year's Eve Party. Several of the couples came to us and asked us to join them. We declined the offer at first because we were in our flight suits and really dirty and tired. Well, their kind persistence won us over, and we walked to the ballroom with them. We were welcomed with open arms. They wouldn't let us buy our refreshments. The ladies grabbed us and before we knew it we were in the middle of the dance floor. We couldn't sit down before another lady would grab us to dance with her. I told one lady that I felt embarrassed by our nasty appearance; and she said, "Nothing is better than to be dancing with a military man still in his uniform, dirty or not, especially when it's soiled from duty." I was glad to hit the sack that night as our day would begin at daylight and not end until 0-Dark-30, the next night. (Sometime in the late evening)

The Air Force always treated us well. We were trained by Air Force Flight Crews to fly the different positions in the C-130 Aircraft. Our pilots and flight engineers not only learned to fly the plane from Air Force crews, we also went through annual recurrent training in their flight simulators. Their maintenance personnel trained many of us. All around the world, the Air Force would provide us with assistance in order for us to complete our missions. Sometimes we would blow a tire on landing or damage a propeller on takeoff at some remote location, and Air Force crews would find a replacement for us. They would loan us an engine or propeller until we could ship the items back to them at their nearest base.

From time to time we would travel to Langley Air Force Base in Virginia. The Air Force team at the pressure chamber would train us in the proper use of oxygen equipment and test us in their chamber to see that we could withstand the effects of high altitude flying and find out if we could manage rapid decompression. They let us feel the physiological effects of oxygen deprivation to get us prepared for the real possibility while flying on our missions. This training would be required every couple of years years. If we were stationed on the west coast, we would travel to McCord Air Force Base in Seattle, Washington, and attend their flight simulator training.

When I first started performing maintenance on the C-130, we had no hangar for work. We would work on the engines and other parts of the aircraft in any weather conditions present at the time. When a rainstorm would come, we would hurry and put the cowling back on the engines and close all the hatches. When the storm would pass, we would begin work all over again. Finally the Aircraft Repair and Supply Base let us use one end of their number two overhaul hangar to perform our periodic maintenance checks. This was the beginning of what we called the Hangar Two check crew. Chief T. V. Linkous was the first in charge. Chief "Alligator" "Rip" Collins, Chief "Dick" Karl and Chief "Shaky" Helms were the first I worked for. Their nicknames fit their characteristics perfectly but we wouldn't dare call the Chief "Alligator" to his face. Chief Collins didn't tell you to get the aircraft repaired "right and right now" but one time. He would gruff up his face and growl and that was enough to scare you out of your wits. Chief "Shaky" had a jitter about him some of the time. I believe Chief "Shaky" had the shakes from a long history of sipping sour mash liquor. His fellow chiefs would call him Shaky but we young fellows wouldn't dare call him anything but "Chief." He and I got along just fine as I worked hard at anything that needed to be done. After a while I became one of his trusted Hangar Two boys. There were only a couple of boys that he would ask for a favor: run to town and get him "a bottle of brown water." Shaky added a little brown water to his coffee every now and then when the shakes got too bad. His sipping never affected his devotion to duty or his memory. Few chiefs had a memory like Shaky had. He could tell you the page number in the maintenance manual where to find a certain maintenance procedure or where to find a certain part number. When a problem developed with the aircraft, he could tell you where to look to find how to correct the problem. These old chiefs showed us pride in our work and pride in the Coast Guard. At the time, political correctness was not heard of and not there to destroy a part of a colorful history I am proud to have experienced and enjoyed. Each chief had his own personality and was not molded from a textbook. They were real men. Most had been in the military since WWII and the Korean War. These old chiefs would fade into history as time passed, but they left us an awesome memory of them in our minds as to the old Coast Guard traditional ways of getting the job done. The knowledge they possessed and passed on to us younger ones is still being passed on today through one Coastie to another Coastie. Their leadership from these chiefs in demanding our aircraft be in perfect operating condition before flight would set my standard throughout my career. Their fearlessness to demand this very high standard would save many lives in the Coast Guard, the lives of our very own rescue crews.

My turn to stand the duty came around again, and this time I had the barracks fire and security watch. I made the rounds: the barracks, gymnasium, the old Q-16 storage building, (presently Hangar 7 All Hands Club) the Officers Club, fuel farm, boat docks, the aircraft ramp and hangar, and back to the barracks. As I was walking in through the watch standers quarters, I noticed Chief Helms lying in one of the watch standers' bunks. The Chiefs' Quarters were located on the second deck. It just didn't look right that he was on the first deck in the watch standers' quarters. One of the men in the quarters said he thought the chief had fallen from the outside stairs leading up to the Chiefs' Quarters. I walked over and asked the chief if he was OK. The chief didn't respond, so I got closer to him in the dimly lit barracks. His face looked as though he had a terrible head injury.

I immediately ran to sickbay and summoned the corpsman to come take a look at Chief Shaky. The corpsman looked at Chief Shaky and said, "Just let him sleep it off. He will be alright by morning." I continued making my rounds and kept a close eye on Chief Shaky throughout the night. After making a couple of rounds, I saw that the chief was getting worse because of the swelling of his head. I again called the corpsman, and this time the corpsman notified the Officer Of the Day (OOD). Immediately, the OOD sounded the alarm to launch the ready HH-52 helicopter. We helped load Chief Shaky into the helicopter. The helicopter crew rushed him to the Naval Hospital in Portsmouth, Virginia. That was the last time I would see Chief Shaky, unconscious but alive. Our station conducted an investigation into Chief Shaky's injuries. Some said he may have fallen from the upper floor landing down onto the cement below, but others say he may have been injured in town. Chief Shaky had a lot of friends. He was a legend in the Coast Guard because of his personality. He was loyal in his duties and the Coast Guard has now lost a massive amount of knowledge and talent. Our air station allowed us to fly a C-130 aircraft to attend his burial at Arlington National Cemetery.

Many of the crew from the now closed Argentia, Newfoundland, Air Detachment were stationed with our unit at Elizabeth City, North Carolina. In our rating were John Moe, Jim Webber, Bill Farling, Fred Carpenter and Bobby Wiese.

Bobby Wiese 1967

Bobby Wiese and Bill Tolson invited me to deer hunt with them on the outer banks. Dogs were not allowed for hunting to run the deer out of the swamp. Bobby and Bill knew of my fearless demeanor around wildlife and slippery creatures, so they let me run back and forth through the swamps trying to get the deer to run out. I would run through the swamps with my shotgun, barking like a dog, jumping over the fallen trees and dodging the thorn bushes. Occasionally I would see a slimy critter. I would just stay clear of them if possible. One day I took a break after running for several hours. I started to sit down on a sand bluff when all of a sudden Bobby and Bill said, "Jump up! Jump up! There's a snake under you!" I must have jumped two feet into the air. They were not teasing. Right where I was just about to sit down was a small rattler with one button on his tail. The rattler was coiled and ready to give me an injection in the buttocks. I instantly whacked the rattler with my shotgun. The boys cracked up with laughter and said if that snake had bitten me in the buttocks that I was going to die. They said that neither one of them was going to try to get the poison from my buttocks. We all chuckled from the entertainment; but, within a very short time, we ran across a full-grown Eastern Diamondback about six feet in length and bigger around than my arm. That was enough close calls with snakes for that day, so we called off the hunt.

Another man that had reported in from Argentia was a man named Greguire. He was married to a girl he had met from Bell's Island while stationed in Newfoundland. He was so used to the cold weather that he wore a short-sleeved shirt in the middle of winter. His name would become famous with the C-130. He called the gas turbine compressor of the auxiliary power unit the "Geest". The APU unit has been called this name since shortly after he named it. As a flight engineer readies starting the unit, he calls out "Clear the Geest" or "Geest Clear?" and waits for a reply from ground safety before he hits the ignition switch. Soon we would give Gregoire a nickname of "GregorGeest." GregorGeest had a pronounced New England accent and was full of energy. I never remembered him sitting down. He was outside while carrying a cup of coffee walking up and down the aircraft-parking ramp looking for something that needed done to the C-130 aircraft. He was full of humor and never stopped talking.

Master Chief Stickney was our chief in charge. He was a good friend to all of us who worked for him. He looked after his men and challenged each one of us to learn and accept more responsibility. He tried to get us all promoted. He was a true outdoorsman who loved fishing and hunting. He built his own boat even without one piece of plywood that had provided a good floor in my buckboard station wagon! He carried the boat to Alaska with him when his orders directed him to report to Kodiak.

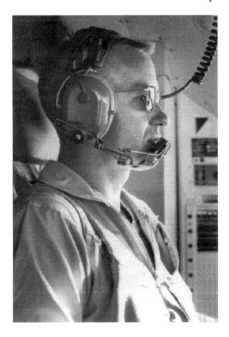

Master Chief Bert Stickney

Master Chief Stickney and wife Carol's home is in Fairlee, Vermont. What a gift to have had the opportunity to serve with such a man!

We were lucky to have quality chiefs at our station to work under. Most were just like you would remember from the old WWII movies. The chiefs controlled everything, and every task was done and done on time. Danny Tosado was another chief assigned to our shop. He was of Puerto Rican heritage. He was always a gentleman and sharply military dressed. Earl Shannon was easy-going but demanded the best of quality aircraft from us. The other chief was Dean Wheat. He was a young chief at the time. He would be the first chief that I had a real misunderstanding with about social engineering.

One day while our shop crew was gathered around in a discussion, Chief Wheat mentioned if there were a black man assigned to the shop, he would promote him over any of us. That didn't sit well with some of the crew and especially not me. I told the chief that he didn't know where any of us came from, our life's misfortunes, or what mixture of nationalities we were. A couple of us had Native American ancestry. One was of Spanish heritage. The chief continued with his explanation of what reasons he made his decision. "Their ancestors were slaves," he declared. The debate became heated as I explained where and how I had grown up and that in our country and our military the person that works the hardest and performs the best gets promoted. The discussion became louder as I explained that promoting anyone in the armed forces ahead of another because of their race, religion or any other preference is purely and simply biased.

Before his insult we thought we all were evaluated on our abilities, conduct and performance. We flew together, sailed together, risked our lives together, bunked in the same barracks, ate at the same tables, and understood we would be promoted on our merits. We respected those that earned their promotions on merits and demonstration. We had no discrimination in our unit, and this biased view only created tension and distrust in a system that we all thought to be fair. There were black men of higher rank with more time in service who had studied hard and had more experience and survived more risks than I. If we had shown our dedication and served equally, then let the testing prove who deserves promotion. Slavery and economics cannot be an excuse for certain races. By no means here in America should I be given any affirmative action promotion over anyone that joins our U.S. Armed Forces.

Good thing our country adopted the Uniform Code of Military Justice (UCMJ) for our service men and women to follow in later years. Even so, we in the military sometimes find ourselves facing double jeopardy. We all volunteered to serve and die, if need be, for our country. We did so on the promise of equal opportunity for advancement without one person being given special favor over another because of social class, religion or political gerrymandering.

After a much-heated argument, the chief and the rest of us had to depart the area to cool our heads.

Several of the men at our air station would receive their orders. Some would be directed to Mobile, Alabama, and be assigned to icebreaker duty. The icebreaker ships each carried two HH-52 helicopters. My friend Mac was transferred with the group of men that were assigned to crew and maintain these helicopters.

Coast Guard cutter *Eastwind* breaking ice in Antarctica. After decommissioning, the ship's bell was put on display at the Chiefs' Quarters in Elizabeth City, North Carolina.

Jack Simpson, Jack Gardner and several others would serve two to three years flying off the decks of these icebreakers. The icebreaker's success determined the survival of the remote scientific research station. Orvil "Mac" McNary would complete several Arctic icebreaking missions while assigned to that unit. While on one mission, Hurricane Camille hit the Gulf Coast with a mighty force. Lots of property was damaged and many people were uncounted for. Mac's family was one of the families that could not be located. The Coast Guard unit, after a massive search for the family, contacted the icebreaker in the Arctic by message stating that his family was missing. His wife Mary Ann had left the area to avoid the storm, but the Coast Guard Unit did not have knowledge of their leaving the area. She had headed to family located in another state, but she had no way to notify Mac while he was in the Arctic. Mac endured much anxiety for a good length of time while the Coast Guard was unaware of Mac's family condition. Finally, with messages between the ship and the home unit, Mary and her son were located at Mac's family home and found to be unharmed. It was quite a helpless feeling for Mac during the crisis period. Thanks to the Coast Guard unit back home, they followed through to ensure safety of one of their own.

Our icebreakers provided access to the scientific research stations in the Antarctic and passage routes for ships in the Arctic. The Antarctic explorations were conducted during our winters and the Arctic expeditions were conducted during our summers.

Modern Coast Guard icebreaker *Polar Sea* with helicopter deck at stern.

Our helicopters provided the icebreaker with a means of transferring supplies and personnel to and from the ship. The helicopters were a valuable aid in forward observation and as a rescue vehicle for the ship.

Chapter Eight

Our station was becoming more and more involved with
the tragedies that plagued the treacherous Atlantic Ocean.
Many ships in the sixties were not built to handle a full
load of cargo and survive the terrible weather systems.
Many ships were lost to Davie Jones' locker. Some went
down with all hands aboard. In our job of air search and
rescue, every effort was put into each disaster to try to get
on the scene as quickly as possible and to save as many
lives and as much property as possible. A ten million
dollar yacht, though, was a lesser priority compared to
saving a single life from the deck of that yacht stranded in
the middle of the Atlantic Ocean.

Our C-130, HU-16 planes and HH-52 helicopter crews
were on the job night and day giving our maximum effort

to respond to the tragedies. Working in joint effort with our boat and ship crews from other units became an awesome force of rescue. Being in a rescue plane circling over a large sinking ship in the middle of a storm gives one an awful feeling of helplessness. Every bone in your body wants to help the ship's passengers and crew get through the rescue attempt alive. Some boats and ships were too far from shore for our helicopters to reach them immediately. A lot of times we were lucky enough to find a US Navy ship or one of our own US Coast Guard cutters that our helicopters could land on for refueling. Many times, our helicopter pilots and crew had a life-threatening experience just trying to land on the storm-tossed ships. At a certain distance from shore there was no choice but to make the landing on the ship or plummet into the sea en-route to Davey Jones' locker. After refueling, the helicopters would continue on a direction to the troubled vessel. They only hoped their rescue would be successful and that they could make another landing for fuel on their return flight to a safe landing area.

HH-52A helicopter landing on deck of USCG cutter for refueling in calm seas.

For most rescue cases when the helicopter was launched on a mission, we would fly overhead in the C-130 or Albatross and direct the helicopter the shortest distance to the rescue scene. The helicopter only had about four hours of fuel and only flew 95 knots for best fuel economy. The HH-52 helicopter had a single engine, so during the rescue operation we were the crews' guardians watching from above. If rescue from a sailing vessel in rough seas was attempted, the crew in the helicopter could be killed if the swinging mast struck the helicopter. If the rescue basket became tangled in the vessel's rigging, the helicopter and crew could be snatched to a certain death unless the cable to the basket was sheared in time. The aircraft having only one engine was another great risk. The engine, gearbox, and tail rotor were known to fail in harsh working conditions. Much of our flying was spent looking after our own as well as looking after others.

Typical HH-52A helicopter rescue with one of three survivors in rescue basket.

In many rescue attempts the ship's mast would rise and fall in tune with the sometimes fifty or sixty feet waves.

Once we were called in the middle of the night during a nor'easter when a ship sent a mayday for help saying that the ship was sinking. We loaded the entire cargo compartment of the C-130 with parachute flares and took off in the direction of the sinking ship. We found the ship and saw that the ship was in real trouble and had settled in the water to a dangerously low level with the seas washing over its deck. Our radioman continuously updated the Fifth Coast Guard District Rescue Center in Portsmouth, Virginia. The center sent out an emergency rescue assistance message to all ships and asked for their positions. One large freighter happened to be en-route in the direction of the sinking ship. At the Coast Guard's request, the freighter responded with haste. We circled overhead and dropped parachute flares as the crew and passengers were trying to abandon the storm battered ship. After many hours, the freighter came within sight and pulled along side the sinking ship. We continued dropping flares until everyone from the sinking ship was on board the freighter. This was a good night when luck was in favor of this crew and ours.

On another night two Norwegian sister ships became victims of the stormy weather in the Atlantic. The weather was unforgiving. One ship just broke in half, but both the bow and the stern were still afloat. A maximum effort rescue attempt was put in place with all available aircraft and cutters in the area put into motion. The C-130s were flying around the clock. The television reporters from Norfolk, Virginia, were arriving, boarding our aircraft and flying to the scene of the disaster. One aircraft would fly until they were exhausted in fuel and forced to land. After refueling, another crew would take off and relieve the plane on scene. As the day went on, every effort to save as many as possible was on the minds of us all.

On another rescue flight the ship was about to sink. Television reporters were in the back of the plane recording the rescue attempt. One pilot wanted so badly to save one more person that he decided to stay over the wreck for a while longer. His fuel was low, and another C-130 was overhead waiting to take its position over the sinking ship. However, his adrenaline pump was fired up and his intelligent thinking, blurred. I happened to be in the C-130 overhead that late afternoon. The television reporters in the back of his aircraft wanted as much coverage as they could get. Finally, he relinquished the control of the mission to the circling aircraft overhead and turned his plane westward towards land. The engineer "Archie" Moore had constantly reminded the pilot of his critical remaining fuel quantity. The pilot had made his mind up that he was going to make one more pass and then one more pass and then one more pass and then one more pass over the sinking ship. Before the plane reached the coast, the low fuel warning lights began coming on. The crew responded with an aircraft emergency mayday and reported to the air station control tower of their emergency. Now one of our own crews had become the victim while their best intentions were to save others.

Our captain had departed for the day but the captain from the Aircraft Repair and Supply Base just happened to get wind of the message. The Repair and Supply Base captain called the air station captain at home and, supposedly in other than nice words, told him that his (-------) plane was coming in, out of fuel, and was probably going to crash. One fuel tank after another was becoming empty as the flight engineer had to turn all the fuel cross-feed valves to open, so that all the engines would be fed from a single manifold by any remaining fuel in any tank. The pilot held the wings as level as possible to aid in prevention of the engines starving for fuel. All of a sudden an engine surged as they crossed the shoreline but got another gasp of fuel to continue operating. The Coast Guard flight crewmembers gave their own life vests and parachutes to the television reporters and assisted them in putting them on correctly. The crew opened the paratrooper doors and instructed the reporters to standby to jump if they felt a large surge in the aircraft movement. Luckily, bailing out was not necessary as the aircraft was able to fly over the Albemarle Sound, up the Pasquotank River and make a safe landing at Elizabeth City.

After the aircraft had landed the Auxiliary Power Unit "Geist" was fired up as part of the normal procedure, but shortly the "Geist" stopped running because of no fuel. No fuel remained in the number two tank that supplies the "Geist" and the number two engine in normal operation. Some very frightened reporters got off that plane. Some said they were glad to be on terra firma and didn't want to cover another rescue such as this again.

Incidents like this didn't happen often in the Coast Guard because we had some of the best-trained pilots and crews in the world. But sometimes incidents did happen, either by miscalculation or by a desire of the crew to risk it all to save another. We trained constantly, and we had some smart people with common sense within our ranks. On the other hand, we were like the rest of the world and the law of averages came into play.

We lived in an atmosphere of "unsung heroes," where doing our job was a good feeling but a part of our normal daily duty. A little thank you from our commanders and a lot of the survivors made you feel gratification. In my early years of aviation, medals were not given often to individuals, but many commendations and awards were given to the entire unit. I really liked being a part of this Coast Guard outfit. Being one of many that would give his all without hesitation, with spirit and with dedication to the task of saving someone in trouble became an awfully powerful stimulant of pride in our duty. Other than lifesaving, we protected our country from the many invasions the average person was unaware of.

After being at my duty station for a while, however, I began receiving some appreciation and recognition for my efforts.

Commanding Officer Captain Brinkmeyer awarding appreciation to Johnny Gray and Fred Tanner.

Captain Brinkmeyer was a super commanding officer (CO). Johnny was a "High Tider" from the North

Carolina's Outer Banks, and he and I would become friends for the rest of our lives.

The more exposure we had in our rescue duties, the more confident and less fearful we were of our operations. We felt more and more as if we were a part of the flying machine we were operating. The aircraft became so familiar that sounds and vibrations would let you know just how each of our planes was operating. Making minor adjustments could keep a plane flying for many more hours on very necessary missions. What we were accomplishing in saving lives was worth more than money could buy. What a great job to have!

U.S. Coast Guard Air Station Elizabeth City
Aircraft parking ramp (late 1960s)

The first C-130 #1340 with the new paint color scheme is located on the left side of ramp. The last remaining Coast Guard R5D, soon to be replaced with the only Coast Guard E-Model #1414, is backed up to the hangar. This aircraft was used around the world, mainly for calibration of Coast Guard LORAN stations' signals. In the late sixties, we were manned to operate four C-130s. Due to a shifting and restaging of aircraft to all of our C-130 stations, we ended up with twice the number of aircraft.

Even with this heavy additional workload, we at our air station proved that we could still maintain and fly twice our normal responsibility.

We learned more and more about how to repair the aircraft. Our Aviation Electrician's Mate (AE) rating was also responsible for operation and maintenance of propellers. We learned how to assemble and test several different types of propellers. Harvey Lawrence, Bill Farling and Harold Lindsey taught us the fine and delicate art of handling and assembling the C-130, HU-16 and R5D (C-54) propellers. Harvey and Bill would challenge our fitness since we had to lift the propellers from the assembly bench and position them on a prop dolly. The C-130 propeller with four blades weighed approximately 800-900 pounds and had a thirteen-foot diameter from one prop tip to the other prop tip. The R5D and HU-16 propellers with three blades weighed 700 and 600 pounds, respectively. Propellers were very critical in the performance of an aircraft. Internal and external hydraulic leakage could cause catastrophic failure. Fine adjustment of the many parts inside the valve control housing could cause the aircraft to operate smoothly and within normal operating range or could cause the engines to overheat or cause improper balanced torque with the other engines. The engine and the propeller had to be adjusted together perfectly in order for the engine to perform at its intended power.

AE 1st Class Harvey Lawrence was the propeller shop supervisor during a great deal of my learning experiences with propellers. Harvey was an extremely sharp military man. One requirement if you worked for him was to have a spotless shop and a super clean workbench where all of the critical internal prop parts were laid out ready for assembly. He liked smoking a little stogie. His work uniform was always neatly pressed. His work hat was even starched and pressed. He taught us how to install new blade deicing boots on the damaged propeller blades. Every prop that left the shop headed for installation on an aircraft looked like new and operated like new. Harvey was a big, strong man who had driven a tractor-trailer truck before he became a Coastie. That physical appearance gave many of us young men a reason to pay close attention to what he was teaching us.

"AE" 1st Class Harold was another who liked his stogies. Only Harold liked the big fat ones. Harold was like a dad to many of the young boys who worked for him. He always tried to talk to you if you had a problem or would show interest in how you were coming with your studies.

"AE" 1st Class Bill had no smoking or drinking vices. I guess it was the way he was raised with his family in Reidsville, North Carolina. Bill was a very strong farm boy. He had a sense of humor in teasing us young boys. He would dare us to compete in all kinds of physical challenges. Once he bet us a one hundred dollar bill that we couldn't carry his mechanics toolbox to Hangar II which was located about two hundred yards away from our shop. A couple of us decided that we wanted to try for the money.

The other boy picked the toolbox up from the deck, took a few steps, then quickly dropped it right back down. I thought that if I could help lift those propellers from the assembly bench, I could surely carry Bill's toolbox two hundred yards. I picked that toolbox up and began walking towards Hangar Two. It was the heaviest toolbox that I had ever attempted to lift. That toolbox had to weigh 200 pounds, but I had my mind made up that I was going to carry it the entire distance and reap my reward. I struggled to find a way to hold on to the box and continue to carry it. My hands became numb and the weight of the toolbox made it difficult to stand up straight while trying to walk. It finally came to a point that I could no longer hold on to the toolbox, and I had only traveled half the distance. I gave it my darn best effort. I had to run and get a tow tractor to carry the toolbox back to the shop!

Sometimes I would help Bill Raynor, Hoot Gibson and Fred Carpenter on the aircraft-parking ramp. As the planes came in from their flights, we would stop by maintenance control and see if any of the planes needed repair. If there were a discrepancy on any one of the planes, then we would try to repair it in time for the next flight. Sometimes the plane was the only one left on standby for rescue use so our urgency in a quick repair was of the most importance. We would carry a small canvas tool satchel with several most-used tools. That way we didn't have to carry our large heavy toolboxes while walking the distance of the ramp, over one hundred yards. We learned a lot from these older men and soon we were challenging Bill to who could get to the aircraft the quickest and get to do the repair. Bill was always ready to hustle so we had a constant challenge to get to the aircraft first.

Frank "Hoot" Gibson was a gentle old country boy from Georgia and had an enjoyable personality. We hit it off well, and he and his wife Helen and I became friends for all the time I knew him. He would show us how to repair the aircraft and let us do most of the work. He loved to talk about how life on the farm was back in Georgia.

Frank "Hoot" Gibson

Fred Carpenter was a New England boy. He was a gentleman with a good sense of humor. He enjoyed working with us southern boys and laughed at our different manner of dialect. It was Fred's old car that I had bought from my friend Mac. Fred spent much time having us use the aircraft technical manuals and having us operate the electronic test equipment. Fred liked calling me by my nickname, Country. If a flight mission were planned, Fred would ask if he could have Country go along as part of his crew. I didn't mind the nickname; just about everyone had one. Besides, that nickname wouldn't be the last nickname that I would have in my career.

I had been dating for some time and I thought time was slipping away. I was already 28 years of age and no telling where I would be ordered to perform my duty next. I had been promoted to second class and was making a few more dollars a month in pay and my flight/hazardous duty pay was more stable so I felt more confident of being able to make ends meet. I let my eagerness to get married overcome me. Not having to live in the barracks anymore seemed to be another benefit from getting married. I dove right into the marriage. I was blessed with a very sweet stepdaughter. However, right away there seemed to be stresses from standing overnight duty and going out on military missions for days, weeks or months. These stresses lead to several separations and some very unhappy times.

One of the master chiefs was Nathan Caddy. Master Chief Caddy invited several of us to go with him to the Loyal Order of the Moose Lodge. We went to the Moose Lodge and met several of the members there. We only had met a few people in town before, and the Moose Lodge had a lot of members. Many of the members worked as civilians in the repair division at the aircraft repair center on base. Several of us decided to join the lodge. As customary of new members we were initiated into the Loyal Order of the Moose.

Before long I began to meet many people around town. Many of the local farmers whose farms we flew over were members there. They treated us with respect for serving our country. Just about all the members had served their country in the military, and knowing that made it more enjoyable to socialize with these fine people. Getting to hear their stories of when they were in WWII or Korea and hearing of the hardships they overcame and survived was interesting. I always made time for a veteran that wanted to tell his story. Others were tradesmen in town. Many members became life long friends: Buddy Fletcher, Bobby Benton, Doug Mercer, Marvin and Beulah Tillett, Donald and Wanda McDougal, Kenneth Bateman, Seth Halstead, Billy Bateman, Big Boy Russell, Earl Jones, Herman and Anita Freeman, Herman's mother Kathleen and many others, just to name a few.

Marvin Tillett, Earl Jones and Robert Russell invited me to the VFW, and I got to know many more of the town's citizens who were also war veterans: Harry Watkins, George and Mildred Williamson, George Askew, Buddy Price, James Gaskins, Calvin Lamb, the Toxey brothers, Harry and Earnest James and many more. These were my real heroes. I grew up during WWII and the Korean War and remembered all too well the sacrifices that this generation of men and women gave to our country so that we might live free. Boy, what a feeling of patriotism. Now it was our turn to show our appreciation to all of these brave men and women and be ready when called to do what duty our country asked of us.

Marvin Tillett

Marvin served during WWII and Korea in three of our armed services, the Army during WWII, the Navy, and in the Coast Guard. He, along with all of his veteran friends demonstrated to us younger men what patriotism was all about. They spoke often of the friends they had lost in combat. Their frequent reminders of never losing sight of what price freedom cost and never letting our country down will always chill me and will always be on my mind. I will forever miss my old Elizabeth City friends who I was fortunate and proud to know.

Harry James fought as a Marine in the Pacific Theatre. His company made one of the landings on the island of Okinawa. This was one of several islands where the fiercest battles against the Japanese took place during

WWII. Harry is a proud veteran. He and his wife Lela Maude have been my family's friends for over forty years. Harry now has a grandson, a paratrooper (Sergeant Cliff Pritchard) serving to protect our country in time of war.

Harry James
US Marine WWII

Selvia Meads worked as a civilian at the base. He was always quiet and never boasted about his sacrifice to our country. Selvia got along with everyone and worked steadily every day for the Coast Guard.

Selvia and members of his tank squad
Korea 1950. L to R: Kernts, McMillan,
Selvia, Levi, Miller

It gave me honor to work around men that risked all to
give us our freedom. Even in their civilian life, something
about men and women that have served in the armed
forces understands just how fragile our country is.

One day I asked Selvia when had he served in the military.
He told me that he had served in the Korean War and
drove a tank. He was wounded several times during the
war and awarded two Purple Hearts. His action in combat
had earned him the Bronze Star. His bravery enabled
many troops to survive what would have been certain
death by the Communist Chinese.

HEADQUARTERS 1st CAVALRY DIVISION

30 December 1950

AWARD OF THE BRONZE STAR By direction of the President

PRIVATE FIRST CLASS SELVIA J MEADS, Armor, United States Army, a member of Company B, 70th Tank Battalion (Heavy), attached 1st Cavalry Division, for gallantry in action against the enemy, on 1 November 1950 near Unson, Korea. While attempting to clear a withdrawal route, through heavy roadblocks, for an infantry battalion, Private Mead's tank came under intense close range fire. Realizing his vision was greatly obstructed with his driver's hatch closed and knowing the importance of picking the right route along the narrow road, Private Meads, unhesitantly and with a complete disregard for his own safety, opened his hatch thus exposing himself to the intense enemy automatic weapons fire and small arms fire. Remaining in his exposed position, though constantly under fire from the enemy, he encountered a burning tank blocking the road. Quickly and without stopping his tank he drove through houses at the side of the road, bypassing the burning tank and opening a route for the vehicles following. By selfless courage and quick thinking in the face of enemy fire, Private Meads opened a route of withdrawal and unitarily aided in the successful withdrawal of the infantry. His heroic action reflects great credit on himself and the military service. Entered federal service from North Carolina.

Selvia Meads
Citation for the Bronze Star
For heroism

George Williamson is another friend I made while stationed in Elizabeth City. George fought in Germany during WWII in the US Army. He and his fellow patriots at VFW Post 6060 never let a day go by that they don't try to present an expression of gratitude for the friends they lost in battle and for the opportunity to fight when their country called on their needed help. If not for this rapidly fading group of heroes, America would not be free today. We should never forget these brave men and women. George and Mildred have just lost a grandson in our ongoing battle against terrorism in Iraq and Afghanistan.

George Williamson, US Army

Chapter Nine

One day I received orders to report to the Coast Guard Air
Station at Barber's Point Hawaii. I had often dreamed of
going to Hawaii. I remembered well the movies made in
Hawaii. I thought of all the beauty in that paradise. I also
remembered all the death and destruction the island had
suffered during WWII. Anyway, I was looking forward to
being assigned to duty in paradise. My wife and I decided
that she and our daughter would remain in North
Carolina until summer when school was not in session. I
took my overseas physical and tied up all the loose ends in
Elizabeth City.

I bought a Volkswagen station wagon and got an auto loan
from the Industrial Bank in Elizabeth City. Melvin
Daniels was the loan manager at the time. He was always

a good friend of the Coast Guard servicemen at the base. Melvin had served in the Armed Forces. Melvin's American family originated on the Outer Banks, and he had family kin in the Coast Guard and family members that made a living on the open seas. Later years, he would become Mayor of Elizabeth City. I drove the car to Norfolk, Virginia, and had it shipped from the Navy Base Pier to the Navy Docks in Pearl Harbor, Hawaii.

After catching a flight out of Norfolk to San Francisco, I was on my way to Hawaii. After arriving in San Francisco, I stayed over at a hotel near the airport awaiting my flight across the pond to Hawaii. I ran into a nice couple that was visiting there named Fred and Juanita MacDonald. They asked where I was headed, and I told them that I had orders to Hawaii. We traveled in uniform at that time. They were very friendly to me and invited me to sit with them at dinner. After dinner the band started playing, and we had a few drinks. Fred and Juanita got up and danced to a few numbers. Then Juanita asked if I would like to dance; and I said, "Sure." So we got up and danced for a couple of numbers at her insistence. I walked her back to her seat and thanked her. She danced a few more numbers with her husband Fred and then asked me to dance again.

We got back out on the floor and began dancing. As we were passing a table, a gentleman spoke to me. He said, "Where are you headed, sailor?" I answered, "I am being transferred to Hawaii." As I turned towards the table again, I recognized the gentleman to be Johnny Mathis sitting there at the table with his girl friend and another gentleman. I stopped dancing, approached the table, and introduced my new friend Juanita and then myself. He asked if I was going over to Viet Nam. I said that I didn't know what I would be doing other than air search and rescue. He offered to buy our group drinks and seemed to be honored to do so for a service man. I was impressed to say the least since I had listened to his music many nights while I was dating in my earlier years. We talked for a while; and before I left, I asked him for his autograph. Only paper napkins were on the table, so I decided to pull out my orders and let him sign my orders. I didn't know if I would get into any kind of trouble for defacing my orders, but at that time of night and being who he was, I didn't think my new commanding officer would mind. He signed my orders and wished me good luck and thanked me for taking the time to talk with him and his friends. Fred, Juanita and I enjoyed the little time we had to share friendship before I had to catch my flight to Hawaii. They gave me their address, but with all of the moving commotion, I soon misplaced it and never was able to contact them again.

I arrived in Honolulu, Hawaii, in December of 1969 and was met by an old friend that I had met in service school in Connecticut. Ray Wolfe was there to be my sponsor. Ray had been in my class when I had propeller training in Windsor Locks, Connecticut. Ray and his wife Anne made me feel welcome. Ray showed me the way around, and I found out that I would be working with him. Ray and Harvey Lawrence were two of the best propeller mechanics that I had known in the Coast Guard. They were also the sharpest dressed and had the cleanest shops that I would ever see.

After I checked in with the personnel office and was shown to my quarters, I realized right away there were strange odors in the barracks and saw that some of the men (mostly the young men) looked as though they had poor military pride.

New Insignia of Coast Guard Air Station
Barber's Point, Hawaii

The room that I would be living in had thick glass blocks
for windows to give light, but you couldn't see clearly
through them. At least the room was clean and had air
conditioning. The younger men lived in rooms that had no
windows, so I felt pretty fortunate. My first night in my
room, I smelled that strange odor. It seemed to be coming
from the room above me. A gap in the ceiling allowed the
air to circulate to the second floor. I found out what the
odor was in due time.

The next day I went to work at the old aircraft nose dock.
We didn't have a hangar to work in; so when we had
maintenance to do on aircraft, we would pull the C-130
under a shelter that was called the nose dock. Most of the
aircraft was sticking out in the hot sun or rain depending
on the weather. Ray introduced me to some of the chiefs
and to the engineering officers. I knew Chief Willie Sutton
from my last duty station in North Carolina, so at least I
knew one chief that I liked. I met Jim Jones, Kevin

Lineweber, Tom Moore, Joe Jellison and Master Chief "Pappy" Young. Pappy was our leading chief. Another master chief was one of the most colorful Coast Guardsmen that I have ever met. His name was Patrick Posey. He was 100% pure Irish-with red hair and a fair complexion. And may I say he had a well-developed belly as some of the older chiefs had. He loved to talk and tell sea stories about the Coast Guard. I met our engineering officer Cdr. Kozlovsky. I met our operations officer, Cdr. Dan Martin. I ran into another Coastie that was in school with me back on the mainland named Phil "Shadow" Thompson. He and Ray were good friends, and they would introduce me to the rest of the crew and tell me how things were run at the base. After work we would all gather at the watering hole located in an old WWII Quonset hut. There wasn't much to the place but some paneling put up and a small bar to get a cold beer or soda after a hot day's work on the aircraft.

I got myself settled in the barracks, and the next day I finished up my check-in list and reported to work with Ray. I had been assigned to the propeller shop. Each one of us was assigned to tasks within our rate structure as one part of our job. The other part of our job was flying as crewmen on the different positions in the aircraft. I would be the last aviation electrician's mate to manage a propeller shop. Coast Guard Aviation Engineering turned over the propeller duties to the aviation machinist mate's rate. Ray had been to propeller school and became one of the first of his rate to take over that job from the aviation electrician's mate rate. I worked with Ray for that year. He would be transferred to another air station within a year, and I would assume the supervisor duties until another trained machinist's mate could fill the billet.

"Nose Dock" where we performed the inspections and repair of our aircraft. Photo from previous years showing R5D C-54 Aircraft.

A couple of months went by, and we had been eagerly trying to find out why our C-130 propellers were failing to come out of feather after we had shut down the engine during engine-out training. After engine shutdown on training flights the propellers must come out of feather when the engines are needed for restart. If the propellers fail to come out of the feather position when commanded, the engine will not start in flight. On long search and rescue missions out over the ocean we would shut down number one engine at 120,000 lbs. gross weight and number four engine at 110,000 lbs. gross weight to allow maximum endurance while in the search area. This allowed fuel for several more hours of search time when we really needed it. Our "B" Model C-130 aircraft did not have external fuel tanks to provide 11,000 lbs of extra fuel like the "E" Model and later aircraft had. It was dangerous to the flight crew when the propellers would not come out of feather so that the engines could be restarted in flight if needed in an emergency. The Air Force was having the same problems at the time with their C-130s. We tore into the internal workings of the propeller; and after many tests, we found the problem: failure of the dome piston seal and failure of the transfer tube seal. We also found domes with structural cracks in the seal area. We turned all of our research over to Cdr. Koslovsky, and he saw to it that the Air Force and the Hamilton Standard Propeller factory received an emergency message about our findings. Immediately, all propellers throughout the services were inspected and repaired. Finally a factory modification of shot peening was done to several critical parts of the propellers to strengthen them, and the dome quad seals and transfer tube seals were re-engineered. Sadly, the Air Force had some catastrophic failures of their propeller domes before they were safely modified. Cdr. Koslovsky could not do enough for Ray and me after our correcting a major flight safety problem with our aircraft.

Once in a while I would stop by the Quonset hut (watering hole) with Ray, Phil, and some of the boys. On occasion I would hear some of the younger men talking badly about the Coast Guard and even running down our country. They seemed to be grouped up with a number of them when they would spout words of dislike for our military.

I walked up to the bar and ordered a drink, and one of them introduced himself and called me "Comrade." Knowing his intention as to the word "Comrade" meaning of the communist persuasion and seeing that he was trying to impress some of his pals by watching my reaction, I decided to let him know my intentions; and I just decked him right there at the bar. That changed the expressions of the contemptuous grins from the faces of the group he was trying to impress by calling me "Comrade" and grinning back to them at their table. They found out right then and there that I was not one to put up with their harassment and that I was willing to respond. This would be just a beginning of the harassment from the draft dodgers who had joined the Coast Guard thinking they could get out of the draft during the Viet Nam War. Any Coastie that did not demonstrate their dislike for the military by creating harassment for those that cared for their service were systematically and frequently threatened with abuse, either verbally or with physical tricks to demean them. I was shocked at this kind of harassment happening on a military base. The base that I had just come from would throw this type people out the aircraft door while in flight.

The next day the group of draft dodgers went to the command and wanted me put on report for decking, what I considered, a traitor. Cdr. Kozlovsky got word of the incident, and I explained to him what had happened. I think he felt that what happened needed to be done, but he couldn't comment on it. Cdr. Martin was assigned to investigate the matter; and I think he, too, thought what had happened needed to be done, but we were in the military and that was against the rules. Well, Cdr. Martin decided that under the circumstances, he didn't think it worthy of any further action so he asked me to try and avoid the hippies.

I stayed clear of the draft dodgers as much as I could even though some of them worked with me or for me during the normal working day and on Ready Crew Alert days. They were on their good behavior when working around the aircraft and when many of the senior men were there during the day. After the working day ended and they had their "dope smoking" hour, it was a different story. Their dastardly and arrogant behavior was exposed to all they were around.

I did my best to stay clear of the barracks after work. I would visit the Navy club with my friends Phil, Ray, Marty Downie or Charlie Logsdon. We enjoyed the local Hawaiian people. My new Hawaiian friend, Mr. Fred Robbins, would introduce me to local Hawaiian villagers. Often we went to the Yoshie Club located on the Eva Beach road. Fred grew up there, so he knew everyone in the area. We had heard of a few military men who were handled pretty roughly for being disrespectful to the local Hawaiian villagers. Thank God, I never had any trouble. I was always mindful of being courteous to all my new friends. Fred was a colorful character and never had any dislike for anyone.

Near Christmas season, several of us would go from house to house uninvited and intentional and visit the chiefs and some of the officers who lived in the Eva Beach housing area. Phil "Shadow" Thompson, Ray Wolfe, Master Chief Pat Posey and I would make the rounds for cheers. This was only after the gang was thoroughly primed, with celebration in mind, at one of the clubs. We would make a stop at Commander "Koz's" house. All of the dedicated crew liked working for the commander. He would stand by his men in thick or thin, and he knew that they respected him and would give their best effort no matter what the mission. Commander "Koz" had a saying about the men that would go out every night and try to keep up with all the nightlife in the paradise of the Hawaiian Islands. He would say, "You boys don't come to work with 'Polynesian Paralysis'." (Meaning being unable to perform at the highest level and having no hangover)

Commander "Koz" (Now Admiral "Koz" Ret.), "Hammering Hank" Wilson, Lcdr. Ret., Master Chief Jerry Sherwood Ret., Okinawa visit.

We then stopped by the commanding officer's house for cheers. The captain had a coffee spill stain on his beautiful white carpet and asked the group if we knew how to clean a stain from a carpet. The gang of us, very influenced by the cheers we had partaken, began giving him our personal advice about how to remove his stain. Irish Pat said a little kerosene ought to lift the stain from the carpet. The captain didn't seem impressed, so Shadow said to try using a little mineral spirits. The captain shook his head and said he didn't think that would work either. I blurted out that we use Menthol Ethel Ketone (MEK) to strip the paint from the prop tips and that would surely take that spot out. It seemed to the captain that we really didn't care if the spot came out or not. He said Mr. Allison (his pilot friend) told him to use warm water. That made sense to me as warm water is used to make the coffee in the first place. Anyhow, in our holiday spirit, we really were not interested in the captain's stain.

Soon we were at Chief Sutton's house. He, Chief Watson and their wives were playing cards, which they often did for recreation. They stopped playing for a while and entertained our gang or shall we say that we entertained them with our behavior. Soon they sat back down and started playing cards again. I said to the boys, "Lets get out of here. These old folks want to play cards, and we have a lot of stops to make." I mean Chief Sutton and Chief Watson must have been at the most in their late thirties. They would talk about how old I thought they were for years to come. I thought highly of both of them and their wives.

Best friends
Master Chief George and Dottie Watson,
Master Chief Grable "Willie" and Edie Sutton
after retirement at daughter Susan's wedding.

Not long after the holidays, I was on my way to Combat Flight Engineer's School with the Air Force in Little Rock, Arkansas. I boarded a plane in Honolulu and flew to Los Angeles, California, where I would catch another plane with connecting flights to Little Rock. At the airport in Los Angeles I went to the men's head (restroom); and as I began to undo the thirteen buttons that held the flap closed on the front of my uniform trousers, a man just reached around to touch me. I threw a punch at him and hustled out of the head and reported to the first police officer I saw on what had happened. He said they had had reports of this before, and he summoned another officer to see if they could catch the culprit. After thinking about it, I'm sure that if the men at the base heard of what had happened, they would get a big laugh out of it. I've heard many times of other service men being humiliated by such disrespectful people, but really I could not let myself believe someone could be so desperate.

Finally I arrived at the Air Force Base in Little Rock. I was assigned to the training barracks and roomed with a young Air Force man who was in training to be a Forward Command Combat Spotter. He would leave soon for Viet Nam. He would be dropped behind enemy lines and direct aircraft fire to the enemy targets. That takes a brave man to give that much for his country. I admired his courage. One day after class, he was gone.

I had to study hard to grasp all of the training that I needed to get through the Combat Flight Engineer's School. We studied in the classroom for a while, and before long I found myself in the flight simulator going through takeoffs and landings. Then there were all of the emergency procedures that I had to demonstrate from memory, even in the dark with simulated fires and multi-engine failures. I had worked on nearly every electrical component in the cockpit including most all of the instruments, but memorizing and demonstrating what to do to stay alive was one big adrenaline rush. I loved what I was doing, and I knew where nearly every valve and relay was located in the aircraft. All of my previous training and years of repairing the C-130 aircraft surely helped me when I had to learn how to handle the emergencies from the flight engineer's seat in the cockpit. In our early years of flying, our checklist had to be learned and cited by memory. In later years, the checklist would be required to be read from a written checklist. I finally accomplished what the Air Force required to receive my certificate. I would go back to my base in Hawaii to complete the flying requirements for my flight engineer's certification.

My family was finally ready to move to Hawaii with me, so we all boarded a plane to California. At the Coast Guard Base in Alameda, we would go through an overseas checklist to see if the family needed any medical or other attention before being stationed in Hawaii.

I made it back to my Coast Guard Air Station in Barber's Point, Hawaii, and began flying with a flight engineer instructor. The instructor, Jake Valdez, was the instructor that I worked with during most of my training. We flew a lot on search and rescue and logistic missions. We flew from Hawaii to Acapulco, Mexico, to monitor the tuna fishing fleet. Jake spoke fluent Spanish, easily communicating with Mexican officials and airport workers, making our tasks easier. We would see that none of the different countries' fishing boats violated the international fishing treaty, including our own US fishing fleet. I felt my hind end was glued to the flight engineer's seat from the many hours of training on active missions. Bill Farling, Dave Richards and Chief Kevin Linewebber were just a few of the other engineers that I would fly with. Jake finally said that I didn't need him anymore to observe me during the many flights, and that I was ready for my flight engineer's check ride.

A few days went by and our station was called on to perform an emergency rescue 1,000 miles southwest to an island in the Pacific called Fanning Island. Chief Lyle Boslau called me and said, "I want you to take the flight." He also said that he would monitor my performance for my flight engineer's check ride. I topped off the fuel tanks on the C-130 B-Model #1340. I performed a good preflight on the aircraft and loaded my toolbox and other necessary extra equipment on the plane. I figured my performance takeoff and landing data for take off and soon we were on our way with chief parachute rigger, Chief Charlie Dugan; navigator, Lcdr. Joe Crowe and radioman, Fred Carlisle. In the sixties and early seventies we were able to use a manual computer called a "whiz wheel," while computing take off and landing data.

We landed at Hickam Air Force Base in Honolulu to pick up a medical doctor and loaded several racks of Jet Assisted Takeoff Rockets (JATO). The Air Force Para Rescue unit at Hickam had previously dropped two of their para-rescuemen on Fanning Island, the island where we were to land. The only runway on the island was built

163

for a small aircraft. A medical doctor used the runway to land his small plane when he would visit the island natives. The Coast Guard had a lighter weight C-130 than the Air Force, so the chances of a successful landing on the island would favor the Coast Guard making the attempt.

The Air Force paramedics on the island, along with information from the previous over flight of their flight crew, decided that the only way to get a C-130 on the island was to cut down many of the coconut trees at one end of the runway so the wings would not strike them on the landing attempt. The natives were reluctant to cut down many of their trees because the cocoanut trees provided them with their livelihood. The runway was measured at thirty feet wide and slightly over two thousand feet long. We had landed on many of the old WWII landing strips on several of the islands, but this one would challenge us all. We would be operating in a tropical environment, and the aircraft's power performance is greatly reduced at higher operating temperatures. The only way off of the island's short runway would be to use the JATO rockets if we were lucky enough to make a successful landing.

We took off from Hickam Air Force Base in Hawaii and proceeded toward Fanning Island. Along the way, the Coast Guard communications stations updated us as to what conditions to expect. The island used a short-wave radio to keep us informed on the condition of the rescue victim and the progress of removing the trees so we could attempt a landing. The weather remained in our favor all the way to the island. Chief Boslau questioned me all the way there about every normal and emergency procedure in the flight manual. After about four hours of flight, we saw the island coming into sight. We began making preparations for a short field landing on the island.

As we flew closer to the island we could see that it was going to be a very risky landing. The trees looked as though they were going to be in the way of our right wing on landing.

Approach to (first time) landing C-130 on 30' wide Fanning Island runway.   Adrenalin rushing! We're going to make it!

The runway was constructed of coral that had been pushed up by a bulldozer and spread out to make the runway.   On both sides of the thirty-foot wide runway, there was a drop-off of several feet where the bulldozer had pushed the coral up to make the runway. Sliding off either side of the thirty-foot wide runway would ensure that the wing contacted the ground and most likely none of us would survive since there was no rescue equipment on the island. At the far end of the runway was the ocean. We circled the landing strip several times in the planning stages of the landing attempt.   The landing data was checked several times, and there was no room for even the slightest error. If every inch of the available runway were not used, we would end up in the ocean.   Finally, the decision was made by the pilot, Albert Allison, and his co-pilot, Art Foster, to put the big "Hercules" C-130 on the landing strip. The plan was to fly the plane in a slide until clear of the coconut trees and then drop the plane down on the coral runway. Performance data was checked and reviewed by the entire crew.   The plan sounded like it would work, so the plane approached the end of the runway with the trees. The pilot kept the right wing high and the plane in a slipping movement. However, when the trees were cleared, the pilot slightly hesitated to put the right wing down as the left wing was nearing impact with the runway. The aircraft was not centered on the narrow runway. Art Foster, the co-pilot, shouted, "I've got it," and took over the throttles and assisted control of the yoke. He slammed the wheels down on the runway and pulled the throttles to maximum reverse as fast as the propellers' speed would allow him while the pilot controlled the nose-wheel steering. When our aircraft finally stopped its forward motion, there was no room at the end of the runway. I had never seen Cdr. Art Foster get excited about anything. That day we all could thank our Maker and Art for allowing us to live to make many more rescue flights. (What an adrenalin rush!) With the narrow runway, we would have to reverse the propellers and back down the runway so we could get ready for takeoff. We opened the rear cargo ramp and door and began putting the engine throttles in reverse while Chief Dugan talked to the pilot and guided us down the runway.

Backing down the runway on Fanning Island.

As we put the engines in reverse, the oil temperatures on the engines exceeded the maximum high oil temperature limits so we would have to move the throttles back to ground idle to try and cool the oil temps. All of the engine oil temps climbed over 140 degrees. That meant the aircraft would be required to have an over-temperature inspection on our return to home base in Hawaii. When we finally reached the other end of the runway where we could take off, we looked the aircraft over really good because of the maximum effort landing.

At that time, we found out more about what our mission was about. The wife of the leader of the native people had stepped on a fish bone. Her leg had become infected and blood poison had set in. She also had sugar diabetes that only aggravated her critical condition. The Air Force paramedics, parachuted in earlier, had done all they could for her. The paramedics were glad to see us and thanked us all for putting the C-130 on the runway.

Four jet-assisted-takeoff bottles mounted on each side air deflector door.

Chief Charlie, Chief Boz and I went about getting our bird ready for take off. We mounted the JATO (Jet Assist Rockets) to the air deflector doors located just forward of the paratroop doors. Charlie used the ignition tester to ensure the rockets would fire when needed on take off. We took a few minutes to cool off from working in the heat; and while we were resting, we had a chance to converse with some of the islanders.

Friendly islanders of Fanning Island

They were overwhelmed by the big plane landing on the tiny runway and asked many questions. One of them wanted to know about the jet bottles we had just hung on the side of the aircraft. We told him that the rocket boosters would help us get off the short runway when it was time for lift off and that we would be dropping them from the sky as soon as we were finished burning them on take off. He wanted to know if he could have them, and we decided to have the pilot fly along the coast near shallow water so that the islander could retrieve them easily.

Soon the island leader was ready to load his wife after the doctor had readied her for transport back to Hawaii. We prepared her a mattress on the cargo floor so that she could stretch out and be as comfortable as possible during the long flight. We said good-by to all the people we had just met and loaded the patient and paramedics. We prepared for the equally demanding take off. The engines had cooled down, and we had control of the oil temps. We all listened carefully to the flight checklist briefing on the use of the jet assist rockets along with the short field takeoff procedures. The throttles were pushed over the gate into the flight range, and all engines checked within normal limits. Then the pilot, backed up by the co-pilot, went full throttle and released the brakes. We were in the no abort mode in a matter of seconds and committed to a take-off even if we experienced an engine failure.

As the big Hercules reached over 50 knots, Boz hit the JATO ignition switches. All eight jet rockets fired at once and everyone felt the thrust of an equivalent power of two extra engines. Within seconds, the aircraft reached a safe takeoff speed and leaped into the air just as it was planned and just before the C-130 aircraft ran out of runway. After our take off, the pilot, not forgetting our promise to the islanders, turned right back towards the island. When we were over the shoreline, we began releasing the jet assist bottles one at a time and we watched through the porthole windows as each one of them landed in the shallows.

H Model demonstration with fired booster
JATO rockets.

What a good feeling we had to have accomplished this rescue. We had made a safe landing and take off on an island runway thirty feet wide and two thousand feet long and one thousand miles from our base. Now we had to finish our mission by getting our patient to a hospital in the fastest time. All this while I was getting my flight engineer's check ride! That's one for the books. We arrived back at the Hickam Air Force Base in Honolulu and transferred our patient to an awaiting ambulance. We took off again and landed back at our base at Barber's Point. When we landed and shut down the engines, Chief Boslau said, "Congratulations Freddy, you are a qualified flight engineer." Our crew was rewarded with a medal for the rescue. Many in our command thought our accomplishment worthy of the Air Medal, but the pilot with the say said that he already had an Air Medal and decided he wanted something else. He decided to put himself in for a Commendation Medal so (in those years) that meant the rest of the crew had to accept a lesser award. We were awarded the Achievement Medal instead.

Admiral Prinze awarding Achievement Medal to crew and me. Chief Boslau behind Fred.

My good feeling about the rescue was much more important than any medal, but it does feel good when you are shown appreciation for risking your life. In those years and years before, we were always under the assumption that rescues were our normal job and that a thank you was your reward. In most cases our commanders thought to do so. Also, if you ever hoped to have a chance at promotion, each medal added points and chances of reaching the next higher rank.

On our days off and sometimes in the evening there was time to relax and unwind. We would drive to Honolulu for nightlife; but during the week, it was a short evening. We had to get back to the base for the next day's duty. Hawaii was a beautiful place, and I enjoyed the people.

One of the most enjoyable was the air station's gardener, Mr. Fred "Robbie" Robins who had retired from the Coast Guard many years ago. He had served on the sailing ships as a cabin boy. Even at his elderly age you could tell that he was once a powerful man. He could still out work many younger men one half his age.

Boatswain's Mate First Class
Fred Kalaeloa Robins

He was a native Hawaiian with a very pleasant personality. He once was the officer in charge of the

Barber's Point Lighthouse. He had been in charge of many lighthouses throughout the islands.

Robbie standing atop Barbers' Point Lighthouse.

Barber's Point Light House beautifully gracing the Oahu shoreline.

Fred would be at work long before the sun rose. He kept the grass, flowers, and palms trimmed. He lived just off base near one of the big sugar cane factories. I would often take Fred to where he wanted to go on the island. His younger son Roy was attending Brigham Young University in Utah. His other son, also named Fred, was a supervisor with Matson Freight Lines at the docks in Honolulu. Sometimes I would drive Fred to the other side of the island where his older son lived. That was near Kaneohe Marine Corps Air Station. Fred's family was the original owners of the land where the Barber's Point Air Station was located. His Hawaiian family name was Kalaeloa. He was a proud man. He talked of his pride in the Coast Guard and when he was in charge of the Barber's Point Lighthouse located just a short distance down the coast from our base at Barber's Point.

A lot of the old timers were transferring back to the mainland. Commander "Koz" Kozlovsky was transferred along with Chief Willie Sutton and Chief George Watson. Commander Koz "sorta" kept the radical draft dodgers in line; but as soon as he left, the radical behavior of these disrespectful troublemakers went on a sharp rise. Immediately, the commanding officer of the Coast Guard Air Station, Barber's Point allowed any men that wanted to grow their hair to their waists. During working hours, the men would roll their hair up and fasten it with bobbie-pins. They would then cover their hair with a wig. They would cut the back out of a work hat (base ball cap) and fasten a bungee cord to hold the two sides together. This would cover their wig. After work every day, as many as eighteen or twenty of these men would walk down by the old Navy bunkers and smoke pot for an hour. They then would walk back by the watering hole and drink a wine cooler to cool their throats. The barracks were full of the smell of incense candles burning as many were smoking pot in their rooms. Every chance many of them had, they would try to harass the men that were adhering to the military rules and traditions. Mostly those who had the misfortune to have to live in the barracks with these losers were harassed. The commanding officer offered an open door policy to his office to these men. He told the

Command Master Chiefs Harry Brown and Patrick Posey that they could not tell a man to get a hair cut. This "freedom" was something unheard of throughout the military service. He did ask the non-conformers to not let their hair down outside of the barracks or until they got outside the guard gate off base. All of this radical behavior brought strenuous tension to the ones of us that knew that the commanding officer was not carrying out his official duties as demanded of his position. He created a living hell for the ones that had a true commitment to our service and to our country. There were constant conflicts between the different cultures.

As I thought predictable, my wife wanted to return back to her home in North Carolina. The Coast Guard allowed me an early shipping return for my family and our household goods back to Carolina, but I would have to stay in Hawaii until my three-year tour of duty was complete. This would end our habitat as a family, and she soon chose another from back home. This marriage experiment was just not going to work for me, so I gave up on the idea for years. I was destined to live a single life while being in the military.

I moved back into the barracks to my old room. It was clean with air conditioning but still with the aroma of incense burning. This was a continuous reminder of the type of people that I would have around me for the remainder of time that I would be stationed at this base.

One morning I was waiting in line for breakfast after I had told the cook how I would like my eggs cooked. The cook who was preparing my eggs was one of the longhaired, hippie troublemakers. I asked for scrambled eggs, so he began to shuffle my eggs across the grill. Then for harassment's sake he raked them off into the used grease and grill scrapings. He then dipped the eggs along with all of the old grease and scrapings and put them on my plate. I had been harassed just about enough and nearly started over the cooking counter after the idiot. About that time I noticed the Chief in Charge, Chief Salanoa, was in the galley. I stopped myself and decided to let the chief see what kind of harassment one of his draft-dodging cooks was doing to some of us. Chief Salanoa had a lot of pride in the Coast Guard and was a regular Coastie. He was from Samoa and a big man. I showed my plate to the chief, and he said, "I will take care of this." The chief walked over to the draft dodger. He picked him up by the front of his shirt and apron with one hand and slammed him against the bulkhead. With the other hand, he balled his fist up and told the man, "If you ever do that to anyone in my galley again, I will kill you." That ended the harassment from this one individual for the rest of the time he was at the unit.

On Sunday morning some of the many decent young men that lived in the barracks were leaving to go to church. Several of the hippie draft-dodgers grouped outside the entrance to the barracks. The draft-dodgers harassed a few of them, and one really good hard-working young man walked out the door to go to his car. As he walked past the group that were verbally harassing him, one of them reached out as if to knock his Bible and papers out of his hand. Witnessing that abuse to the young man was all I needed to let my bloody English, Scotch-Irish, North Carolinian, Cherokee, and All American brawn rule my brain; and I let into them.

Not one of them wanted any part of my furry. They cowered down just like the less-than-men they were. I called them all "Hippie Draft Dodging cowards," and they should be ashamed to stoop so low as to try and insult a young man trying to get to church.

I often thought that the very freedoms my and their forefathers fought and died for, they were destroying by joining in a subculture to take it all away. I'm sure they were still under the effects of drugs to make them so brazen and disrespectful of others' freedoms, especially religious freedom as they often spouted their misguided belief in Communism in order to impress their peers. I'm sure they just wanted to fit in with the anti-war movement scene that many of them had been subjected to before entering the Coast Guard. Each time I saw these men act in that way, I would jump in the middle. I was risking my future in the service that I loved so much, but I felt it was my duty to stand up to these Hanoi Jane Fonda Haden follower types. I have seen, with disgust, these people in action against our country. I made up my mind that if one of them tried to urinate on me as they were doing to some of our returning heroes from Viet Nam, that person would have given me the invitation to terminate him. There was no doubt in my mind that at that time and place it could very well happen. A lot of this built-up hatred among many of us patriots could have been avoided if one man (the commanding officer) would just carry out his sworn duty to uphold the military standards that we all were trained and expected to maintain while accomplishing our missions in the military, no matter what mission was requested of us. No other base in the Coast Guard was so out of control in an attempt to pacify the draft-dodgers and impress their parents back in California for political ambitions.

The word spread through the barracks of me standing up to these troublemakers, and the hippie draft-dodgers just became more brazen in their harassment. The commanding officer was too busy with his politicking with several of their parents from California to even care about the ones of us that were living in the barracks, holding the line and keeping his aircraft safely flying. Some of them worked well at their assigned job, but they would hang with the undesirable group after work, smoke dope, and mimic the cowardly behavior of a few that had no loyalty to our country. My new harassment nickname would become "Hippie." They started writing my name on the latrine bulkheads and in the electrical panels and on the inside of all the aircraft access panels. They would write "Fred is a Hippie," and it spread to everywhere we would fly-all the way to Southeast Asia and every island in between. They would correspond with their friends at other bases to spread the word "Fred is a Hippie" for harassment's sake. My name would become famous in the Coast Guard even though many would not understand the origin or reason of my now famous notoriety. I continued to hold my head high and demonstrate to the draft-dodgers at each of their undermining efforts, that I had no intention of cowering down to their drug infested and un-American rhetoric. Being from my bloodline and where I was born and raised, "coward" was not a word used to describe a man from the breed of North Carolinians I came from.

We were heavily involved in flying missions. We were regularly flying to Southeast Asia, Viet Nam, Mexico, Midway, Marcus, Kwajalein, Iwo Jima, Kure, Saipan, Wake, Johnston Island, Yap, Pago Pago, Manila, Alaska and many other places.

Wake Island, a frequent refueling stopover for
Coast Guard C-130s transiting the Pacific.

We had a lot of responsible duties to perform, and these troublemakers were making it very difficult for many of us. But still, the commanding officer refused to hear of or see any problems with these draft-dodgers' actions.

The long range aids to navigation (LORAN) station located on the island of Iwo Jima was manned by the Coast Guard. Part of our duty was to re-supply the station's needs, and we did so with frequent flights in our C-130 aircraft. Normally a dozen or more men were stationed on isolated duty to operate and maintain the equipment that sent out LORAN signals needed to guide ships and aircraft across the Pacific. Once in a while we would have time to drive up to Mount Suribachi where the Japanese had dug in during the WWII invasion of the island and where they fired their weapons in the slaying of so many of our US Marines. In an attempted beach landing during WWII, the US Marines were trying to come ashore in their efforts to rid the Japanese from the island. Thousands of US Marines lost their lives at this very place while in a desperate struggle to stop the Japanese and save our homeland.

All throughout the WWII Pacific Campaign by US Forces our Coast Guard, under direction of the Navy, operated landing craft and manned ships to do battle with our enemies. On one particular island landing, Coastguardsman Douglas Monroe steered his landing craft through the coral reefs and delivered his load of US Marines on shore. As he was returning to the ship to load another group of Marines, he looked back and saw that the Marines he had just put ashore were pinned down by enemy machine guns and all were going to perish. Monroe turned his landing craft about face and headed to the beach to try to save the Marines. He maneuvered his craft in the surf to provide a shield for the Marines until they could receive fire support from other Marines. Many of his group of Marines died before he could provide them cover, but many of them survived by his unselfish and brave action. Coastie Monroe's life-saving instincts were part of his character, and he did what was necessary. He was killed by the Japanese machine gun fire meant for the Marines, but saved many Marines by his unselfish action and sense of loyalty. He was awarded the Congressional Medal of Honor (Posthumously) for his bravery.

Memorial of US Marines on Iwo Jima

Beachhead landing site of invasion force with destroyed landing craft still present in the shallows.

I guess I could leave this story out and make it read politically correct, but then I would be like some writers and not tell the real story of what the military is really like. I want to tell the experiences that a trooper might really face while serving.

One evening, a couple of other men and I were sitting at a table in the galley eating our evening meal. In comes one of the draft-dodgers with his hair frizzed out and down to the middle of his back. We knew that this was just another chance to harass anyone who cared about proper military grooming. Well, I didn't take kindly to the man pulling up a chair at the table right next to where we were sitting. Two of his friends were sitting there, and they were really enjoying the obvious dislike showing on our faces. The hippie flipped his hair in an obvious attempt to antagonize us. I told the two men sitting with me, "Something had to be done and that this was a military base and ought to be run like one, whether the draft-dodgers liked it or not." I told them that this man looked like a cave man. The commanding officer had said they could grow their hair as long as they wanted, but politely asked them if they would not leave the barracks with their hair not rolled up in bobbie pins. (It was sickening. It was disgusting.)

We finished with our dinner and the other two left ahead of me. I walked out of the galley door and was walking towards the barracks. I heard the three men sitting on the barracks steps saying, "Cave man," and they continued to repeat the words as I walked closer to the steps where they were sitting. I knew right away that the man that came into the galley with his hair down his back had heard what I had said to the two men I was sitting with. I asked who they were calling a cave man and they all three said, "We are calling you a cave man." With them blocking the steps into the barracks and deliberately calling me the name, I decided that I had no other choice but to take a licking from the three of them or be man enough to single them out one at a time and do my best at standing up to them. I guess it reflected back to my childhood when standing up to bullies and taking a licking made you feel better than cowering down and taking a licking anyhow. At least those three would know that there would be no free lunch at my expense.

Needless to say, I stood up to these troublemakers and paid the price for my actions. The old man's political ambitions influenced and controlled his actions.

One of the first class petty officers that was always cozy with many of these draft-dodgers was transferred. Only after he was transferred to Coast Guard Air Station Miami, Florida, was he arrested for selling narcotics to the junior men. He could get by with it at our base in Hawaii. The commanding officer liked liberal-minded people of his character and thought highly of him. While he was stationed at our base he only encouraged the troublemakers. With us not knowing of his devious character and his trying to make friends with the drug users, he aided in the draft-dodgers' opportunity to make many of our lives miserable that lived in the barracks.

The commanding officer continued to entertain certain parents from California, as we found out he had political intentions upon his return to California. The draft-dodgers increased their drug use even more openly until the next commanding officer ordered the doors removed from rooms in the barracks after this commanding officer was later transferred.

We had many rescue helicopter pilots in the Coast Guard that volunteered to exchange duty with our Air Force men serving in Viet Nam. The Coast Guard pilots would fly the Air Force rescue helicopters and let Air Force pilots have a break from combat to fly rescue missions with the Coast Guard.

Lcdr. Joe Crowe volunteered to go to Viet Nam to rescue downed flight crews behind enemy lines. Considering my frustration with the way things were going in my life and at this base, I was ready to go as a crewman on the rescue helicopters. I had already been through weapons training in the army, and I had the gumption to do the job. I asked the commanding officer if he would allow me to volunteer to go with Lcdr. Crowe as a rescue crewman. He said there was no provision for exchange of air rescue crewman between the Air Force and Coast Guard. What a let down!

My good retired Coastie Hawaiian friend Fred "Kalaeloa" Robbins would talk to me when times seemed a little desperate in dealing with some of the type of men with whom I had regrettably been assigned duty with. He would always say, "When you know you are in the right and doing the right thing, don't let yourself down; feel good about yourself." He always said that, "he felt so good that he could not express himself." He really did give me inspiration and appreciated my courage in trying to do things the right way. He showed me how to have the true Hawaiian spirit and live life to the fullest.

Even if I couldn't be assigned on the rescue helicopters in Viet Nam, I could be assigned with a river or coastal patrol crew. The recruiter that signed me up in the Coast Guard was serving there, and I would gladly join his or another crew. Chief Hope Beacham was patrolling the rivers and delta, fighting Viet Cong junks that were carrying ammunition and enemy troops.

Chief Hope Beacham on patrol in Viet Nam,

Hope's crew kept a pet leopard onboard to discourage the enemy from trying to sneak aboard their patrol craft. The enemy wanted nothing to do with this creature.

We had twenty-six pilots volunteer to go to Viet Nam to rescue flight crews behind enemy lines. We were very fortunate to lose only one. That was Lt. Jack Ritticher. Many of us had flown with Lt. Ritticher back in Elizabeth City, North Carolina. I still remember him today as if he were rushing out to his helicopter on the flight line to rescue mariners in distress. Once in a while he would fly the old Albatross seaplane on a rescue mission. Pilots were required to be qualified in two different aircraft.

Lt. Jack Rittichier, HH-52 rescue pilot, United States Coast Guard Air Station Elizabeth City, North Carolina.

Jack Rittichier Lt. USCG MIA Viet Nam, located and finally brought home for burial on American soil.

Lt. Rittichier found his Marine Corps pilot and while receiving hostile enemy fire, rescued him only to have his helicopter blown to bits while trying to evacuate the downed pilot from the jungle. It would be over thirty years before the remains of Lt. Rittichier, the Marine pilot and Jack's crew were found and brought home to America. "WELCOME HOME PATRIOTS"

Chapter Ten

I flew on many flights with the commanding officer as his flight engineer, sitting between and just aft of him and the co-pilot. I kept his aircraft in excellent mechanical flying condition and performed my flight engineer's duties for him as we flew as far as Southeast Asia, to many islands near the Equator, Alaska, Mexico and the US mainland. He did everything he could to impress the admiral when we escorted the admiral to his many remote destinations.

We had a Coast Guard LORAN station on the island of Saipan, and we flew there once in a while to provide logistic support. On one flight carrying the admiral, the commanding officer was copilot; and Lcdr. Glasgow was the pilot. When we taxied up the ramp to the terminal to disembark the admiral, the commanding officer wanted the big C-130 parked on the sloping taxiway leading to the level-parking ramp instead of parking on the level-parking ramp. He said that it would be more impressive for the admiral to face the door as he walked back to the plane the next day. The Captain also said that the crew had a very difficult time removing the chocks from between the main landing gear wheels the last time he parked in this position. After a period of time when the hydraulic pressure bleeds off, the brakes become free and the aircraft will roll until stopped when the wheels contact the chocks. The aircraft was on an incline, so I told the crew to put chocks, piles of cargo tie-down chain and anything else they thought necessary to stop the aircraft from rolling. If the aircraft rolled straight back, it would end up dropping off a cliff and into the Pacific Ocean just below. I went with the first crew van to the hotel, and later the rest of the crew arrived. We were tired and ready for a swim in the lagoon. Old military landing craft were in the water, still there from our WWII invasion of the island. We swam out to the vehicles and looked at where they had been hit by artillery. I had a feeling of sorrow for the servicemen that gave their lives on this spot for our freedom. We swam back to shore and were relaxing on the beautiful beach when all of a sudden someone from the hotel came running out and shouted: "Your airplane has rolled off the parking area back at the airport!"

Lieutenant Duane Jefts and Andy Viscondi in Chang-Mai, Northern Thailand, relaxing before their next mission.

Co-pilot Duane Jefts, Chief Bob Powers and we others ran for the crew van and drove as fast as we could back to the airport. We thought for sure that the aircraft had rolled off the cliff. Our adrenalin was pumping overtime. When we pulled on to the aircraft-parking ramp, the big C-130 sat down in a sloping gully. The wheels had sunk in the mud and the belly of the aircraft was touching mud from the nose to the cargo ramp in the rear. We quickly looked the aircraft over for any structural damage and it looked as though the landing gear doors were possibly undamaged, even though they were down in the mud.

The crew put their wits together and tried to think of the safest way to get our plane out of that muddy draw. I was relieved to see the aircraft where it had rolled and stopped. Even though we still had a problem, we wouldn't have to tell the admiral that his plane had rolled over the cliff and exploded. We discussed finding a large enough tractor and pulling the plane out of the ditch with our cargo chains. We decided there might be a chance of structural damage to the aircraft if we tried towing it with chains. I told the co-pilot that if we cranked all four engines, lower the flaps to give the aircraft lift and put the throttles to full power that we might be able to break the suction from the mud and roll out of the gully. So we all agreed to try with Chief Powers watching the propellers to warn us of them striking the ground.

Chief Powers

Ltjg. Jefts and I started the engines, lowered the flaps and put the throttles to full power. The aircraft began to shake all over but only moved a very little. Mr. Jefts said, "Maybe I should let the plane roll back and try to rock it out of the mud." I suggested, "Hold the throttles. If you let the plane roll back it probably will sink deeper in the mud or damage the bottom of the aircraft. Keep the throttles to take off and let the plane fly itself out of the gully." Within another minute the aircraft broke free of the mud, and we taxied back up the ramp but this time to a level parking spot. We never saw any chocks for our aircraft wheels where they should have been, nor could we find ours. Just maybe the flight line crew moved them after our plane rolled over them. I will never forget the shock of my being responsible for nearly losing an eight million dollar aircraft.

There were just enough breezes pushing on the large vertical stabilizer and rudder to cause the nose wheel to turn as the aircraft rolled down the taxiway. Luckily for us the plane's nose wheel turned in the right direction. We spent the next several hours wiping the mud from the bottom of the aircraft. The only damage we could find was on take-off as the nose wheel shimmied while we were rolling down the runway. We were able to repair that problem on our next stop in Thailand. We contacted the US Air Force Base in Udorn and Utipou to see if they had the part we needed, and sure enough they sent us the part. The Air Force, as always, was kind enough to provide us with a nose wheel steering valve; and we were back in good operating condition.

Years later I convinced the C-130 standardization team at the Elizabeth City Coast Guard Air Station to print on the written checklist "INSTALL CHOCKS Upon Engine Shutdown." I would always tell the story to the pilots I flew with, in case they were in a remote area and found themselves off the pavement and in the mud. Several incidents would arise in later years. Vice Commandant Vivian Crea (when a young Lieutenant pilot) rescued a C-130 from the mud in Elizabeth City by powering the plane back onto the runway.

Sometimes we had a day off at places like Bangkok, Hong Kong, Taiwan, or Yakoto, Japan and were able to shop on our return leg of the flight. Sometimes all of the available room in the cargo compartment of the aircraft was taken by what the crew and passengers bought. Some lighter items were tied to the overhead.

Hong Kong Harbor
Boats are called "junks"

On one of our flights when we were escorting the district admiral and his wife, we were always aware of sabotage efforts by some around the world that would do us harm. We would lock our aircraft up when we departed the ramp parking area. We pinned all of the emergency escape hatches from the inside. When we returned to the aircraft for the next flight we would remove the locking pins when we did our preflight. The locking pin for the center overhead escape hatch was missing so we used a screwdriver in place of the pin. I guess whoever did the inside preflight forgot to check the overhead escape hatch and remove the screwdriver as a ladder was required to reach the hatch. We had taken off and flown some distance over the ocean when the admiral's wife stood up from her seat and walked to the rear of the aircraft to stretch her legs. She stopped directly under the escape hatch and began talking to a few of the crew. I was on break from the cockpit and engaged in conversation with the admiral's wife. All of a sudden I saw the screwdriver whiz by her head as it brushed her clothing and fell to the deck of the cargo compartment. I quickly nudged it out of sight with my flight boot. As I did, I just smiled and continued to engage her in conversation as if everything were normal. The screwdriver had worked its way out of the pinhole due to the vibration of the aircraft. She never mentioned a word, as she didn't know just how close she had come to being seriously wounded because of our neglect. We were responsible to see that she had a safe journey, and we nearly failed. Here we had almost lost a Coast Guard C-130 aircraft by nearly letting it roll off of a cliff and almost killed one of our most important passengers. The reality of my responsibility was sinking in!

Lt. Bill Ricks was our assistant engineering officer. He was a tall, very humble man who grew up near Elizabeth City, North Carolina. We all knew him from having been stationed with him at our last duty station in Elizabeth City. I had previously flown with him on the old HU-16E seaplane we called the "Goat." He had flown search and rescue in the "Goat" at Miami, Florida; Biloxi, Mississippi and in the Philippines. Now he was flying the C-130B here at Barber's Point. Once in a while he would be assigned a mission to Viet Nam. His flight engineer on one particular flight was Bill Farling. They landed at Cam Ranh Bay, Viet Nam; and after they had parked their C-130, they were able to get a photo shot of an ordinance explosion in front of their plane. They weren't for sure if the enemy had sent in a mortar or what, but it got their attention.

Naval Air Facility Cam Ranh Bay, Viet Nam
(Coast Guard C-130 tail in front of cloud)

Bill said the men stationed there were used to excitement of this sort.

Lt. Bill Ricks
Flying over Viet Nam

Lt. Ricks had married a beautiful Pasquotank County girl named Billie. She was always a welcome sight at our station functions in Hawaii. I had several friends from North Carolina who made my miserable time living in the barracks somewhat enjoyable each time we were at work or at a social event. There was my good friend Carol Hill, now a Structural Mechanic, but he used to be the seaman on the rescue boat that I ran-when we stood duty together back in Elizabeth City, North Carolina. I knew Bill "Fearless" Farling, Bill "Brutus" and Shirley Lewis, Dave "WD" and Marge Richards and Kirby "High Tider" Bowden. I didn't feel totally overwhelmed when some of them were still on the base.

Lcdr. Bill and Billie Ricks
(Carolina Pride)
Aviation Engineering Officer

We flew often to the island of Midway and to the Coast Guard LORAN Station on Kure Island. We supported the Coast Guard personnel assigned to isolated duty for a year on the island of Kure. We flew in personnel as they exchanged duty and carried in cargo of food and equipment. The islands of Kure and Midway were notorious for millions of Gooney birds that made this part of the Pacific their home. These birds would fly out to sea for several years, returning to the Kure and Midway islands to nest and raise their young. Gooney birds were aggressive when we would walk near their nests. Their peck was more like a small dog bite. The birds were very large and very clumsy when on land, although while in flight, they were very graceful. They could catch the gentle breezes and glide low over the water. Often it looked as if one of their wing tips was touching the water. When they would come in for a landing, however, they seemed to forget how to put their feet down in a manner to support the body. Most of the time, they would crash land on their bellies and their beaks. Being so large (nearly seven feet of wing span) and flying so slow, they really became a danger to us and our aircraft each time we wanted to land and takeoff on Kure and Midway Islands. Oftentimes we would have to replace a propeller, windshield or leading edge panel on our wing. The birds weighed enough to tear a hole into the metal leading edge of our wing when we would collide with one of them in flight. Sometimes the impact would cause our propeller blades to warp.

Lt. Bill Ricks, Lt. Denny Morrissey and flight engineer pointing to stenciled birds.

Upon return of one flight from Kure Island, I replaced two propellers because of Gooney Bird strike damage. They unfortunately scored eight strikes on one landing and takeoff at Kure Island.

Flying missions were long at times as flight time and crew mission restraints were flexible except every seventh day. Even then, if we were needed for search and rescue duty, that day was overridden. One day the alarm went off for a ship in trouble half way to Japan. We ran to the aircraft and prepared to start the plane. One of the engines didn't pass a performance check for takeoff, so we had to return to the aircraft ramp and work on that engine before the plane was safe for flight. We worked for about eight hours before we could get the engine to perform satisfactorily. We topped off the aircraft with fuel; and when the aircraft passed the performance checks at the end of the runway, we took off for the ship in trouble. It was already evening time. We were the only available aircraft at the base. We were young and every call for assistance from us was answered with the same enthusiasm. I was proud to go and be able to help someone, no matter how many hours it took to complete a successful rescue. We flew into the sunset and then darkness. The aircraft engines purred. I kept a close watch on the one that we had had trouble with. I watched every movement on the instruments of the four engines. I watched the fuel use from each wing tank closely and balanced the wings fuel tanks as needed, making sure to use the auxiliary tank fuel first. If one of our boost pumps failed in the auxiliary tanks, that fuel would become useless and we might have needed it to reach our destination at another distant island where we could refuel. We flew late into the night to reach our refueling stop on another island.

We refueled and immediately took off in the direction of the ship in trouble. The red instrument lights in our cockpit were making our eyes tired. On occasion, I would have to clear my eyes as the instruments seemed to look doubled. Instead of four engines to monitor, on occasion there seemed to be flashes of eight engines. I wet a red rag (maintenance rag) and rubbed my eyes from time to time to be sure I was alert. Once in a while I would tap one of the pilots on the shoulder to be sure he was awake. They would take turns controlling the aircraft while one would get a short rest.

We reached our rescue target in the wee hours of the morning. After making contact with the ship, we found them to be underway again. The ship's captain radioed us that he was able to get control of his emergency and had changed his course for safe harbor at the closest island. After seeing that the ship's captain was confident he could make it to safe harbor we turned, this time into the sun, towards our refueling island destination. After refueling, we again took off back towards our home base at Barber's Point in Hawaii. I never thought land looked so good. On approach I gave myself one more face wash so that I would be alert for landing. When we shut down our engines, we had just finished a thirty-four hour crew mission day. I turned the plane over to the ready crew in the duty section, as we all were exhausted. I went by the galley and grabbed a small bite to eat and then went to my room in the barracks. I stayed there for two days trying to rest as I could and regain my energy and straight thinking.

Not long after that incident when one of the engineers stepped off of the flight deck accidentally and broke his leg, the flight rules were limited. Several times since then the flight-time rules have been modified for certain conditions, only to be extended by the District Commander for Search and Rescue emergencies. Even in these conditions, I would volunteer to do it again if needed. I have always felt pride and a since of loyalty to our mission when I was allowed to be a part of doing something good for my Coast Guard and my country. I loved my job!

Coast Guard LORAN Long Range Aids to Navigation Stations dotted the Pacific Ocean. Some islands were located in very remote areas. Our C-130 aircraft made frequent landings on these islands.

Welcome sign at Coast Guard LORAN Station, Kure Island. Gooney bird standing beneath sign.

Gooney Bird chick.

We landed on Yap Island to bring support supplies to the LORAN Station. The inhabitants of each island had their own way of doing things. On Yap, the natives chewed beetle-nut; and their teeth were stained by the nut juices. They also used stones as symbols of value in front of their homes.   There were downed aircraft from the battles during WWII still visible in the jungle growth.

Occasionally we would land on a man-made runway on French Frigate Shoals. The Navy built a base on top of a volcanic reef during WWII. The Coast Guard was using it for a LORAN Navigation Transmission Site. The Coast Guard had a dozen or more men stationed on the site, and we would re-supply and transfer men to and from Hawaii to the site. Sometimes the men would have to be removed if there was a forecast of a typhoon putting them in harm's way. The men would stay on the site for a period of twelve months before they would be relieved.   They would be allowed a break sometime in the twelve months.   Years later I heard that a rogue wave from a typhoon smashed over the entire island. Damage was extensive.

Approach to landing on French Frigate Shoals
Coast Guard LORAN Navigation Station (Pacific).

The LORAN Station on the island of Palau was the southernmost station.

Flight Crew riding on Angaur, Palau LORAN Station's aircraft crash rescue vehicle.

Palau had the most beautiful vegetation and other scenery.

On some flights we would fly to Japan and load a repair crew of Japanese workers. We would fly to different island LORAN stations. The Japanese repair crews would climb the tall LORAN towers with a bundle of wires and some protective paint in a small basket-like rig with a cable attachment tied to it. These small men would attach their rigs to the top of the support cables and begin sliding down the tower support cables. As they descended, they would splice in pieces of the support cable where corrosion had weakened the cable. Then they would paint the area and slide down to the next spot needing attention. Some of the LORAN towers were two thousand feet in the air. Our C-130's were the main source of transportation in support for Coast Guard LORAN stations around the world. The long hours of hard work serving in the Coast Guard were rewarding in getting to experience the many remote areas of our beautiful world.

More than once we received an emergency mayday call from a pilot that transferred small, single engine aircraft from California to New Zealand or Australia. The pilot would remove all but the pilot seat and carry extra gasoline inside the cabin in five-gallon containers. Several times we had been out to assist him and guide him in to the Islands.

We received another call and our rescue crew responded. This time the pilot indicated that he had lost oil pressure. This is definitely not a good thing to happen anytime whether over water or over land and especially over the ocean. With losing the only engine, the pilot's survival became a critical situation for us. Our radioman made contact with the aircraft and communicated with him in an effort to locate his aircraft. Our rescue crew talked with the pilot as his engine had frozen up from lack of oil press. The pilot talked with the rescue crew and told them everything he could in hopes that the rescue crew could locate him and get a rescue ship to him when he crashed into the water. The pilot didn't panic as he told our rescue crew he was going through the clouds and when he could see the water. He had hoped we could be there to know his location, but sadly our aircraft did not get there in time. The pilot's radio went silent, and there was no response after numerous calls to try and locate him. An all out search was called to try and locate the downed pilot using his last known radio directional signals, intercepted from our rescue center. After a massive effort to cover the area, the small plane was never to be found.

Failure to find a pilot or a mariner in distress can leave you feeling sorrow for the person and their family. That ocean is tremendous in size; and even in good weather sun reflections on the water, whitecaps, wave shadows and the mere size of the area to cover, all play a part in our chances of locating a victim.

One day our rescue alarm sounded and the Commands were to prepare two C-130 Aircraft for maximum effort search northeast of Midway Island. A Danish ship had gone down; and the Air Force, Navy, and Coast Guard would combine efforts to rescue the Danish mariners. Two additional C-130 aircraft were summoned from the mainland in San Francisco, California. The crews flew all day to Hawaii, refueled, grabbed a bite to eat in the galley, and then flew on to Midway Island. My crew flew all day; and after we landed, I was able to visit with the San Francisco crew in the galley. I knew the pilots and some of the crew on the aircraft #1348. I talked to pilot Lcdr. Matt Ahern and co-pilot Lt. Kirk Colvin. I knew the flight engineer, Lou Sliter from duty together in Elizabeth City, North Carolina, and the navigator/radioman Chief Roger Schmidt. After resting, eating and having their plane refueled, they left on their search mission to Midway.

Four Coast Guard C-130 aircraft, two Air Force C-130 aircraft and two Navy P3 aircraft were searching in an area controlled by a Coast Guard cutter. Ragged ceilings from 500 to 1500 feet and low visibility because of scattered rain-showers throughout the search area made conditions for multi-aircraft search marginal at best. To further complicate matters, several navigational aids on the CG #1348 aircraft were inoperative. Chief Schmidt had invited Navy Chief Norm Elliot, stationed on Midway Island, to fly with the Coast Guard crew for this flight. After three hours of searching in bad weather, the Coast Guard C-130 #1348 and a Navy P3 collided while flying in "IFR" (surface controlled because of visibility) conditions. An Air Force C-130 escorted the Navy P3 back to Midway Island, and a Coast Guard C-130 escorted the damaged CG #1348 C-130 back to the island. Miraculously both planes made it back to Midway Island without loss of life. The Navy P3 aircraft had shut down its number one engine to conserve fuel. Had the engine been in operation, the number one propeller on the Navy P3 and the number two propeller on the C-130 would probably have made contact; and most likely, no one from either aircraft would have survived.

The Coast Guard plane sustained damage on its underside and on one aileron. The belly was ripped open from the crew entrance door to the cargo ramp.

Belly of CG1348 C-130 looking forward.

Belly of CG1348 C-130 looking aft.

The Navy P3 aircraft lost twelve feet of its wing on impact with the belly of the C-130. Also, the Navy plane sustained damage to the top of the vertical stabilizer.

The Navy P3 had twelve feet of left wing missing.

Coast Guard C-130 flight crew standing. Navy P3 flight crew seated. Celebrating a chance to fly for their country, another day.

I thought about just how close we came to losing another crew of our brothers, both Navy and Coast Guard. We have had many fatal and near fatal disasters, but this was one accident where we beat the odds. Sometimes I think God is protecting us from the dangers we face while we give our all in our efforts to saving others. Thoughts of tragedies and respect for those brothers lost are always on our minds. When the call for help comes to us, we momentarily put those thoughts aside and give the same effort as our lost brothers did while trying to save another life.

If we continue to work to have the best maintained aircraft and ships and we train to be the best, then the rest is all about attitude, pride, luck and our almighty God.

Our Coast Guard Air Station in Barber's Point and the Engineering Office in Washington performed an investigation of the collision between the two planes. The

Coast Guard, Navy, and Air Force thoroughly followed every aircraft's movement and made recommendations for safety in the future.

After their investigation, crews to repair the Coast Guard were selected from what personnel were available from our air station in Hawaii. Many hours of labor were performed by groups of mechanics with different specialties, mainly structural mechanics. The plane was patched up strong enough to make a flight back to Hawaii but had been damaged enough that it could no longer be pressurized for high altitude flight.

Coast Guard C-130 #1348 structural repair crew.

After a final thorough inspection and repair, the aircraft would be flown to California for a major repair. The crew would have to pre-breathe oxygen for a period of time before they could start engines and begin their flight takeoff. The crew would be on oxygen on the long flight from Hawaii to California. Once the crew began their pre-breathing, they could not remove their masks. If they removed their masks, they would be susceptible to getting the bends because the plane wasn't pressurized during the high flight altitude required to make the ocean crossing. The gas turbine compressor that is used to start the aircraft would not start when the switch was energized. Bill Farling, the flight engineer, removed his mask to step off the aircraft and get the gas turbine started. He was off oxygen for just a very short time so the crew decided to continue on their mission. They took off and headed to California. They climbed slowly to an altitude planned for optimal fuel consumption to reach the mainland. Sometime during mid-flight, Bill began experiencing pain in his limbs. The crew tried to comfort him as he was suspected to have come down with the bends. Sure enough, Bill had the bends; and the radioman made arrangements in advance for the medical team in California to take Bill to a dive chamber upon the plane's landing. Bill survived the bends and returned to aviation duty.

That wasn't the first time that the Coast Guard C-130 #1348 had to be flown to California for major repair. We originally had the plane in Hawaii before it was assigned to Coast Guard Air Station, San Francisco. I was assigned the flight engineer duty on a planned training flight one morning. I had completed most of my preflight inspections and began doing my fuselage and wing walk-around checks. Cdr. Koslovsky was the pilot for our training flight, and he joined me in the outside walk-around inspection. We were walking under the wing looking up for fuel leaks and flight control damage. All of a sudden something hit the commander on his cap. He took his cap off and found a rivet head from the bottom of the wing.

Coast Guard C-130#1348 graced with Hawaiian Lei (Aloha).

The rivet head had popped off due to corrosion. We looked around on the ramp and found other rivet heads lying under the wing area. Looking closer, we saw that the wing looked like it might be settling downward because the metal skin on the bottom of the wing was rippled in places. The commander cancelled the training flight and rounded up all of his structural mechanic specialists. They de-fueled the aircraft and found that the wing's internal metal structural components had corroded so badly that the wing was ready to break off. In fact, if we had taken off, the wing would have come off the aircraft. Now that kind of near fatal experience can get your ticker pumping!

The older B-Model C-130 aircraft did not have primer corrosion protection like the later models. In Hawaii, corrosion was bad on the older C-130B aircraft due to the ocean's saltwater mist. A team of men was assigned to try to keep the corrosion at bay. All year long the crew worked at corrosion control with the work beginning after the normal workday.

Coast Guard C-130 #1348 flying over Diamond Head, Oahu.

A special repair team was called in from the Lockheed Aircraft Company in Ontario, California. They replaced all the necessary pieces so that the plane could be flown safely across the "big pond" to California. After the aircraft was temporarily repaired, the plane was allowed a one-time flight to the mainland; and a major repair was accomplished. The plane then was assigned to the Coast Guard Air Station in San Francisco. This is how the #1348 became the plane to fly back to Hawaii and to Midway Island before the midair collision with a Navy P-3. Fate would have it that I would be the last flight engineer to fly on the #1348 C-130 as I rode in it to the bone yard in Arizona from my next assigned base in Elizabeth City, North Carolina.

One day we received a radio call from the Big Island of Hawaii. One of our C-130 planes had to make an emergency landing after one of its propellers had failed. They had been out on a rescue mission. Since no more planes were ready to fly at our base in Barber's Point, we would have to call on our Air Force friends at the air rescue unit at Hickam Field in Honolulu. The air rescue unit gladly agreed to carry our spare propeller and tools to the Big Island. The Air Force crew flew out to our base, we loaded our propeller and Bill and I flew off with them to Hawaii. After the short flight, we unloaded our gear and began searching for a crane that could lift the propeller while we were exchanging the old for the new. We finally were able to find an old auto wrecker with a long enough boom to lift the propeller from the wing. Bill "Pitts" Pittsenbarger and I had the propeller replaced and ready for run-up and in-flight shutdown check in a record time of two hours and thirty minutes. Air Station Barber's Point was, once again, back in the C-130 rescue business thanks to our Air Force rescue brothers and the helpful Hawaiians living on the Big Island.

Many times we were ordered to remote places around the world. Sometimes an engine or a propeller was needed. Sometimes we had to make do with any kind of lifting equipment that was available in the remote areas. Each of our flight engineer/plane captains was required to know how to change a propeller, engine, tire, and brake because of the remote missions around the world we were sent to perform. Time after time our Air Force and Navy brothers would assist us, and we were able to continue our mission.

Experiencing more and more aircraft failures and finding that I could repair my aircraft anywhere made me feel very proud. I felt good that I was becoming more valuable to the Coast Guard. I wanted to be called on and to be able to perform any mission my country needed. I just couldn't wait for my next adrenalin rush while doing my job. The Coast Guard had become my family, and each mission was accomplished with family pride attached to it. I couldn't fathom having a more rewarding and likeable occupation.

I often thought of my orphan brothers and where they might be performing their assigned duty all over this big world. I wondered just how many were serving in Viet Nam, Alaska or maybe one of the remote Air Force or Coast Guard stations in the far Pacific or even on a Navy ship. I wondered if our paths would cross during one of my many journeys. I found out later many of the boys were serving close to places I had traveled during my duty. Richard Evans and Doug Beatty from the orphanage was a couple of years younger than I and were now serving in Viet Nam. Earl Wade had just come to the orphanage after I had left. He was serving in Viet Nam at this time with the 35th Combat Engineers before being assigned to the 1st Calvary. He was serving in the Binh Dinh Province in the Bon Son Plains.

Earl Wade ready for what might come next.

Johnny Tuttle was near my age and graduated from high school the year before I did. We were in a group of orphans that had grown up together. Johnny volunteered to serve in the US Army. Johnny was assigned to serve in a headquarters specialty field. He served several years in Asia during the Viet Nam War. Johnny was well read, patriotic, quiet and shy. He had an impressive memory.

Johnny Tuttle with friends in Japan

James Hope joined the Marines and later served with Air America. James was a couple of years younger than I; but, believe me, he was just as daring and adventurous. James fought in Viet Nam and nearly didn't make it home to his lovely young wife. His flight crew crashed their helicopter after taking hostile fire, and he nearly burned to death in the fire. He has been in a life-long battle with his injuries received from the war.

US Marine James Hope with wife Ethelda.

At times our station would put on a luau. Fred "Robbie" Robbins would show the crew how to cook a pig, Hawaiian style. We would dig a pit for Robbie, and he would build a fire in the pit. Eventually the pig wrapped in banana leaves would be placed in the pit. The event would last all day and into the night. Everyone would be dressed in gala Hawaiian attire with flowered leis around their necks, and the ladies wore flowers in their hair. I loved the spirit and the music. I wished all of my friends back home could experience an event like this.

The sandy beach with the moon glimmering on the slow rippling waves lightly touching the shore would leave a lasting impression on me. Sometimes I would sit there on the beach till the wee hours in the morning, maybe wishing a beautiful Polynesian friend would appear to sit down beside me and keep me company. Going back to the barracks after a day like this was a distasteful matter of necessity. I can see how some of the men would get "Polynesian Paralysis," just by wishing to live in this enticing imaginary world. It was fun.

Several of us volunteered to help build a nicer recreational club in one of the old WWII Quonset huts. We visited our Navy friends at the Explosive Ordinance Depot base at

West Lock. They handled the ammunition as it came off of the ships. The ammo on the ships was shored up with large pine planks. We were able to get enough planks to build a very nice bar. We put glass mirrors behind the bar and paneling around the room. After adding air conditioning, we had a comfortable place to get out of the barracks. We could get a sandwich or a cool drink and socialize with other Coasties or our visiting friends from the Navy base. We had several nice people that operated the club for us. The club turned out to be nice enough for all the families at our station to have get togethers.

Other times we would go to other beaches and military recreational areas on the island. The Army sponsored a military rest area on a beach in the village of Waianae not far from our base. With waves that grew about six feet high, the beach was nice for swimming. Before W. D. Richards and his wife Marge had left the island, they invited my wife and me to go to a picnic there. W. D. didn't like to body surf in the tall waves, but Marge and I would take on the challenge. It was dangerous though, as the waves crashed hard onto the beach. If you went head first into the beach, there was enough force to break your neck on impact with the sand. Some people over the years did just that. We were careful and enjoyed the water, the sand and the sun.

W.D. and Marge Richards with Andy leaving
Hawaii with orders to North Carolina.

Another place was popular for the nature lovers to gather
in the buff. On occasion different people tried to entice me
to join in with them at the buff beach located on the other
side of the island. No way was I going to get naked in
public, not this man!

As time passed, I would see my friends leave the island,
some more celebrated than others. The Aloha sendoffs
were entertaining and joyful, but the person that you
worked with for several years and their family would be
missed. Lt. Ricks, his wife Billie and their children
departed Aloha Tower by ship. They decided to relax and
take the ship voyage back to the mainland instead of
flying. We all prepared them a nice sendoff with tons of
leis and lots of hugs and kisses from friends and co-
workers.

Billie and Bill Ricks with many leis of affection and love from crew and families. Aloha!

Aloha, as lines are cast off. Until we meet again. Mahalo

Eventually, my three years of duty at this station were over. What could have been one of the most enjoyable, hardworking and relaxing tours of duty turned into a nightmare at times. I would forever hate men of my own country that persistently tried to undermine the USCG service and our country while they wore the uniform of a

United States military man. I have the same affection for the men of higher ranking that cowed to their rhetoric.

One of the men thought it a good idea to write a major Massachusetts newspaper. He wrote that he didn't know why the rest of the Coast Guard stations on the mainland, could not be like our USCG Air Station in Barber's Point, Hawaii. He wrote along with other topics: At USCG Air Station in Barber's Point, Hawaii, we men can wear our hair down to our waist.

The CO allowed the men to let their hair grow as long as they wished. The men would then wear a short wig over the rolled and bobbie-pinned hair. The commanding officer ordered that the command master chief could not tell any man to get a hair cut. Many were frequent users of drugs. I received word that this individual helped end his and the other losers reign of disrespect to the Coast Guard Air Station in Hawaii. I heard changes came swiftly after word was received in headquarters in Washington, DC. I wished I could have gotten a copy of the letter sent to the newspaper.

I would hear of the changes that finally came about with a new commanding officer. Doors were removed from the draft dodgers' rooms in the barracks in an effort to deter the use of drugs. Burning incense was banned from the barracks. Order and discipline was once again being orchestrated to regain control of the base. Hearing of this somehow relieved part of my frustration and pain, especially when I heard of the drug dealer who gave us so much trouble in Hawaii being held accountable by his arrest for selling drugs to young Coasties. Coast Guard intelligence took the sorry Coast Guard impersonator out of his drug business and stopped his selling drugs to our young men in uniform after his transfer to Coast Guard Air Station in Miami. What a blessing to see that the rest of the Coast Guard had not succumbed to this draft-dodger's rhetoric. Shortly after this man's arrest, the Coast Guard started implementing an anti-drug education and a drug surveillance policy.

My friendship with my good Hawaiian friend Fred Robbins, "Robbie" as we called him, will never be far from my mind. I appreciated getting to know his family. On occasion, I have made contact with his younger son Roy, one of the managers at the Hale Koa military rest center in Hawaii. I enjoyed the moments of time I spent with the native Hawaiians. Everyone could learn something from the true Hawaiian spirit. The way they talk and the way they enjoy what nature has provided them brings a certain feeling of freedom to relax and be a part of their lives.

It wouldn't be long Master Chief Posey would be retiring. His young son Pat would soon be carrying on the Posey family name in the Coast Guard. The old timers were gradually fading away. A lot of them would never be heard from again unless you remained in contact or lived in their neighborhood. As they retired, many would return to their original home area from where they joined the Coast Guard. MCPO Posey retired to the local area of Eva Beach, Hawaii, with his wife Mary, son Pat and daughter Kitty.

MCPO Pat "POZ" Posey, wife Mary and Captain Leo Donahue.

Chapter Eleven

One day I received a call from a chief that I had been stationed with at my last base in Elizabeth City, North Carolina. He had been assigned the Aviation Rating Detailer in Washington DC. He wanted to know how I was doing and said that he had a couple of openings for my rate. He said that I could have my choice between Elizabeth City, North Carolina and San Francisco, California. Without hesitation, I told him that I would take Elizabeth City. He also said that he had an apology to make to me from when he was my chief in Elizabeth City. He apologized for saying that he would promote a black man before me because that person's ancestors came from slavery. He must have looked at my personnel record while he had been in Washington, DC, and noted that I had come from very humble beginnings. Even with our past disagreement, I always thought the chief a decent man; and his apology proved to me that he really was.

Soon I was on my way back to North Carolina. What a breath of fresh air. Not that I didn't enjoy my friends in Hawaii, but I would not be living in a barracks with people that didn't want to be in the Coast Guard and did everything they could to disrupt the lives of the ones that wanted to serve their country. I knew many of the men stationed there in Carolina; and now, women were beginning to come into the Coast Guard.

The Coast Guard would have some getting used to dealing with women serving. Many small stations dotted our coastline and isolated duty stations were located around the world. There were innocent young women vulnerable to the attraction of older men in authoritative roles. Several years of training would be required for that connection to be broken. In some cases the problem is still challenging. Many careers ended and punishment administered because of this attraction.

The equal opportunity era began being applied. Special instruction to all of our troops on being fair to each other no matter what color, religion, or sex soon became a topic in our weekly training sessions. This instruction would be only a front to the intentions of the politically correct. In the near future, each section of the instruction would be manipulated to the advantage of color, religion, or sex. As for color, a program would be invented to give special education at Coast Guard expense and promotion to Blacks, women and others of non-Western European (Caucasian male) ethnicity. As for religion, steeple crosses would be removed from all military chapels throughout all military branches. As for sex, homosexual conduct would be allowed if one didn't tell and didn't get caught. The liberals in congress and the current president Obama are preparing to order our military to accept open homosexuality within its ranks. In my opinion from past experiences of attempted abuse as an innocent teen to my adult years, what a terrible mistake!

I'll always contend that the Coast Guard had a good record of working together. No matter the color or religion, we all had the same opportunities for promotion and duty assignments during our careers until now. Everything was based on our performances and abilities. Albeit, tales were heard of a few men being promoted because of their friendship and special acquaintance with those of higher authority. Now that's just hearsay, mind you!

After the Coast Guard instituted this civil rights program, I saw the beginning of distrust and dislike of what was being mandated. The ones delivering the message would become more and more bullish in their demands. Many of them belonged to political groups outside the Coast Guard and used their bully pulpits to push the outside agenda on our servicemen. No one could complain through the chain of command because his or her career would be ended or drastically hurt if they didn't act as though they were involved and agreed with every detail of the civil rights ideological program. This program would be a perfect example of how an outside race-based political consortium could dominate a military service.

This was only the beginning of what would be called affirmative action. The civil rights manipulators would make race and sex a reverse discriminating issue and call it fairness. Non-white male and female troops would be given special instruction and free college in order for them to be promoted over white males. From the time I joined the service to defend my country, I had been told that the military system of promotion was fair and equal. Each person had the same opportunity for advancement based on that person's duty performance, testing and their own willingness to achieve. We all had the real equal opportunity of dying.

I observed the civil rights program in the military become a tool to institute any program from many radical outside organizations. In the beginning, the program was supposed to create harmony with all races or sexes and teach those that had dislike for one race or the other to mellow out and get along. The program was full of deception from its beginning with key personnel carrying out continuing deceptive practices as mandated from outside the service. The program began with basic demands; and as outside interest groups thought up new tactics to gain advantage, little by little their tactics were instituted by military members of the outside organizations or by senior officers looking to be a standout with proper political correctness towards affirmative action. The result for these officers was selection to high-ranking positions often decided on by members of the liberal congressional caucuses and elected politicians.

I watched the civil rights program grow from harmony between the races to one of the most abusive "Give Me" Socialist programs. No one in authority will tell you that certain people would be selected and advanced based entirely on the color of their skin or the anatomy of their body. Growing up poor without equal opportunity has no bearing on getting special instruction to become an officer in the military unless you are non-white. I advocate that the military should return to its color-blind equality for all before it is too late and the Socialist-minded have enough power to make all the rules to favor themselves and to make those rules permanent.

Anyway, I was glad to be back around familiar surroundings and a lot of Coasties and towns' people that I knew. I had to live in the barracks for a few weeks until I could find a place to stay. I brought an old Chevy pickup truck with me from Hawaii. Finally I was able to settle down outside the base in a mobile home that I had bought from friends Harry and Faye Putnam. Harry and I worked on and flew as rescue crewmen on the old seaplane called the "Goat." What a relief, being able to have my own little place of privacy and peace.

I drove to Delaware to visit my sister, and she helped me set up house with furniture and new carpet. She sold furniture for a living. My little place looked really nice when I finished with the furnishings.

The crew I worked with at the air station would sometimes take a break from their work, and we all would go fishing at a catfish pond in Camden County. When we caught enough fish, we would return to my place and have a fish fry. Chief Pete Davis would bring his deep fry cooker and we would unwind until late in the night.

After one fish fry, it became so late when everyone left that I just piled the dishes in the sink and added the soap and water. I thought I would clean them the next day. Well, the next morning I was called out on a rescue mission out of the country for nearly a week. Of course, the dishes didn't get washed as I had planned; and they sat there getting slimier as the days went on. Finally, a friend of mine stopped to check on my perfectly clean home and found those dishes still in the sink. She didn't want to touch them but suffered through the distasteful chore of washing the dishes anyway. I would hear of leaving those dishes for the rest of my life.

Quite often I would go fishing or hunting with more friends from my base, Everett Taylor and Claude Fightmaster. We always seemed to find some sort of entertainment to keep us busy.

I found out that one of my orphan sisters had moved to Elizabeth City with her husband, Sonny Hill. Joyce had been a couple of years behind me in school. Getting to see someone from where I called home and that I had grown up with was great. Her husband loved to fish, so I had another friend to fish with.

Life was wide open in those years, as political correctness and affirmative action had not totally stained the colorful, long-time traditions that made our Coast Guard service great. We worked, sometimes for sixty, seventy, or eighty or more hours a week. We left on missions, not knowing when we would return. We flew rescue missions, illegal alien interdiction missions, illegal drugs smuggling missions, fisheries treaty missions, and International Ice Patrol missions. We stayed busy keeping our planes in perfect flying condition and ready for any mission since we worked on the plane and would also fly on the plane. (A good incentive to be perfect, don't you think?) We inspected the C-130s using the check system during these years. We would bring a plane into the hangar and completely disrobe it of its access panels and cowling. We would perform a complete inspection of the entire aircraft that usually took about two weeks. When we had finished the inspection, the aircraft was ready to fly around the world; and in some cases that was a requirement. After working and flying as we did, breaking lose with heavy relaxation was often on the agenda. In the early seventies we played just as hard as we worked. If we rescued an unfortunate mariner or pilot from the ocean that day, it was customary for the pilot to buy the crew a case of beer. During these years every crewmember wanted to be the first to find a victim in the water. The beer wasn't necessary because we all had that rescue spirit; but for the crew, it seemed to give us a good friendship and loyalty connection.

One afternoon while relaxing, we began to discuss the possibility of constructing a beach on the base riverfront. My good friend, Conley Beacham, and several of his duty section crewmembers decided to construct the beach site during their Saturday duty. The project was going along smoothly until the Officer of the Day noticed the operation and shut the operation down. That shutdown lasted until Sunday morning when Conley and his crew showed up again to start the conveniently positioned bulldozer.

I, along with some of my Atlantic Strike Team friends had already partially completed a boat ramp from which the crew could launch their private boats. Fred Ellinwood, his teammates and I would pull the old concrete from the new boat ramp area on the banks of the Pasqoutank River with chains tied to an old bulldozer. Old concrete with rebar extending from it and rotted wooden piers were piled up on the shore. We cleaned the debris as far as the bulldozer would go into the water. All of a sudden we got just a little too deep, and the bulldozer shut itself down. We were in a fix so we decided to go borrow the newer, larger bulldozer and pull the small bulldozer back to the shop. Well, we finally made a large enough ramp for one boat to launch so the crew was happy. We would continue the project at a later date. We wanted to improve the area a little at a time so that those that could make our lives miserable for doing so wouldn't notice our progress. A little mischievous, no doubt, but that was the way to get things done without a whole bunch of red tape. Within the group of us we had the knowledge to get things done and "get things done" was the way we lived every day in the Coast Guard. We always operated on a limited budget, but that didn't deter us from accomplishing our missions.

As I said, the weekend waterfront morale improvement project was about to get even better. Conley and his crew began to carve out the broken concrete piled along the shoreline. This time they would have the larger bulldozer as the base had bought another newer one to replace that old one. He pushed and pushed on that debris on the riverbank until early into the next morning. He worked his way closer and closer to the water until he was pushing the concrete out of the water itself. The crew was enjoying the hard work, as that was the norm in our own everyday life. While pushing on a pile of concrete in the water, the bulldozer's tracks began to spin, digging deeper and deeper into the bed of the river. That was the limit for this bulldozer, and the crew was in a fix just as we had been on the boat-ramp project. Everyone was in a spirited mood so they decided to go borrow the new bulldozer and pull this one out of the river so they could get on with the business of building a recreational beach for the crew and families. Conley, Butch, George and other secret gremlins worked all day on the project and when finished returned the bulldozers to their same positions as they had found them with hopes no one would notice they had been slightly used in a weekend covert operation.

As the sun rose on Monday morning and everyone drove past what used to be a pile of rubble on the way to work, there seemed to be quite a stir in their interest. People looked in amazement at the new swimming beach that suddenly appeared over the weekend. It was a miracle.

Oh! But the commanding officer of the air base was to come by that same road on his way to his office. He finally did ride by and noticed something was a little different with the looks of his waterfront. He got out of his car and investigated the scene to see what had suddenly appeared over the weekend. He was not at all amused as he arrived at his office. He called around to the different commands on the base to see who the perpetrators were. I believe that he already had suspicions of the rowdy air rescue crews from the air station being the culprits.

Word came back that the air station men were responsible for cleaning up and moving the debris from the shoreline. He immediately asked the commanding officer of the air station, Captain Petterson, for the names of the "misguided nincompoops," that tore up his shoreline. The commanding officer of the air base told Captain Petterson that he was going to court martial each and every one of those men. Captain Petterson told him that he would investigate the matter. Captain Petterson asked Master Chief George Watson to check into the matter. Master Chief Watson talked with Conley, and Conley told him that they had built the beach in good faith for the morale of the crew. Master Chief Watson reported back to Captain Petterson, and they both decided that it was a good idea that just didn't go through proper channels. Getting things done that may never have been approved and answering to its fury later was an age-old tradition in the Coast Guard. Courts-martial were certainly in order for those involved; but the beach was good for the morale of the families. Courts-martial sometimes would be worth it to benefit so many people. What the heck! Risk of courts-martial was always there to those with colorful personalities who were willing to get things accomplished, even though those in command would never approve knowing the project. Sometimes I felt like (even though Coast Guard) we were the real McCale's Navy.

Captain Petterson called the base commanding officer and tried to negotiate a way out for his crew. The base Commander was having nothing to do with letting this matter go, and he wanted the names of those "misguided nincompoops" so he could begin courts-martial proceedings. Captain Petterson stood his ground and told the commander that he was not going to court martial his men. What a man to remember that stood up for his crew. What a relief for us about to face courts-martial. Over the history of our service, men and women have chanced facing courts-martial when they thought they were right and will continue to face the same in the future.

The beach would become the most popular place on base for all of the children and spouses. During the day they played in the sand and on weekends their husbands would join them with a grilled cookout. The beach would continually be improved over the years and provided the air-rescue crews with a safe place for rescue and pyrotechnics training.

General horseplay and trickery were a way of life to us in those years. It seemed to keep everyone on their toes and laughter in the air. Every time someone would be promoted, one tradition was to throw the new promoted man overboard into the river. If we were not on the ship, then the closest boat dock with water would be sufficient. Sometimes just the bank of the river would do.

One day big "Tiny" Zambrinski was promoted. The crew he worked with took the occasion to initiate Tiny in good fashion. Tiny was a gentle giant, and everyone liked him for his easy-going personality. He stood well over six feet tall and weighed in at well over 200 pounds. The crew grabbed him and forced him down onto a freight dolly. They used aircraft cargo tie-down straps and chains to secure him to the heavy wooden dolly. Tiny was helpless and at the mercy of his friends. The crew rolled the dolly towards the river and down the old seaplane ramp. They continued letting the rolling dolly slip into the water so that Tiny would sense the dolly was going to sink. Someone decided to use a chain to tie the dolly to a cleat on the side of the ramp and then walk off to frighten Tiny.

The crew walked off, and I was the only one left as I sensed a slight bit of danger in this initiation. Tiny began trying to free himself when all of a sudden the chain became loose from the tie-down cleat, and the dolly rolled even deeper into the water. The dolly was not going to float at all with all of the weight of the tie-down chains holding Tiny tightly to the dolly. I jumped in the water behind the dolly and began pushing the dolly back up the ramp, all the time shouting as loud as I could to the crew to come back as I needed help. Luckily, I had stayed to be sure Tiny was safe. The crew was still within hearing distance and came running back to the water's edge. Things were quieter when Tiny was finally released from the cargo dolly. A lot of lives would have been ruined by the thought of the tragedy of losing a good Coastie friend, all because of a risky friendly initiation gone wrong. Often we lived on the edge with teasing and joking being the norm. Sometimes because of our friendship with one another, we nearly killed or severely injured each other by our horseplay.

On another occasion I would be promoted to first class and the crew had their turn with me. This time they would just carry me to the edge of the river and toss me over into the water. A half dozen of the men fought my struggle all the way to the river and swung me a couple of times and let me go heading into the river. Well the water was not very deep and they couldn't get me far enough into the river in deep enough water. I landed on the protruding rocks lining the shore. I landed (shins first) and that was not a good feeling at all, but I had to show my appreciation for their interest in me and tried to laugh it off. I would have to nurse one of my shins for the next couple of months and while on my next mission to Alaska.

Chapter Twelve

One day Chief Pete Davis asked if I would help him with a flight to Alaska that would last approximately two months. I had nothing holding me back, so I volunteered to be the second flight engineer along with Chief Pete on the LORAN Calibration Mission. We gathered all the spare parts and support equipment we thought we might need for the duration of the flight. One thing no one would forget to bring was a fishing pole. Lcdr. Harvey Orr was our aircraft commander and Lcdr. Doug Herlihy was the second pilot. Navigating was Ensign Jim Boetlier. Several of the crew brought their motorcycles as we would be flying into the remote areas of Alaska and there was no transportation at many of the remote Eskimo villages. Chief Pete, Danny Bowden, Tony Strollo, Wayne Triplett, Scotty Huffman, and Radioman Heath were the rest of the crew. We strapped all of the motorcycles to the cargo ramp.

I left my house key with my good friend Buddy Fletcher. He farmed close by and offered to look after my place while I would be gone. Lots of times our farmer neighbor friends would offer to send vegetables to our other Coast Guard troops serving in distant bases around the world. We would carry potatoes, cabbage and collards grown in Weeksville, North Carolina, to Hawaii, Alaska, and Puerto Rica. The crews there would send back fish, king crab or pineapple. Bobby Benton, Billy and Kenneth Bateman, the Small family, Doug Mercer, Buddy Fletcher and others farmed just outside the base. Farmer Earnest James was a retired Navy chief, farmer Carl Dinger a retired US Marine and Harry James fought during WWII as a US Marine. Farmer Frank Hollowell retired as commander from the Navy. All of the Weeksville families made us Coasties who were away from home feel welcome and would do anything they could for our Coast Guard families.

Crew ready to load for LORAN flight to Alaska.

Soon we took off for Andrews AFB and on to Wildwood, New Jersey, where the Headquarters Electronics unit was located. There we loaded the LORAN monitoring van and accompanying antenna trailer. We spent the night and rested for the long next day's flight. Several of the LORAN calibration experts would travel with us and operate the equipment that we were carrying. The next day we took off from the Wildwood Airport. It was a very hot day, and we were loaded to our maximum on weight. It would require every inch of runway to take off and clear the pine thicket on the other end of the runway.

We turned off the bleed air from the engines to allow the engines to perform to their maximum power. Our pilot Lcdr. Harvey Orr applied maximum power with the throttles being careful not to over-temp the four turbine engines. With having the older T-56-7 engines, it took all the power that the four engines could muster to get the aircraft up to take-off speed.

On this particular E-model C-130 #1414, we had external fuel tanks hanging under the wings between the engines. Those tanks increased the aircraft drag enough to affect the take-off speed and distance. With all of these elements working against us we were still able to make take-off speed. When we reached past the point of no stopping on the runway, we all grunted and strained to help the aircraft get into the air. We were coming closer and closer to the end of the runway and the pines were becoming more and more clear. As we reached our necessary take-off speed, both pilots pulled back on the yoke; but the aircraft's reaction was slow as if it didn't want to leave the ground. If we cleared the pines trees on take-off, it couldn't have been more than an inch.

Doug and Harvey
Whew! We made it.

With the air temperature being so warm and with us being heavily loaded, we were having difficulty making our assigned altitude as planned by the National Aircraft Control Center. We continued to make our best effort until we could burn off some of our fuel. The bleed air had to be turned on to provide pressurization so that our crew and passengers could breathe enough oxygen. The bleed air would take some of the power from the engines but we had no other choice. We finally made our assigned altitude after several waypoint delays, and we were on our way to Edmonton, Alberta, Canada. We would land in Edmonton, refuel and spend the night. When we landed and began our post-flight inspection of the aircraft, we noticed pine branches hanging from the wheel wells. We cleaned the debris from the wheel wells and found that some of the branches were as large as one inch in diameter. We had carried the pine treetops that we had struck on take-off from Wildwood, New Jersey.

The next day we would take off heading to Alaska, only this take-off would be a little less stressful. The temperature was cooler, and the runway was several times longer than the one back in Wildwood. The flight to Anchorage, Alaska, would go smoothly.

Lcdr. Harvey and Chief Pete

The next day we prepared the aircraft for takeoff to different remote landing strips. We would fly to McGrath and unload the large van and antenna. The electronics crew would set up the equipment for monitoring the LORAN tower signals coming from different Coast Guard LORAN stations that affected navigation in that particular area. While they were setting up and calibrating their gear, we would repair any discrepancies on our aircraft. If we were ready to fly and had spare time, we could tour the area on our bikes. McGrath was a Forestry Service Firefighting Base. There was a general store that caught my interest with wolf skins hanging on the wall. There were all sorts of hardware supplies in the store that were needed in the backwoods by trappers, miners and other frontiersmen. We would load up and fly to the next landing strip where the LORAN signals needed to be calibrated. Each place would have its own unique character. Some places had good fishing streams, but a lot of places also had large Alaskan brown bears. We landed at many Eskimo villages.

Forestry Service Fire Fighting Base McGrath,
Alaska.

At one place after we had landed, we were fishing in the
stream while the electronics people were doing their
calibrating. The whole crew was catching Dolley Varden
trout and salmon. We saw a big brown bear approaching
the other side of the stream. This bear was the prettiest I
has ever seen. The bear's fur coat was a beautiful light
blonde.

We decided to play a trick on Ensign Botelier by walking
away from the stream and leaving him there fishing.
When we got far enough away we all shouted, "Lookout for
the bear." By that time the bear was just across the
stream from Jim. As Jim looked up, he saw the bear and
looked as though he had seen a ghost. He still tried to
show his bravery while he scrambled away from the
stream as fast as he could; and from then on, he looked
every direction for any sign of a bear.

Wild Alaska brown bear.   Jim was the
bear's next meal!

At one fishing stream, the game warden asked us to leave
because too many bears were gathering across the stream
from where we were fishing. There must have been six or
eight bears there that were eating the fish heads that
some of the smarter crew were throwing across the stream
to the bears. Some of the bears were grabbing the salmon
that we were fighting to pull in to the shore. He was right
to ask us to leave and probably just in time.

We landed at Unakaleet and stayed in the dorm the kids
usually use during school months. This was a nice place
to fish. The postmaster let Harvey use his vehicle so we
were able to check out some of the good fishing spots.

Danny, Wayne and Harvey
Got supper!

Doug, Danny and Wayne
Don't tell anybody there're fish in Alaska!

Many nights we slept on the aircraft troop seats, as there was no other place. We carried Chief Pete's cooking gear, and he was the master chef. We would catch the fish and cook them right after they came from the water. With Pete's ingenuity, we had great outdoor meals when it wasn't raining.

We landed at the Coast Guard station at North East Cape, St. Lawrence Island. This was one cold place and even colder in the winter as the walkways between the buildings were covered for safety reasons.

Summer at NE Cape, St Lawrence Island
Burrrr!

We landed at Mekoryuk Village on Nunivak Island. Large herds of musk ox live on this island.

Mekoryuk dirt landing strip on Nunivak Island.

This landing strip was too narrow to turn our big C-130 around so we backed it down the runway to get into position for take-off. While we were parked at the end of the runway, a bush pilot landed on the same runway. The bush pilot crossed the tail of our plane and dropped his aircraft down onto the runway as if we were not even parked there. The tail clearance of our plane is 38 feet. While we were parked there our wheels started sinking down into the mud. The permafrost was melting from underneath the weight on the aircraft wheels. We kept a close eye on the aircraft so that we didn't sink too deep into the turf. During the cold weather months the runway remains frozen but during the summer the turf begins to thaw on top.

Kids gathered at Mayor's house. Friendly and always full of humor!

Soon we were off to another destination. We were headed to a place called Dutch Harbor. This was a very important harbor in the Aleutian Island Chain that provided safe harbor for our troops during WWII and for our Alaskan Fishing Fleet to the present day. The present day landing strip in Dutch Harbor is nicely paved and the rock hill along side the runway has been graded away, but when we used the landing strip the runway was paved with the large rocks that had been dug away from the hillside and spread so that a plane could land on the strip.

Landing at Dutch Harbor, Alaska, must be
a perfect landing, the first time.

As we made our approach to the runway, we took photos
of the different approach ends while we made a decision
on which end would be the safest to land. We made that
decision and landed on the rock runway, which proved as
hazardous as we had thought. The wings on our aircraft
stretched wide, and striking the hillside was a dangerous
threat. There was no room for error. As we attempted our
landing, the rocks from the runway pounding on the
bottom of the aircraft sounded as though we had
destroyed our plane. The landing gear wheels picked up
the large rocks as we rolled down the runway and
scattered the stones as if they were mere grains of sand.
After we landed, we all went outside for a damage
assessment. The damage was quite extensive, but we
thought that we could repair the damage and return the
aircraft to a manageable flight operating condition. The
rocks had pounded the landing gear struts, but the struts
did not rupture. The entire brake anti-skid wiring was
torn away. The brake lines were damaged, but we had
prepared for that and had brought new lines with us. I
had brought wiring and accessories and began rewiring
the wheel wells on both sides of the aircraft. We had
predicted that many landing sites could create damage to
our aircraft. We removed the inner landing gear doors as
the rocks had torn them apart to an unfixable condition.
We stayed there in Dutch Harbor until our mission was
complete.

One of the fishing fleet captains offered to give our flight crew some king crabs. He told us that the Coast Guard rescue crews had saved his life twice and that he was eternally grateful. He said that the Coast Guard ships and aircraft are ever-present keeping watch over the fishing fleet during the dangerous fishing season in the Bearing Sea. He called us his angel that assumed the same risks as his crew in the most dangerous occupation in America. His words would continue to ring true as more of my Coast Guard friends would perish, giving their lives so others may live, in one of the most dangerous environments in the world. Along with my Coast Guard friends, many of the fishing captain's friends would also perish in efforts to provide America with delicious Alaskan seafood while making a living fishing in the Bearing Sea. On average, one crewman a week would perish during this fishing season.

Lcdr. Doug Herlihy and Bearing Sea fishing boat captain.

We roamed the island looking at all the old WWII sights. There were several old war buildings still standing and much interesting junk lying about. Since our mission to Dutch Harbor, the rock hillside has been removed and the runway paved.

After leaving Dutch Harbor, we needed to make a repair stop at our Coast Guard Air Station in Kodiak. The bottom of our aircraft needed much attention. We borrowed a couple of inner landing gear doors from one of the planes stationed in Kodiak. We were able to repair any discrepancies in our electronics/navigation gear, which is a must while flying in the dangerous environment of Alaska. We restocked our spare parts kit; and when the plane was ready to complete our mission, we were able to take a couple of days off.

We knew most of the crew stationed in Kodiak, and they offered to take us fishing and king crabbing. Master Chief Bert Stickney, Bill Berkinbile and others showed us a good time while we were visiting their base. We left in the boat with a dozen king crab net rings and our fishing gear. The nets were made of a circular metal ring with netting tied to the ring. A place to tie bait was in the middle of the ring. Also, four lines were tied to the ring and they came together to one line at about three feet. Then the one line was tied to a buoy float. We baited the crab nets and sent them overboard every fifty feet or so. We began fishing for halibut, giving the crab traps plenty of time to attract the large crabs. We started hooking into some big halibut. The halibut seemed as though they had a hold onto the bottom as we struggled to pull them to the surface. We caught several large halibut and then started pulling up our crab nets. I have never seen so many crabs. We pulled one after the other, and the boat was becoming full.

We pulled in one net, and there were nine crabs that joined the pile already in the boat. Each one of them weighed about nine pounds. We had the time of our lives fishing and crabbing that day. We carried the crabs and halibut to the mess hall and put them in the freezer. We would be back later in our mission and be able to take them back to Carolina with us. This was turning out to be one of the best missions that I possibly could have been assigned.

After a couple of days' rest, we departed for Nome, Alaska. Nome was a very interesting town. There were interesting people of all kinds who still worked the beaches and gold mines in the area: fishermen, tradesmen, and prospectors.

There were native Eskimos all about. Everything was flown in by air until the seas thawed in the mid summer. A Coast Guard buoy tender was tied up at the docks. The buoy tender crew's job was to repair any navigational structures that were damaged during the bitter winter.

Nome, Alaska
Summertime

Abandoned gold dredge at Ophir, Alaska

A private pilot invited Harvey and Doug on a little side trip. The pilot let them use his cabin.

Harvey and Doug relaxing in the wilderness.

Harvey splitting firewood.

Harvey after the trout.

We socialized with the crew from the buoy tender for a couple of days while our electronics monitoring crew completed their calibration of LORAN signals.

Soon we were off to another village on the island of Kiska. Kiska was an island held by the Japanese during WWII. We would land at Port Heiden. The beaches at Port Heiden were loaded with glass balls that had been torn from the Japanese fishing nets and had made their way to the black sand beaches. The crew would team up on their motorcycles and explore the area. I went with Pete as we headed to the beaches. We parked our bike and crossed the huge dunes. We started walking the beach looking for the best spot to gather glass fishnet balls. We found several huge deposits of balls and began picking them up and stowing them into several large sacks.

Doug showing glass balls trapped in the sand.

Once in a while out of the corner of my eye I would see an arctic fox cautiously creeping through the sea grass. We picked up all the glass balls that we thought we could possibly carry on the back of Pete's bike and turned back toward the way we had come. We walked for a while and looked down at our tracks. A set of bear tracks were following our tracks! A large bear with a small cub had smelled our tracks. We were in a predicament as the bears were going in and out of the dunes as they followed us down the beach. We didn't know where they were, and we didn't want to surprise them as we crossed the dunes to get back to the motorbike. We tried to reason where they might be and hoped we made the right choice, or we both would be mauled to death by the big mother bear. We picked a crossing point near where we had parked the bike and made a cautious crossing of the dune. When we saw we were in the clear, we jumped on that bike as quickly as we could and tried starting the bike. Pete was in a big hurry, and the bike didn't start as quickly as he would have liked; but, finally, the bike did start, and off we charged down the rocky road. I thought for sure that the tires were going to blow out with all the weight on the bike. If the big bear had seen all we were carrying on the bike, she might have been more likely to run from the odd sight.

Pete and I rode back to the aircraft and loaded the glass balls onto the plane and rode off for more adventure. We found several boats beached nearly covered with sand and beginning to decay, but they had some nice nautical equipment still attached to them so we asked the Elder in charge if we could have the old parts. He said to take all you want. We went back to the aircraft and brought back some tools and removed what items we wanted. We gathered some portholes, propellers, cleats and steering wheels. This was a great day for gathering artifacts.

Good thing Cdr. Orr allowed us to bring motorcycles along on our mission, as we were able to explore many remote sights. Some isolated areas had no vehicles for transportation. Cdr. Orr was good about keeping morale high among the men and women that made up his aircrews. Our dedication to whatever mission we were assigned made our pilots look good. We never believed that we could not successfully complete every task we were asked to perform. Failure was not an allowable word amongst us Coasties.

Time passed quickly during our month and a half mission. It seemed as though we calibrated the LORAN signals at nearly every landing site in Alaska. It was an experience of a lifetime, but now it was time to return to our base back in Elizabeth City, North Carolina. We worked on our plane to repair what damages and discrepancies had occurred and performed a good inspection in preparation for our return flight. The next day we loaded the ramp with all the king crab and fish that we had caught. It had been frozen solid while in the freezers at the air station. We said good-bye to all of our friends stationed there at Kodiak. We took off and climbed to altitude as soon as the aircraft controller approved the highest altitude we could fly (near 32 thousand feet). We turned the air-conditioning and heat system off in the cargo compartment and the temperature continued to drop below freezing in there. This would keep the crab and fish frozen all the way home. We would not have to stop for fuel half way because the winds from a westerly to easterly direction at our altitude were strong enough that we could make the distance. When we landed, the temperature was in the high eighties so we had to make quick arrangements to get the frozen crab and fish to their proper destination.

We would have salmon and king crab for our friends and family for months. The memories experienced on this trip would become some of my greatest adventure stories to pass on to other Coasties and my children and grandchildren. Crewmembers on the mission seemed like brothers, and sharing the adventures together made tighter bonds between us in our everyday flying duties once back home. We had traveled more than 45,000 miles on this mission (nearly twice the distance around the center of the earth.)

Chapter Thirteen

We were back at our normal work and flying schedule after a couple of days off at home for rest. In Coast Guard aviation, each of us is assigned to a specific responsibility while we are not flying. We are assigned the duty for a period of time and then rotated to another duty to gain knowledge of the many support functions that make a rescue air station work. These duty assignments prepare an individual to really understand and be able to care for an aircraft anywhere in the world and to qualify as a flight engineer/plane captain. The same steps are taken with the radio/navigators and pilots in their command roles.

One day while repairing a C-130 aircraft parked on the ramp, we heard and saw a Navy E-2 doing touch and go training on our runway. The Navy plane was using the runway, passing just behind the tail of the plane we were working on. On one practice touch and go, the aircraft seemed not to be able to get back into the air when its wheels touched the runway. The aircraft tried to lift off several times and couldn't. As the pilot tried to maintain his runway heading, he began to lose control after each attempt to get airborne. He ran off the runway and crashed into one of the Aircraft Repair Center's overhaul shops. The crash truck took off in the direction of the crashed plane. The driver/operator was a man that grew up not far from where I grew up in Winston-Salem. Jim Lambert, the driver, was from Andy Griffin's hometown of Mt. Airy, North Carolina.

Jim, with parents Ruby and Fred, honored with Achievement Medal for Professionalism in crisis.

Steve Bronke was the other co-operator. Immediately, the crash alarm sounded with a response on the public address system. "Navy E-2 crash at repair center. All hands respond."

I shouted to my crew to come with me on our big tow tractor that we called a "mule." We drove as fast as we could to the repair center and took our directions from our fire chiefs, Tick Farmer and John Tatum. Most of us were sent up to the roof of the building to fight the fire from that position. The building was being used as a fiberglass repair shop, and many workers were working inside when the plane had struck the building without warning. The heat was draining, and the smoke and odor were really getting to many of us. We had no breathing equipment as there was none to be had, but our job was to put that fire out. We fought the fire for some time, and some of us were being overcome by the smoke fumes and heat. I helped several men who were no longer able to stand get off the roof. Then I felt myself becoming disoriented and asked the men on the ground to send up some water for us to drink. Before we could get a drink of water, I was getting dizzy and started to step on the ladder rung to come down off of the roof. The next thing I knew I was going head first down the ladder. Luckily there were several men at the bottom of the ladder who saw me falling. They grabbed me and were able to break my fall. They took off my fire jacket. I was overheated, soaking wet from perspiration, and had inhaled a lot of fumes. All I wanted was a cold drink of water and a cool place to sit down for a few minutes. Before I knew it, the corpsmen had striped me of all my clothes down to my under shorts and had me in an ambulance. I told them that I was doing better and that I didn't need to go to the hospital, but they would not listen to me. They put two of us in the back of the ambulance and off we went to the hospital. After a chest x-ray and a little time for the nurses to monitor our vitals, we were held for a while; and then we were given a ride to our base. We received word that four had perished in the crash. One of the pilots, Lcdr. Lynge, was killed along with three of our aircraft overhaul employees, Joe Spruill, Gilbert Spitzer and Maylon Jones. Following is an article by Bessie Culpepper and Leo Boatright from the Daily Advance Newspaper

Plane Strikes Building
At Coast Guard Air Base

By Bessie Culpepper
And
Leo Boatright

An undetermined number of people were killed this morning and at least 10 injured when a Norfolk based Navy plane crashed into a building at the U.S. Coast Guard Air Base in Elizabeth City.

Three persons are thought to be dead but the actual number of people in the building has not been determined. The identity of the dead and injured has not been released. The accident occurred at 9:20 a. m.

The plane has been identified as a Navy ET2, a submarine chaser.

Albemarle Hospital implemented its Disaster Plan, which is used for major emergencies, immediately after notification of the crash, Dr. Bob Poston went to the base to aid Capt. William Thomas, M.D.

The hospital was notified to anticipate between 20 and 40 people. One person was dead on arrival and 10 people were treated for lacerations, smoke inhalation and abrasions.

Dr. T. P. Nash implemented the disaster plan and every physician in Elizabeth City responded including the two new pediatricians who are not beginning practice until Monday.

When the initial reports of the crash were received by the hospital, the operating rooms were cleared and patients who were prepared for surgery were returned to their rooms, Dr. Nash said. Norfolk General was in contact with local hospital officials and was ready to accept any overflow of patients.

Preliminary reports indicate the plane, which was practicing take-offs and landings when it struck the Aircraft Repair and Supply Center. The plane was flying from west to east. A Coast Guard Fireman Fred Tanner said he was working on a plane when he saw the crash. "We jumped on the mule (fire engine) and went."

Tanner fought the fire from the roof of the building, along with others, and was overcome with smoke. He was treated for smoke inhalation and released.

All emergency equipment in the area and law enforcement agencies responded as established in the disaster plan.

Local policemen and other law enforcement officers aided with routine patients as they were brought to the emergency entrance in an effort to expedite treatment for the injured.

No further information was released pending arrival of Navy investigators from Norfolk. The crash of the Navy training plane is the same type that took five lives in a crash just off Ocean View in Norfolk June 19, 1973.

Crew responding to assist Navy
(The Daily Advance, Elizabeth City, North Carolina)

I would go back to performing aircraft inspections and find that a lot of our planes were severely in need of rewiring in many critical areas of the aircraft. We actually had an engine shut itself down in-flight all because of faulty wiring. With engines shutting themselves down in flight, fuel quantity unreliable in many fuel tanks and landing gear indicators showing unsafe positions during flight, it was time to do a major rewiring to those areas before we lost one of our own flight crews. This kind of rewiring is something that should be done during an overhaul of the aircraft and is not normally accomplished during a routine inspection. We knew we could do the job, and we knew the serious consequences if we didn't do the job--and soon. The wiring was so bad on those old "B" Model C-130 aircraft that for sure, one of our crews might go down, probably in bad weather when everything was needed to work and indicate correctly. Master Chief Pete gave us the go ahead to strip out the old wiring and replace it with new. We set up our wire marking machine, ordered new connector plugs and put in a lot of overtime to complete the job along with our regular inspections to have the aircraft ready in the allowed time for the inspection. By making the efforts to correct the serious problem with our aircraft, we virtually eliminated many failures that had been constant problems on those aircraft, previously consuming many hours of repair time after each flight. Irvin Derr, Nate Watson, Jim Sarri and I worked continuously until the job was complete.

We made such a difference that we attempted rewiring every "B" Model C-130 at our station. We took on a refurbishing job to clean up the cockpit as we rewired the instrument wiring. With help from the parachute riggers and ordinance men, we had the seats recovered in the process. After refurbishing one C-130, we heard comments from the admiral indicating that he thought he was flying on one of our new planes. That made us feel good, but if he only knew just how close all of his fleet was becoming to a near disaster just waiting to happen. Our reward for all of the many hours of hard work and eliminating a catastrophe wasn't recognized formally by our command. Our reward came as we were flying and heard crew members speak of how good the plane looked and how well all of the electrical instruments performed. We not only stopped many constant flight discrepancies, we made the planes much more reliable and safe. Most all of us Coasties took pride in our flying machines, and during the sixties and seventies we were known world wide for our reputation of having the best safety record.

I always had the attitude that all of our aircraft and equipment should be the best-kept possible. Most Coasties carried out their duties in the same manner; however, a few didn't seem to have the same mindset and had the notion that as long as it would operate for now, that was good enough. Well, my constant approach to doing the best job possible irritated several of the leftovers from the hippie generation. Many of them had not released themselves from the "don't care" attitude. Some were still smoking wacky weed and engaged in other illicit drugs.

For my demanding excellent performance, several of them came up with a new name for me and started calling me "Red Neck" instead of "Hippie," the nickname I so honorably earned while stationed with the draft-dodgers in

Hawaii. They began writing "Fred Is a Red Neck" everywhere they could write the slogan. I demonstrated my patriotism and pride everyday and that seemed to attract some that had peer pressure on them to act in a different manner. I could not do anything about what they were calling me, but I would not let them get by with less than excellent performance while they worked on our aircraft. When we operated in foreign lands, some would come back with suggestive photos to try and intimidate me; but they were wasting their time.

Typical teasing

Communist Mig on display.

Once one of these misguided men threw a screwdriver at the aircraft and the screwdriver stuck into the metal skin of the plane. That kind of behavior had to stop, and I would be one of several that wouldn't fear retaliation and stand up to the foolish behavior of these men. I didn't care what they called me. Several didn't like me for what I stood for and would again spread the word throughout the service. Other people that worked with me and for me learned that there was only one way to perform maintenance on the aircraft. I would show them myself the deterioration of the aircraft we were risking our lives in and the only way to keep our crews alive. Thank God, they had the maturity to see that we had a choice of living or dying, and they chose the better of the two. So Chief Davis and Chief Cox, Chief McNealy and other crew leaders and I mandated being the best in keeping our aircraft and equipment in the finest operational state as I had been taught from the Coasties that were my superiors. We worked extremely hard to put out the best operating and reliable C-130s possible. After an average of two weeks of performing inspections and repair on the aircraft, we sometimes would get together for an early liberty afternoon and unwind, but never before our aircraft was operationally ground-tested and an in-flight test performed.

Crew happy with job well done blowing off steam. Kneeling: Archie, Charlie, Verle Standing: Fred, Steve, Mike, Chief Johnny McNealy, Bob

After a weekend break, Monday morning came; and we started the inspection and repair process all over again with another C-130.

Chapter Fourteen

When we were flying in our C-130s, we worked closely with our brothers crewing the helicopters. A new helicopter had shown up at Air Station, Elizabeth City. We now had a larger, higher performance helicopter called the HH-3F named the Pelican. The Pelican had twin engines instead of the single engine installed on our older HH-52A Guardian. The extra engine made the helicopter more reliable for offshore rescues. That meant the C-130 aircraft that had flown cover for the smaller helicopter in the past would not be needed as often for rescues closer to shore. We continued to provide cover and assistance for the Pelican for rescues further off shore as mechanical problems occasionally occurred even with these newer helicopters. The Pelican, being more powerful with a larger cabin, could also rescue more survivors in a single flight. Cdr. John Rice, Cdr. Don Winchester, Lcdr. Steve Helvig, Lcdr. Bruce Drahos and Lcdr. Terry Beacham were some of the HH52 or HH3F helicopter pilots. Our rescue statistics continued to climb but now we had a slightly better flying machine.

HH-3F (Pelican)
Training with 40' rescue boat

Terry Beacham with brother Hope.

Most of the pilots and rescue crewmen that flew the Guardian were retrained to crew the newer Pelican. Many of these crews were dual qualified to also fly the HU-16E seaplane or the C-130.

We all continued to answer the call when we were needed as members of a flight crew. We would be sent on missions in every direction. Sometimes we would go north to help our Canadian friends to look for an overdue fishing boat from Halifax, Nova Scotia, or St. Johns, Newfoundland. We had a brotherhood of common interest with the Canadians forces, as we would assist them with any maritime emergency; and, in turn, they would assist us in our search and rescue efforts. Sometimes we would be sent on an International Ice Patrol.

Every iceberg a different beautiful monster.

En-route to the Canadian Provinces, we would make a stopover in Groton, Connecticut, to pick up our Coast Guard Marine Science Technicians (MST) personnel. Another name we used for them was "Ice Picks." The MST personnel would be responsible for the documentation and the reporting of the icebergs to the ships. On these iceberg patrols we would operate out of different bases in the Canadian Maritimes. Sometimes we would operate out of Summerside, Prince Edward Island. We worked with the Canadian forces in our efforts to keep the North Atlantic shipping lanes safe for all mariners. The Canadians flew a patrol plane, larger but similar to the US Navy P-3, called the Argus. Prince Edward Island was a beautiful place. The Canadian forces were fun to work with and the local people were very hospitable to our flight crews. We enjoyed our time visiting with the townspeople. We would drive to Charlottetown when we would have time off from flying. We took in their music culture, and it seemed to somehow be in my blood as I felt every note run through my body. "Foot Stomping Tom" always gave a stimulating performance. The old English and Irish tunes were always entertaining. Then hearing the beautiful voice of Anne Murray made us want to be back home with our loved ones.

That is enough of acknowledging that every hour of military duty is not working, but sometimes getting to enjoy different cultures around the world. Now it was time to get our minds back on our job. We had a lot of patrolling to do. We would work hard at our jobs of flying and keeping our plane in tip-top operating condition, but also we would play hard to keep our morale high.

Most of the times we worked in freezing/icy conditions that required much more precaution and preparation before each flight. If we couldn't borrow space in the hangar for our aircraft overnight, then we usually had to completely de-ice our plane before flight. The slightest amount of ice on top of the wing or flight controls could create lift failure or control failure on take-off. With an estimated 15-minute survival time in perfect conditions after crashing in that freezing water, failure was not an option for our crews.

While on patrol one day, a flight crew decided to shut down their two outboard engines to conserve fuel during their long patrol over the icebergs. The only way you can safely shut down the engines and have them ready for restart if needed in an emergency is to assure that there is no moisture in the airspace in which you are flying and the outside air temperature is above freezing. Any thin cloud layers can have moisture. The other thing that is important is to assure that the engine anti-icing hot bleed air valves remain open to the engine to ensure no ice will build up within the engine.

Sometimes humans are forgetful, and on this flight the engineer's forgetting to leave the bleeds open for the engine anti-ice almost caused a flight crew to crash into the frigid water.

Flying by large iceberg on International Ice Patrol.

The crew experienced an engine failure on one of their operating inboard engines, and that engine had to be shut down. This meant that the aircraft was flying on one of its four engines. The engineer immediately pushed the two outboard engine condition levers to air start, and neither engine propeller would rotate to air start the engines. The crew was in a perilous situation and must find a way to keep the plane flying until they could find a runway to land on. Immediately, the engineer dumped all unnecessary fuel to lighten the load. With only one engine operating, the pilot pushed the throttle to maximum power. The crew was still out over the frigid ocean. With all their efforts, they made it to shore and could barely maintain a controlled decent to the runway. If they had been on the other end of the patrol leg, then they would have all perished. When the plane landed, the inside of both outboard engines was a solid block of ice throughout. It takes overnight with heaters blowing into the intake and into the exhaust to thaw a frozen engine. I know, as I experienced an engine anti-icing problem in flight and iced up an engine. The crew was lucky this day and can thank Allison-General Motors, Lockheed Aircraft and God for giving them another chance.

Sometimes we would conduct our flight operations out of Gander, Newfoundland. This field was famous for the launching of many trans-Atlantic record-seeking flights in the early years of aviation history. Now the airfield is used for a major crossroads of international travel along with the Canadian domestic airliners. During the Cold-War era, it was normal to use the airfield with Soviet and East German Aircraft transiting to Cuba from Russia.

Other times we would operate out of St. Johns, Newfoundland. We would often stay at the Airport Inn overnight. The crews in those years often held a traditional initiation we called "Screeching" for the crewmembers that made their first flight over the North Atlantic icebergs. Screech is a local drink that if not used cautiously will alter your normal way of thinking and acting. You may not remember all that happened to you as you consumed the traditional amount of doses. Most of the time it was a joyous occasion during the initiation, with laughter and high spirits within the whole group of Coasties. The local citizens loved to help introduce new Coasties to their long standing tradition of initiation. Once a newly "Screeched" air crewman had survived his initiation, his name patch from his flight suit was proudly posted on the wall behind the bar.

Once in the happy spirit of things, one flight crew with "Happy Jim" Comito and Floyd "Butch" Hampton decided to give Sir Irving a ride back to the good ole USA and let him travel from one Coast Guard base to another until Sir Irving reached as many bases as possible before the crew would bring him back to Newfoundland. Sir Irvin was dressed in a Coast Guard flight suit as he now had been qualified to fly on a Coast Guard C-130 as a crewmember.

"Tonto" Doug and friend preparing Sir Irving for his excursion aboard a Coast Guard C-130 for destinations in the good ole USA and other places.

I believe Sir Irving traveled all the way to Florida and Puerto Rica before his vacation was over and time for him to travel back to his home in St. Johns, Newfoundland. The local citizens missed Sir Irving, for quite some time while he was on his mysterious adventure. You see, Sir Irving was a large metal statue of an English Knight that stood in the Airport Inn's lobby. Sir Irving was their mascot that welcomed guests to the inn. Humor was a big part of each mission as some days were long and tiring.

Sir Irving being welcomed with royalty at
Happy Jim Comito's house.

Over the years, a few romances developed; and some of
the Coasties would continue those relationships and bring
their new wives to the States.

After the planned time of our crew's mission was
completed, we would return back to our base in Elizabeth
City, North Carolina. Another crew would be preparing to
go back to Newfoundland to resume patrolling the North
Atlantic shipping lanes. The icebergs, sometimes
tremendous in size, would drift south into the shipping
channels; and new data would be prepared by the flight
crews and sent to the mariners sailing in the dangerous
waters where the Titanic had met her fate. As the other
crew left for their mission, we would assume the
maintenance of the many aircraft at our unit and stand by
for our next assignments along with our normal rescue
duty. I really don't know of another job that I would have
been as satisfied to do. I don't think I could have found a
greater group of Coasties to have worked and flown with.

Each year we would take time to honor those that
perished in the tragic Titanic disaster. One of our crews
would prepare a wreath; and during our patrol, we would

drop the wreath from our aircraft over the exact position where the Titanic submerged beneath the waves.

I had been dating the same girl for several years, and we had a mutual agreement that neither one of us ever wanted to get married again. Wanda was about to lose the house she had been renting for many years, because of the owner wanting to sell. She tried to find a place that was safe for the children and a place that she could afford while working as a designer at the florist. The only place that she could afford was unsafe. I understood the desperate situation and offered to build a house for her to rent and in a decent neighborhood. The payment on a brand new house was much cheaper than what she would have to pay for rent at the unsafe dwelling.

Building house for Wanda to rent.

A few of the boys at the base wanted to earn extra money so I hired several of them to help me with building the house. Floyd "Butch" Hampton, Zeke Everly and Chief Ron Cox helped me as they could. There was one other young Coastie from Iowa, and I wish I could remember his name. Sometimes one of my orphan brothers would drive in from Winston-Salem to visit his sister Joyce living next door. He would come over for a visit; and I would let him help me, just as Tom Sawyer did. James would help me drive nails while he was visiting. That was the only way we could spend a few quality hours together as time was important. My friend and high school classmate of Wanda's, Virgil Frazier, helped me with my electrical tasks.

Wanda's Central high school friend Tommy Brothers helped me with putting in our septic system and clearing trees. He even left me a tractor to use. Tommy had served his country in the US Army's 82nd Airborne and had been sent to fight for his country in Viet Nam. He was one of the proudest American war veterans that I have ever met and I have been around many proud American veterans.

US Army volunteer, Tommy Brothers

Tommy continues to serve his country through his dedication to church work and support of our US Forces. Tommy and his friends travel to military bases and offer support to young troops now fighting our wars to keep us safe from terrorist. His love of God and country gives him the adrenalin needed to spend many long hours in support of our troops offering to pray with them before and after they return from battle. Tommy knows first hand how irresponsible and cowardly our country treated our returning Viet Nam War troops. In the forty years that I have known him, Tommy has demonstrated his continued love and concern for our troops and their families. When he could help a young Coast Guard family get started in building a new home or repair the septic system of an older home, he always tried to give them the best break possible.

As the house building was nearing completion, we both questioned the idea of getting married. She had two wonderful daughters, and it was hard thinking of not having a family of my own. Marriage worked for many men and women in the military, but for me I just didn't want to chance another failure. After convincing myself to stay single until I retired from the military, I changed my mind after being single for nearly a decade. I felt more positive about the outcome of my decision. So, I took the big plunge with a wonderful lady that seemed to understand my commitment to duty. Nearly exhausted, I closed on the house with the bank on Friday, was married on Saturday, and moved in on Monday after a very short honeymoon in Virginia Beach. Wanda always claims that she had to take over from the orphanage homemothers, as I was still full of energy as well as being proud and spirited. Two wonderful children were also part of the commitment.

We lucked out to find a great neighborhood to build our house in. Mr. Eugene and Shirley Meads were very thoughtful in helping me get my first start in having our own home. Gene and Shirley were very lenient and helpful to young Coast Guard families. Their son Terry would stop by in later years as I was building our second house and offer to help even after he had been working all day.

I couldn't have found better neighbors or a better neighborhood anywhere. My neighbors were Lt. McMillan,

Captain Donahue from my last base in Hawaii, Lcdr. Bob and Mary Mueller, Cdr. Don and Linda Jensen, Bill and Fatie Johnson and a retired Navy chief named Leonard Guest. Leonard and his wife Dot came from Franklin, NC, and the same part of the mountains as my family. He joined at seventeen during WWII and became a sub-sailor. He served on submarines and surface warships during WWII and the Korean War. I knew I was in good company with the many loyal servicemen and their families living next door.

Len Guest at seventeen "ready to serve."

Len Guest in torpedo room.

Once again I was lucky to be around people of pride. Many more military men and women lived in the neighborhood but also hard working civilians. Sonny Hill and his wife Joyce lived behind me. Joyce and I had grown up together at the orphanage in Winston-Salem. Sonny was an awesome fisherman, and he would invite me on occasional trips with his many friends.

I flew with Lcdr. Mueller on many flights, and he also headed up the Flight Standardization Team. Being neighbors, our children would play together; and Bob and I would cut firewood. Bob had just finished a tour in Kodiak, Alaska. Occasionally we would fly from our base in Elizabeth City, North Carolina to Kodiak. Flying in Alaska is often times even more dangerous as the environment is unforgiving.

Lt. Bob Mueller, chilling out at Cold Bay, Alaska

Flying into the air station at Kodiak, Alaska was no easy task. Thorough training in practice approach and landings was a must before a flight crew was ready for landing on this airfield. Pictured below is what the aircrews faced each time they had to land on this runway. Now add darkness! Now add Alaska fog and rain! Now add gusty winds!   Now you have the conditions that Alaska flight crews fly in on many occasions.   The flight crew must abort their approach before the end of the runway if they feel they can't possibly make the landing. The mountain at the other end of the runway demands the best in flying skills and has snatched servicemen's lives.

Approach to landing at Coast Guard Air Station Kodiak, Alaska.   Pyramid shaped Barometer Mountain can be seen at end of runway.

Wanda and Fred

Now married to Wanda, we would have a decent place to start our lives together.

I was proud to be part of Wanda's family with so many patriotic veterans that had proudly served their country in the military. Her dad "Jake" James Tillett and friends Frank Ludford and Gardner Pritchard were life-long pals

and had served in France and Germany during WWII and
had also served during the Korean War.

"Jake" with M1 Carbine, Korean War era.

"Jake" and best friend Frank, Ft. Benning, Ga.

Wanda's uncle Cecil fought in the battle for Okinawa during WWII while serving in the US Army.

Uncle Cecil WWII US Army

Wanda's Uncle Bill served during the Korean and Viet-Nam Wars. He made a career in the US Air Force. Patriotism was always noticed at any of her family gatherings. As I got to know more of her family, I found many had served our country during difficult times of war.

Uncle Bill Tillett
Career Air Force

Wanda's Uncle Eugene Handy served several tours in Viet Nam in the Navy Combat Sea Bees. His small children started calling Eugene "Handy," and the rest of the family uses that name today. While Handy was in Viet Nam, his Sea Bees constructed bases and runways for our fighting troops. Many times he and his men came under attack while working, and he and his men had to stop working and take up the fight with the enemy. Shortly after his return from Viet Nam, he became almost paralyzed in his legs. He couldn't prove to the Veteran's Administration that his war efforts contributed to his illness.

Chief Eugene Handy
US Navy "Seabees"

My brother-in-law John had just returned from duty in the Air Force. He continued using his military skills overhauling the electronics equipment that was installed on the aircraft that I flew.

John McMahon
Lifetime of service to country

Christmas season arrived, and as many men and women that the unit could afford to let go on leave went to their homes. We always maintained enough personnel to man all of our emergency crew positions. Some Christmases I would volunteer to stand the ready aircrew duty for the married crewmen so that they could stay home Christmas morning and be with their children at that special time.

One Christmas morning, one of our flight crews could not get their aircraft started; and they were stuck in frigid Minneapolis, St. Paul, Minnesota. They had been patrolling the Great Lakes for ice conditions, assisting the Coast Guard icebreaker ships and our marine science personnel. They were due back at home base on Christmas Eve but ran into maintenance problems. On Christmas morning Captain Dave Bosomworth told me to grab a radioman and prepare one of our C-130 aircraft for the flight to Minnesota. The captain said "We will not leave our flight crew with a broken aircraft over

Christmas." I gathered what parts I thought we might need to get their aircraft flying again and grabbed my toolbox. I quickly prepared our aircraft for takeoff, and we flew to Minnesota. When we landed, we left our engines running and Captain Boz told the stranded flight crew to go home and wished them all a Merry Christmas before they boarded the warm aircraft.

The weather was below freezing, and the broken aircraft had problems with several systems due to the cold weather. I had only worn my flight suit and my leather flight jacket. I soon realized I had made a mistake with my choice of clothing. We borrowed a heater from the airport flight line, and I began trying to thaw the parts necessary to get our aircraft operating. Wow! Was it cold! The valves to our auxiliary generator were frozen, and our wing flaps were also frozen. I worked for several hours trying to rid the ice from the frozen lines; and finally, I was able to get the valves to operate. When I was able to get the auxiliary power unit operating, I started my engines to be sure each system would operate properly. I turned the heat up inside the aircraft in hopes of heating up the hydraulic lines that serviced our wing flaps. Our wing flaps were just not going to cooperate. I was definitely not going to shut down any engines and take a chance of another problem developing, so I sent word to Captain Boz of our problem. Captain Boz suggested we make a no flap take off and fly the aircraft home without using our flaps. As we were on our approach to Elizabeth City, Captain Boz decided to try the flaps since we were not in freezing conditions. He moved the flap lever towards the down direction one increment at a time and the flaps responded normally. We carefully monitored the flaps to ensure they were not out of alignment and would send us into a rollover.

Captain Bosomworth was just one of many fine Coast Guard commanding officers that really did care about their men and women under their command. He was always an excellent airman in the various different types of aircraft that he piloted. The crew enjoyed being part of his flight team.

Captain Boz loved to coon hunt with his dogs and several local men in his hunt club. He loved his dog Bruno. Bruno would come to work with the captain, and Bruno became a hit to a lot of the men and women of the air station. That coonhound became part of the crew, and the crew loved to pet him. That dog fit right in with the captain's easy going personality.

Captain David Bosomworth with companion and "Honorary Aircrew Canine Bruno."

The aircraft propeller in background is the last C-54/R5D propeller ever to be assembled by the Coast Guard Air Station as the Coast Guard transitioned into the C-130 Aircraft. Captain Bosomworth retired as many great COs before him, but when he departed the Air Station he would be missed by many of the crew. Only the captain would retire within our local community, and we could see him on his frequent visits back to the base to attend many of his shipmates' retirements.

It seemed our aircraft were on missions on a daily basis. One day we were asked to fly to Andrews AFB to load food and then carry the food to Cincinnati, Ohio. The Ohio River was iced over and the surrounding area was hit with the largest blizzard in memory. The roads were impassable, and rural areas were isolated without power and without food. The American Red Cross needed our assistance, and we intended to deliver whatever they needed. Ltjg. Odom and Lcdr. Hibbard were assigned as our pilots, and no time was wasted getting our plane into the air.

We landed at Andrews AFB and met with Red Cross personnel. We immediately began loading food rations by hand onto our aircraft. We were able to load 32 thousand pounds of food and secured the food to the cargo deck. We took off and headed to Cincinnati. We arrived in Cincinnati; and with the help of many volunteers, we unloaded the many boxes of food into cargo vans. Everything was done by hand as the food was not palletized. The community was in dire need of the food items, and we wanted to be able to make another round trip to Andrews AFB before we ran out of crew mission time. The movement of the cargo by hand slowed us down to a point that we would have to make our return trip with another load the next day. After we finally were able to deliver the first load of food, we flew back to Andrews AFB and waited until morning to fly the next load of food to Cincinnati.

After our mission was completed, we had delivered 60 thousand pounds of food to the strickened Ohio area. It was just another mission that we loved to be asked to help out. What a rewarding job to have!

Richard Bullock and Fred securing food before take-off.

Coast Guard crew unloading emergency
food supplies with help from volunteers.

Then we were off to Panama to carry repair parts for one of
our cutters. We then would take off to the Gulf and
Caribbean to patrol in our year round struggle against
illegal aliens and the criminals of the drug trafficking
trade. This is another massive responsibility for the US
Coast Guard and the Drug Enforcement Administration
(DEA). This is a responsibility we take just as seriously as
our many other tasks.

A friend of mine, Guy Raby, served as a US Marine and had joined the Coast Guard as many others and I had from other services. Guy had served in Viet Nam, and he wore his American pride on his shoulders every day. We often flew on the same flight crew. When time for him to re-enlist for another tour of duty, he wanted to re-enlist while at altitude inside a C-130 aircraft. Commander Ricks was well liked by most men that served under him, so Guy asked Commander Ricks if he would do the honors while in flight.

Guy Raby being sworn in by Commander Ricks.

Chapter Sixteen

I received my orders to the US Coast Guard Aviation Technical Training Center. I would become an instructor in the Aviation Electrician's Mate School. I had been in the active flying duty for many years, and now it was time for me to help train the new men and women in becoming aircraft specialists. A new building had been built on the base in Elizabeth City for the purpose of combining all of the aviation related rate training. It became a very excellent facility. Modern classrooms and training equipment made it a nice building in which to teach. Many of my old shipmates and friends were teaching at the Training Center. Mack, Jim, Ron and Don were there in our section of the school. Many others I knew in the other rating schools. I would meet many others that had been serving at bases all over the Coast Guard and now assigned here. I left for instructor school at the Navy base in Norfolk, Virginia. After practice fire drills, just about every night while living in their barracks, I decided to drive back and forth to school every day. I was glad to finish their school and get back to our unit. We had three phases of classes where the students would learn a certain material and then be advanced to the next phase. We had modern learning labs where the students could get supervised hands-on experience with equipment and technical procedures that they would be responsible for at their units when reassigned after graduation. Each student had to pass both practical and written exams in each phase before they met the requirements to graduate.

Soon I was promoted to chief, and that was a big step to make in the Coast Guard. Much to-do was made of this event. My students, after some encouragement, picked me up and carried me out back of school, but not without a good struggle from me to try and free myself. Then they thoroughly watered me down.

At this time in the Coast Guard, an initiation was in order for those that were promoted to the rank of chief. The initiation process would consume an entire day of events. Being somewhat unaware of just what was in store for me made me be on constant alert of what was to take place.

I would be required to get as many other chiefs' comments written in my charge book, a book that I had to have on my person at all times until my judgment day was over. Judgment day is what we called our "Initiation" for becoming a chief. What a fanfare it would be. I was kind of apprehensive of what the older chiefs' might have in store for me. It began early in the morning as I prepared my containers of coffee, my special recipe, to be served to every chief on the base that I could locate. Afterward I would attend my initiation in the chiefs' club. What a frightening thought. It didn't take long to find out who had control of my person for several hours. Things were happening that I was not really prepared for but I was a chief now and had to endure my initiation. I am proud to have gone through such a traditional function after making the chief ranking.

Knowing of my continued fight against drug use within our ranks and of my distaste of the way draft-dodging hippies harassed our troops during the Viet-Nam conflict, most chiefs had me dress as a hippie to teach me to understand humility and its importance at certain times.

Ordered by older chiefs to come dressed this way for my initiation.

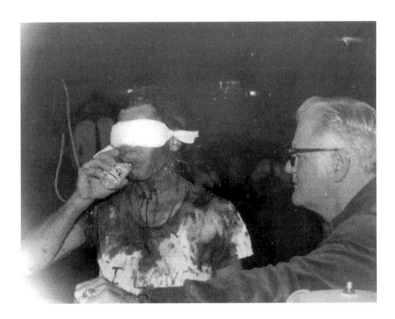

Chief Frank Darling, my defense council.

I had previously worked for Chief Darling for a period of time when I was stationed at the air station, and I asked him to be my defense during my initiation. He did his job well as my defense/offence council, as I will never forget my experiences. Some experiences are only to be known, if you yourself have attained the rank to be honored by them. Once my initiation was over, I soon realized what expectations were required of me and understood the greater responsibilities that came with the promotion. We had been demonstrating our ability to be promoted to chief for years in our knowledge, performance and military bearing. There was a closer bonding with the older chiefs and a greater commitment to supporting the men and women in the Coast Guard. There also was a commitment to our communities where we were stationed. We would get involved in fund-raisers for different organizations such as needy children's Toys for Christmas, Special Olympics and the Red Cross. The pride of being with a group of Coasties that go beyond their duty and volunteer to help others would bring a lifelong commitment. The list of charities we would help was endless. A few were Parks and Recreation, Girls Club-Boys Club, the Salvation Army and CPOA College Scholarship Fund.

Back at the Training Center, we continued to produce the best aircrew/specialists possible. We knew that in just a very short time these Coasties would be working and flying on the very aircraft that we previously maintained. They would be the ones that would be launched in the middle of the night to save lives. The aircraft they maintain would either greatly ensure their chances of returning home safely due to their good maintenance or bring about the worst possible outcome if they failed to do their best. Either case, these Coasties working on the aircraft would also be the flight crews on the aircraft. This is the Coast Guard Aviation Rule. Reputations will be assigned to each individual as that individual demonstrates loyalty and quality of technical performance on their aircraft. Our goal was set that every one of our students would have the qualifications and decency to be able to perform on the highest level.

At one period of time, I found that our teaching of technical subjects was being taught in an excellent manner; but some would become slack in their own demonstration of Coast Guard pride and especially attitude. During this period, I found it a difficult challenge to change a person's mindset when popularity was gained from the students from his nonconformity in pride and attitude. Due to internal familiarity within our chain of command, changing one's outlook and performance was almost impossible without being retaliated against. Once again in my career, I would stand my ground in trying to protect our students from developing a care-less attitude. As I expected, attempted retaliation by one of my seniors came about. Once again, a senior, if at any operational unit would have been supportive, but for over friendliness and familiarity between junior and senior, this would not be the norm.

Luckily for me, men from other sections in our school knew of my performance and pride. They knew what I was dealing with and were proud enough to give me some assistance. I guess these types of problems happen in every kind of business; only in our business, you had better get one's attitude and their head turned in the right direction or someone is going to die.

Even though we were instructors at the Aviation Training Center, we still were allowed to participate in flights at the Elizabeth City Coast Guard Air Station.

Sometimes there was the distasteful duty of thinning out some of the students that couldn't quite grip the requirements needed to pass their exams. It was never a pleasant task to send a hard-working and loyal Coastie back to where he or she had been stationed before. We always hoped to see them return for another try after time to study a little on their own. Sometimes others had the ability but were discipline problems. These were not so troubling to see walk out the door.

We instructors at the Training Center gave our best to each student. Now it was time to see that individual graduate, go to a unit somewhere in the world, and listen to reports of our student's success. Some students would be recognized for their superior performance as part of a successful and heroic flight crew. Others would be commended for their part in keeping our planes ready so that more lives could be saved. Either way we would have many years to watch our students give their best to the many missions of Coast Guard aviation.

Chapter Seventeen

I enjoyed my experience of teaching at the training center, but after three years I was glad to receive my orders back to the Air Station. I always liked the action part of the Coast Guard, knowing though that someone had to take their turn at teaching and overhauling our aircraft.

Being back at an air rescue station filled me with enthusiasm and pride. "What needed to be done and what could I do to make things better" were thoughts often on my mind!

Due to my rank of chief, I mainly would be in a supervisory role while at my home base. However, my hopes were to continue flying as flight engineer on the C-130 aircraft. I really didn't want to fly a desk; I wanted to fly on a plane. I was only in my early forties and too young to give up the excitement and the adrenalin rushes.

The Coast Guard began training young men to be rescue swimmers. Always before, the flight mechanic or co-pilot was sent down by hoist from the helicopter to the ship or put into the water to help rescue victims. The first group of rescue swimmer trainees would receive their instruction with the Navy Seals in Pensacola, Florida. A friend of mine, Chief Larry Farmer was the leader of the Coast Guard training. Air Station Elizabeth City was the first unit to deploy rescue swimmers. I knew all five very well and found that these men had a special pride and courage in what they were trained to do. They continued with their main job of assuring that the parachutes and rescue equipment used aboard our planes were in excellent condition. They also had to remain in perfect physical condition to be prepared for deployment from a helicopter into the sea. At first there was some complaining from some of the crew of these men training in their physical conditioning while the other men were doing all hands tasks. However after a couple of courageous live rescues and the crew witnessing these rescue swimmers being dropped into the ocean, the crew respected their time to condition themselves. They are a hardworking, brave group of men, and now we have a female rescue swimmer.

Coast Guard's first Rescue Swimmers assigned to Air Station Elizabeth City. Seated: Kelly Gordon, Steve Ober Standing: Joseph "Butch" Flythe, Matt Fithian, Rick Woolford.

The Elizabeth City Coast Guard Air Station was greatly deteriorated from when I was last assigned to this unit in the seventies. Rat infestation and birds nesting in the hangar were not only unsightly but they were becoming a health risk to our crews. Many of the shops were equipped with poor lighting and the air-conditioning, if available, unhealthy.

The commanding officer, Captain Paul Resnik, was not pleased with the appearance of his air station. The unsanitary conditions, poor lighting, inefficient workspaces, and appearances were just too much to bear. With years of operating on a shoestring budget, there was never money beyond necessary operation costs to allow for the hundreds of thousands of dollars to complete the project of a total rebuild. This was a problem throughout the Coast Guard during the sixties and seventies. Captain Resnick and Commander Rice, our engineering officer, put their heads together and came up with a plan. Commander Rice informed the captain that we could get the air station renovated by doing the job as a self-help project. He suggested to the captain that we could use only small amounts of available funds, as they became available, to complete the work. The commander told the captain he knew of one coastguardsman who had the talents, fortitude and willingness to complete such a massive project and that man fortunately was stationed at their Air Station command.

Commander John Rice knew of my talent as a builder since I had built several houses in the area. He asked if I would be willing to take on a lengthy and major overhaul and cleanup of our air station hangar, shops, and offices. I told him that whatever he wanted done to make our air station a more presentable, healthy and efficient place to operate, he could consider it done under one condition, that I be allowed to continue with flying at every convenience during the construction period. I loved flying and being a part of accomplishing our Coast Guard missions. Being allowed to continue being an active part of our mission would also give me a break from the stresses of hard labor, planning, and managing such a project.

Lcdr. "Pug" Guthridge laid out a plan, shop-by-shop, and office-by-office with the commander's priority wishes. Money for the refurbishing projects was begged from our accounting managers as the Coast Guard had little but dire operating monies available.

Not only were the shops and offices being overhauled, but also safety features were added to the aircraft hangar and adjoining grounds. Friendships I had made with base civilian workers during my past tours of duty in Elizabeth City greatly benefited me when I asked for assistance with materials and equipment while taking on such a massive project. Construction approval and assistance with materials was provided by the Public Works Department at the Support Center. Earl Bundy, Big Boy and John gave me access to all of their equipment in the carpenter shop. Bill Grant, Jernigan, Clay Basnight, Doug Simpson, Donald McDougal and others assisted me with a complete electrical upgrade of the entire reconstructed areas. Selvia Meads provided the paint and Carl Spruill, Bruce Huffman, Roy Chappell, Johnny Forbes and his co-workers provided the plumbing supplies.

Most all of the hard work of tearing out the old rat infested structures and rebuilding them to a decent and efficient work space was done by our air station self-help crew. One or sometimes two crewmembers were sent to work with me each morning. For a couple of years we steadily worked to clean up the old and rebuild a bright new station. The results of our efforts increased security in sensitive work areas. Lighting and appearance improved greatly' but most importantly, we provided our crews with a safe and healthy environment to perform their duties.

Working in this construction environment was not without the normal hazards of injuries from falling debris, rusty nails, hammered fingernails and environmental dust and fumes. One day I came down from a ladder and stepped on a sheetrock nail. The nail penetrated my boot and stuck into a bone in my foot. The nail was hard to pull out because of the grooves in the nail's shank. I stopped by to see a corpsman at sickbay, and the corpsman said there was nothing much that could be done but to be sure that I had a current tetanus shot. I went on back to work. A few weeks later I would take the family on vacation to Florida. As we were walking around in Disneyworld, I began noticing pain in my foot. That evening my foot began to swell, so I called back to my home base and told them that I was going to drive back from Florida to see the doctor at my unit. I drove back to my unit; and an X-ray revealed that where the nail had penetrated my foot, there was a definite disturbance in the bone that the nail had penetrated. Our Coast Guard doctor made arrangements with a surgeon in town to evaluate the problem, and the surgeon decided to operate. Well, I didn't need to hear what the surgeon told me at the hospital. He said that he was going to take a biopsy from the bone. However, when the nurse rolled me into the operating room, he said that he decided to take an inch of bone from my foot to be sure that he removed any possible damaged bone. That didn't sound good, and when the surgery was over it surely didn't feel good for some time afterward as they had forgotten to give me any pain medicine. My wife Wanda and my daughters, Pam and Amy, looked after me as if I were royalty.

It wasn't long though before I was back to work where I liked to be. I soon was able to pass my flight physical restrictions and allowed to continue my flying career. My foot would never be stable again but I continued with my life as if it were normal. I continued with my ambitions, my pride, my willingness, and my spirit.

Throughout our service, Coast Guard men and women had unimaginable talents gained from their experiences at different units throughout their careers and from the Coast Guard's and other military's training schools. Someone usually knew how to do anything that needed to be done. Many stations were small, and many stations were isolated on small islands or in very remote lands all over the world. With all of our multitalented men and women, we were able to function with a very small budget and still keep our equipment operating.

David Perham, Senior Chief Fred Tanner, Larry Creasy volunteering self-help improvements around aircraft hangar.

Many different Coasties were assigned to help me with the project at different times. David and Larry were students of mine when I was teaching at the Aviation Training Center and both were great Coasties. One day a young female seaman was sent to work for me. I looked at the young woman and saw that she was no bigger than a toothpick and couldn't have weighed more than eighty pounds. I thought, "If I am going to get any work done, I am going to have to get better help." I decided to get started on my planned project. I assigned different task for the young lady to perform, and each task was surprisingly on time and done with good quality. After a few days I was impressed with the young lady's spirit and abilities. In fact, she had out-performed several of the men that had been sent to help me. Allison Chandler was raised in Smithfield, North Carolina.

Seaman Apprentice Allison Chandler

I was able to borrow her from the Air Station's lifeboat crew to finish my project. I could see that she would do well in the Coast Guard as she had the right attitude and personal pride. As years passed, I would hear of her duty performance, pride and advancements to chief and then progressing to be a chief warrant officer. I was proud to know her and to get to watch her in her performance during her different assigned duties. She always spoke highly of the Coast Guard without grumbling that a task was too dirty or too hot or tiring. Attitude was everything in our business of being prepared or dying.

Chief Allison Chandler being pinned with her Warrant Officer's insignias.

Soon I would be back in the air, flying to many places all over the globe. I would volunteer to fly anywhere anytime that I was needed. I flew International Ice Patrols during our annual ice observance season. We were operating out of the same bases and airports in Newfoundland. Each patrol was a little different in events but basically the same mission: locate and chart icebergs and notify all mariners of the impending danger in the shipping lanes. It was a good experience to sense the extreme change in climate. We would leave Elizabeth City, North Carolina, with a mild climate and land in Newfoundland dressed for winter. Winter hits hard where we operated at times; but during the spring and summer months, weather at times was pleasant in Newfoundland and Labrador.

Sometimes I would fly to the Caribbean in our efforts to curb the illicit drug smuggling into our country. On occasion I would be able to fly with the operations officer, Mont Smith. It was always enjoyable to crew with Commander Smith as he had the attitude about being the best. We lost an engine and encountered several maintenance problems on one patrol; but as always, we overcame those obstacles and made good progress in our mission. While waiting for a new engine, we washed the salt spray from our aircraft as this helped protect our aircraft from the corrosion elements ever present in our ocean-flying environment.

The commander was even perfect in delivering mail to one of our Coast Guard Cutters while on patrol during the Christmas season. We were tasked with making the mail drop by parachute from our aircraft to the cutter's deck. The commander checked the wind direction, adjusted his approach to the cutter, and at the right time called for the drop-master to drop the mail from the lowered cargo ramp in the rear of the aircraft. The mail was contained in a pump drop can with a parachute attached to the can. His call to drop was timed perfectly as the container landed on the deck of the cutter and slid directly to the hatch where the mail was to be carried inside the cutter. One mistake of miscalculating the wind, and the container and parachute would tangle in the navigational antennas and radar or land in the Gulf waters. That was just one more feeling of doing something good for our shipmates on our cutters as they spend a lot of time away from their families while patrolling our shores and the seas. A lot of our efforts to keep our country safe require us to continue conducting operations during the Christmas season.

Another thing we could do for our friends on duty in the islands working throughout Christmas was to put on a Christmas party for them. Not only would we give them a party, we arranged that our next aircrew would bring them a Christmas tree and all the makings of a real Christmas party donated by our station and our crew back at Elizabeth City. That was just one more reason for enjoying flying with a pilot such as Commander Mont Smith. Commander Smith would go on to be promoted to captain and assume the commanding officer duties at Kodiak, Alaska and would be there during the Exxon Valdez oil spill. The Coast Guard was blessed to have many fine men and women as leaders such as Commander Mont.

We crewed our aircraft both night and day to accomplish our mission, and we were successful in keeping thousands of pounds of drugs off our streets and out of the hands of America's drug pushers. We operated in very remote areas and most times were a great distance from any help if we encountered trouble and ever needed assistance. One crew would fly days, and the next crew would take over at night. We did our job as usual, and we were appreciated for our efforts. What more could you want in a job? We were always happy to return home to our families safely, but we were also always ready to take off again on another mission.

Elizabeth City public schools and parks and recreation always needed volunteers. My wife and I had been volunteering for many years in activities within the Elizabeth City community after weekday work and on weekends. If I wasn't deployed on a mission, we were busy volunteering at some activity. We always had a full schedule with following the girls and their activities, but also, we had events where the whole family pitched in.

In nineteen eighty-seven my command recommended me for the Fifth Coast Guard District, "Coast Guardsman of the Year." What a surprise that they had done so. I was very honored to receive the award.

My family would be the first ever selected to be the Elizabeth City Chamber of Commerce's "Coast Guard Family of the Year." The Chamber, Mayor Melvin Daniels, the Recreation Department, Sandy Davis with Special Olympics and other organizations honored our family. Mayor Daniels expressed to Wanda and me that we created such a stir among his other city leaders and chamber members that the chamber had to begin recognizing the contributions our Coast Guard families made to the Elizabeth City community. The men and women and their spouses stationed at the local Coast Guard base were involved in many volunteer activities throughout the city.

Amy, Pam, Wanda and Fred
Elizabeth City's first "Coast Guard
Family of the Year"

We had worked with the Elizabeth City Recreational Department's youth sports events for several years and also been volunteers to help in the Special Olympics program. Wanda had worked for years as a volunteer with the school system, and the girls helped wherever we would be. I had been awarded the "Special Olympics Volunteer of the Year" for the entire state of North Carolina. What a treat as I really enjoyed helping people that truly appreciated everything you did for them.

Fred accepting award from Governor Jim
Martin.   Special Olympics director Sandy
Davis behind.

One day we decided to attempt an improvement project on
our recreational boat ramp. I talked it over with several of
my chief friends, and all agreed that we needed to improve
the ramp for safety and convenience.   The single ramp
area was still cluttered with broken concrete and rebar
sticking up in the air.   Several people had been injured
while using the ramp putting their boats in the water.
Several boats were also damaged while loading and
unloading.

I drew up a set of plans with all of our agreements and
inputs.   Only before we could do anything to the
waterfront, there had to be approval from our base
Engineering department and commanding officer.   This
project could not be attempted without approval as years
before. Before, we knew nothing of permits required, but
now every detail must be completed before the first stone
was rolled out of the way.   Captain Cecil Berry was the
Support Center commanding officer at the beginning of
our planning stage, but soon Captain Donald Hibbard

assumed the command. He, along with my commanding officer, Bill Barker, allowed us to proceed with the project as a self-help project.

Again we used our chief's training to accumulate what expenses we needed to begin our project. Commander Tom Dunn and his assistant engineering officer assisted us with the engineering drawing and securing our necessary permits from the state.

CWO Butch Hubbard allowed Chief Major free time to help with our project. A good friend and fellow Chief Boatswain's Mate, Bert Major, would help me with the project. Bert was in charge of the Morale and Recreation Office. He was a big man and surely came in handy with many of the arduous tasks in the building process. Some of the time was spent under water while chaining the huge slabs of concrete to be lifted out by our crane.

Joe Coleman was a young seaman that worked with Bert at the recreation locker. He would also help us with the entire project. A young Army sergeant from Camden County assigned to the base on a Humanitarian Assignment, Claude "Sarge" Sexton, would also assist us in the construction. Sergeant Sexton was able to help us through nearly the entire construction operation.

We were finally back to the project that we had started many years before. It was bringing back memories of when my Strike Team friends helped with getting the first ramp started. Also it brought back memories of my friend Conley Beacham when he led the charge in getting our very own beach, even though accomplished when the "old man" (Base commander) was home on his weekend off. I just had to see this project completed before I would be transferred to another air station somewhere else in or out of the country.

We worked at clearing the entire area of debris before we started with any construction. This time we were going to build two boat-launching ramps with a loading pier in the center. Around the out side of the boat basin we would build a walkway on top of the bulkhead. On one side we would build a pier leading to a recreational fishing platform over the river. We borrowed the Support Center's bulldozer and graded the area we needed to begin.

Next we had to come up with a cost of the project, and this is where we had to use all of our chiefs' training in how to influence those above you in getting a job completed with an impossible amount of funds available. Bert and I combined forces and joined Captain Hibbard at the Officer's Club located above his office. We talked with him for a bit while we were relaxing with a Sasparillo. We talked with him about how we could construct our project with an affordable amount of money. As time was spent relaxing, the more it seemed to the captain that things were looking good.

Before the evening was over, we were able to get permission to spend about three thousand dollars for materials. We had our materials delivered, and we borrowed a pump from the firefighters at our Crash/Fire Station. Soon we began washing down our first pilings. I made sure we would have good sturdy pilings so I only used eight-inch thick pressure-treated wood. I made sure that our piles were a minimum of six feet down into the soil; and as we entered deeper water, we would wash them down as far as we could. Every one was having a good time with washing the pilings into the soil and a lot of fun was being had when Joe and Sarge were both hanging on top of the piles trying to keep them from floating until we could pump the sand back into the holes to hold the piles. Bert and I would take turns with operating the crane, as sometimes it would take big Bert's strength to hold on to the pilings as I would lower them down into the water. Captain Hibbard came by to view our progress and was impressed with our accomplishments so far.

Soon we ran out of building materials and had to join Captain Hibbard in the Officer's Club for relaxing, explaining that we needed a tiny bit more money to continue with our project. Of course, we used our chief's training to let the captain know just how well the project was going and how important it was to continue. The captain had seen just how much we had accomplished with our first amount of money. Finally the captain came around to asking, "Chiefs, how much do we need to complete this project?"

I said, "Well, Captain, I figure we can get far along with a lot of materials with another five thousand." I wouldn't lie to him and tell him we could finish the project with the five thousand, so I just commented to him that we could get "far along." The captain thought it wonderful and authorized us the funds to continue.

We worked hard on our project, and the winter season was fast approaching. The water was getting colder so we had to take more breaks and protect each other from hypothermia. The winds from the north were unbearable when we came out of the water. We continued with the project on into the winter and worked a few days while it was snowing. Big Bert was more comfortable as he had proper diving clothing to wear while working in the cold water. Although the cold water made us much slower, we pushed on. We ran out of materials again, and again we would join Captain Hibbard for relaxation at the Officer's Club after work. He was impressed at what we were able to accomplish each time he came by to view our progress. By this time, it took less encouragement to sway him to authorize more funds for us. He was pleased with what was being done and was standing by us to the end. It would be spring before we finally completed the project, but what a nice recreational boat and fishing area our crew would have access to use from now on. It turned out so well that our boating-rescue team began using the ramp to launch and retrieve their boat. One of our Coast Guard buoy tenders stationed in Hatteras would make a voyage from Hatteras to assist us in some of our final construction and install a Navigation light at the entrance to our boat basin. Our small service and personal friendships were sometimes beneficial in getting help to complete a project like this. CWO Larry Gray was the commanding officer of the *Kinnebeck*, the ship that helped complete our project. Larry was one of many in the Outer-Banks' Gray family.

My friends Conley, Bert, my crew, and I were honored by Captain Hibbard upon our completion of our project. The Coast Guard Commander of the Support Center, Captain Hibbard, named the boat basin and the beach after Conley, Bert and me: Beacham's Beach and Tanner-Major Docks. Did I forget to mention that we finally stopped using our "Chief's Influence" on our wonderful Captain Hibbard? Not, however, until we accomplished our mission and had separated him from about thirty thousand dollars.

Recreational Beach and Boating Docks

The captain was well pleased and certainly got his money's worth for the Coast Guard. The project was one more morale benefit completed that Captain Hibbard wanted for his troops.

Captain Hibbard was a personable individual who cared for the morale of his troops. He had begun his career as a Coast Guard corpsman, was accepted to OCS, and became a Coast Guard rescue pilot. His humor made long flights more enjoyable.

Captain Donald C. Hibbard
Piloting C-130 over the Pacific

I would crew one more pre-season ice patrol and fly north to the Arctic. Wouldn't you know the weather was unusually cold in Newfoundland, and we lost a cockpit window due to the cold temperature shattering the glass. We would have to return to our base in Elizabeth City to replace our window. Upon completion of our window repair, we started our mission over. We flew to Goose Bay, Labrador; and while flying in to Goose Bay, the radioman told me he had just received a message from home station that I had been promoted to master chief. What a nice surprise. That evening, I went with my crew to the watering hole to celebrate. Goose Bay is a place where when the snow falls, it falls forever. I have seen the snow blown from the runways deeper than the height of our aircraft. Tunnels are built to the building's doors to enable access to their buildings. Soon it was time to venture further north to Sonderstrom, Greenland.

Unforgiving terrain

On descent to landing in Greenland, our number one propeller's rubber hydraulic blade seals blew out. The outside air temperature at the altitude was cold enough to shrink the rubber seals, and that allowed the hydraulic pressure to blow by the seals. The red hydraulic fluid covered the engine nacelle, and after a pitch lock check we secured our number one engine. We landed our aircraft and found that the airbase was on extreme cold weather alert. Everyone had to be shuttled from one point to another by drivers because of the danger of being outdoors in the extreme cold weather. The temperature was down to –30 to –47 degrees on the ground.

The extreme cold would also make it difficult for our crew to replace the failed propeller. We had to adjust our maintenance time with the extreme temperature. We could only work between five and ten minutes and then have to try to get warm. The Air Force Base Commander saw that we were not fully protected from the unusually cold temperature. He called his supply sergeant and the sergeant supplied us with better clothing, suitable for that severe weather conditions. The weather was so cold that the Air Force plane's landing gear struts were collapsing on landing. We struggled on with our propeller replacement; and finally we were able to finish the job.

Our new propeller wasn't satisfactory. We called home base for another propeller and "Tonto" Dunn accompanied another propeller on the transportation flight provided by the US Air Force. The Air Force always came through with assistance in getting our mission accomplished. With Tonto's assistance we were able to ready our aircraft for a test flight.

The cold temperatures were still present and dangerous. Our radioman placed a Pepsi Cola on the steps of the crew entrance door: and before we could push our aircraft out of the frozen hangar, less than five minutes, the Pepsi burst and covered our steps with frozen cola. When we pushed our aircraft to our starting position, we began using heaters to warm the hydraulic fluid in our propellers before starting our engines. We performed our engine run and propeller test for the replacement prop. We finally were ready for our test flight and in-flight shutdown checks. As we were going through our cockpit checklist before starting engines, actions and responses from the other flight crewmembers began to feel slow and mumbled, and I couldn't keep up with the pace. Our pilot, Lcdr. Flood, spoke to me as he could sense something was wrong but making sense of what he was saying was difficult for me. With all of the efforts to get our plane back in the air, I had stayed too long outside in the cold and had begun to feel the effects of the extreme cold. I asked one of the other flight engineers to take my position, as there was no way I could safely be in the flight engineer's seat for this flight.

Aircraft parking ramp –30 to –47 degrees Fahrenheit
Sonderstrom, Greenland

We finally were able to get back in the air and fly to New
England. By the time we landed there, my body seemed to
have overcome my near hypothermic condition. By the
time we returned to home base, I noticed my finger and
my nose had some minor cold exposure and soon after I
was coughing up small amounts of blood and beginning to
get slight nose bleeds. I knew what was happening. I
had stayed too long in the cold, and the cold dry air had
damaged the tissue in my nose and throat. Problems from
this exposure would never completely clear up.

After all the years of my flying in the north country since
the sixties and never experiencing any injuries except for a
little frosted finger and a busted rump from slipping on
the ice, I finally got a taste of what we always tried to train
ourselves not to get. I will tell any aircrew the importance
of being aware of the dangers that cold weather can bring
on you when you least expect it. I will have to volunteer
for my next flight to the Caribbean just to warm up.

Since I had been promoted to master chief and had been
at this air station for over five years, it was time for me to
be transferred to another air station; and for a while I

didn't know exactly where we would be transferred. Headquarters notified me that they wanted me to go to Corpus Christi, Texas, and take over the factory representative job with the Falcon Jet Aircraft. I had never worked on nor crewed the aircraft, but they said that I was their number one choice and thought I would represent the Coast Guard well. My orders directed me to Arizona to attend the factory Maintenance Officer School where I enjoyed the training; but in my mind, I was not the best choice for the job because I had been a flight engineer on a C-130 for twenty years. I would do the best job possible, no matter what my assignment.

A short time after I returned from school, my orders were changed because the person I was to replace decided to remain in the job for a longer stay. My orders were now to report to Air Station Sacramento, California.

This change in plans caused a lot of stress in the Tanner household because one daughter was getting married and another would be left behind to attend college at the University of North Carolina at Chapel Hill. Being transferred was always a challenge to military men and women, but something necessary to gain experience and refresh the chain of command from over familiarity. There was always the feeling of not knowing what to expect from our new command.

Stress on the military wife is sometimes unbearable. Having to leave children behind to attend school and move across country brings a feeling of helplessness and loss. Worrying about the child's safety and unable to help from such a distance is something many spouses face. Packing and moving into an unknown neighborhood is just one more doubting issue.

Chapter Seventeen

We prepared for our move to Sacramento, California. We rented our house in North Carolina to Captain Terry Beacham and his wife Jean. Our daughter Pam was just married. We checked on our daughter Amy two dozen times, as she was working at the beach for the summer before entering college. Her mother may have checked on her a couple of more times before we drove out of town headed to California. Wanda's tears slowed down only after I pulled over somewhere in Tennessee and unloaded her car from the tow dolly. I pointed her in the easterly direction of Interstate 40 and handed her a map. I told her that my orders said for me to report by a certain day, and I didn't intend not to be there. She cried a while longer as I comforted her, but she really missed knowing how her girls were doing. She finally said that I could load her car back onto the car dolly and that she was ready to continue our trip to California. We had a great trip across country, stopping to see family along the way. We visited Elvis' home, the Grand Canyon, and rested in Vegas.

Finally we arrived in Sacramento to the welcoming of Chief Brian Denison. Brian helped us get introduced to some of the crew that I had not been stationed with before. There were many that I knew and a few that I had heard of.

This air station was opened in Sacramento because the C-130 aircraft located at the Coast Guard Air Station in San Francisco were being delayed in their necessary takeoff time to respond to critical needs of mariners. The increased growth in airline traffic and scheduled takeoff priorities created unsatisfactory delays in our missions. Also, with the growth of the San Francisco airport facilities, the Coast Guard was being pressured. McClellan Air Force Base offered the use of one of their hangars and the access to their support facilities for the C-130 flight crews and support personnel. Thus Sacramento Coast Guard Air Station was born. The Air Force offered priority takeoff for our planes responding to maritime emergencies. The crew renovated the hangar with self-help volunteers and made an excellent operational base much as we had done at my last command. When I reported aboard, I found a physically great operating facility with medical and family support in the class of all Air Force installations that I have been privileged to visit.

Coast Guard Air Station, Sacramento, California, station patch with mascot "Yosemite Sam."

The next parts are not intentionally written to undermine my fellow Coasties and the Coast Guard, but I feel it is important to bring light to the facts that may help all flight crews and maintenance personnel abide by a special code of conduct.

Your actions are as serious as a skilled surgeon and your inactions are as deadly, to not only one patient but to a flight crew or many passengers, whether working on a civilian or military aircraft. Never let a few people or even one person grow a pattern of neglect and allow that to be the norm. Remember, you never hear complaints about things that are right, only excuses for not doing what is right?

At the Coast Guard Day picnic, I met my old Coastie aircrew buddy Vern Erickson from our times flying back in

Elizabeth City. Now retired, he gave me shocking advice which I had never expected to hear while I was in the Coast Guard.

Vern knew of the reputation I had acquired throughout my career of Aircraft safety first and doing all things possible to make the Coast Guard a better and safer place to perform our duty. He couldn't believe what some of the men at this unit had conspiring. First off, what they were doing, if at the right base, would be a cause for courts martial. Vern just happened to be in an engineering meeting before he retired and was privy to conversation by members present. Several in the meeting were friends of my (I thought) enemies from past encounters while performing my duty in the Coast Guard. The small group of engineering personnel had plotted on how to lower my performance evaluation, low enough to have me removed from the Coast Guard. They had discussed my reputation for demanding perfect aircraft maintenance, only falsely presenting my reputation as something negative. They discussed my reputation for my aggression against drug-heads that were working on our planes and those that discouraged basic military values. They misinformed the engineering officer that I knew nothing about the C-130 aircraft and that all I ever did was construction. Every good thing that I had done for the Coast Guard and on my free time, my volunteering within the community, they distorted to make me look bad in front of the engineering officer. One statement Vern reported was, "We can have him out of the Coast Guard within six months."

What a surprise! Where do you turn and what do you do when you get that kind of reception? What kind of negative impact would be created on our young troops with this kind of aggression being played out while trying to operate in our demanding mission? I had spent most of my adult life dedicated to giving my best efforts in support of the Coast Guard mission. I had a proven record of tackling any job, no matter how difficult, dangerous or dirty. Now I would have to continue my performance to prove myself all over again. I would do just that!

I tried to lay low for a period of time to feel out these plotters. Vern was willing to come forward and expose these few, but I would not create a disruption for the sake of our Coast Guard unit until I knew there was more than hearsay.

Vern and his beautiful Native Hawaiian wife Claudette were always cordial and inviting to the Coasties that he shared duty with. She was gleaming with the Hawaiian spirit that I had experienced while I was stationed in Hawaii. We enjoyed our friendship and their kindness.

Fred, Vern
Wanda, Claudette

The following documentation is of a very short period in my career showing that a total lack of direction affected our entire operation and nearly with tragic results. This is not the normal or traditional way of the Coast Guard. I had always worked around Coast Guard men and women that demanded the best of safety practices while engaged in the upkeep and operation of their aircraft. But something was wrong here, really wrong. Again I stress to all in aviation to pay attention to bad habits and inappropriate influence to perform maintenance based on popularity. There is only one way to allow a plane to fly and that is if it is safe.

I took over the supervisor duties of the C-130 engine, propeller and maintenance shop. Immediately I was shocked with how this station was allowed to run. The maintenance officer was granting early liberty to my work force nearly every day and at every opportunity possible. Upon beginning my duty, we had no spare propellers built up and tested. We had no spare engines built up and tested, and the one engine they were working on was doomed to fail because of the un-cleanliness of the work area. It seemed everyone was in competition to be popular with the maintenance crew. I tried changing the ultraliberal liberty policy and only award liberty when we accomplished our work and had our engines and propellers ready in case of an emergency. My efforts brought out the depth of the real problem as some older men were misleading the younger ones to thinking their misleading maintenance practices were the right way to do things. This was a perfect recipe for disaster. It wasn't going to happen on my watch!

I was called into the engineering officer's office, and he began to have his spill about what he had been told. He told me that the maintenance officer was running things and that I would follow his directions. He told me that he did not want me to be assigned to his air station because he had heard I was nothing but a carpenter and I knew nothing about the C-130 aircraft. I explained that I did have an extensive knowledge of the aircraft. I gave him my history! When the propeller responsibilities changed from my rate to the machinist rate twenty years before, I was the last prop mechanic in my rate to teach the machinist rate how to assemble, test, install on the engine and how to perform proper run-up testing of C-130 propellers. I told him that I had been performing major maintenance and flying on the C-130 for nearly twenty-five years and had been flying as flight engineer for twenty years. I explained to him that I had been in a working supervisory position for many of those years. He continued to enlighten me on what he had heard of me, and I told him to call any of the commanders and every one of my engineering officers of every base where I had been stationed. I took a firm stand with him.

Before I left, I told him that Jesus was a carpenter also. He and his plotters had created an environment of juniors showing disrespect and when corrected they would run to the maintenance officer and complain. It was like kindergarten, and I had a responsibility to ensure safety of our aircraft and of our crews. I was intent on doing just that, as that was what should be expected of every civilian or military man or woman in my position. This was a military unit and something just had to be turned around.

Thankfully, I was able to get a break from this nightmare temporarily and go on a mission. I would volunteer to fly anywhere to get away from this misguided group. We found that we would assist in the drug war operations in South America. This was right up my alley as I always felt a special desire to help, and I had many years of experience in fighting the entry of illegal drugs into our country. I had previously experienced seeing friends destroying themselves after being tripped up on drugs by an acquaintance that my friends had trusted.

I had been flying missions in this war against drugs since the sixties; and each time I go on a mission, there always seems to be new tactics to beat our efforts. I would still enjoy my duty as I would cover new terrain and meet good people in many foreign countries.

Stacy Appel in hat with Peruvian anti-drug workers.

Crossing the Andean Mountains

Being in places you've only seen in pictures was a real treat, but we needed to remain focused on our task at hand. Flying over the top of the Andes was awesome. The lush jungles in the river valleys just ahead were beautiful. But what was hiding inside was an invisible dreaded danger to our brave warriors fighting our continuous war against the scourge of drugs headed to our shores. After a refreshing break, it was time for me to return to my base and be unimpressed with what maintenance practices were being performed on our aircraft.

As flight discrepancies were reported after each flight, the Engineering department was authorizing minimum and temporary repairs. As I became more familiar with the normal maintenance practices being performed at this unit, I became alarmed. Some propellers were leaking so bad that the propeller hydraulic fluid was running down the blade and dripping on the deck. Brush blocks supposedly conducting current to de-ice and anti-ice the propeller blades and spinner were electrically shorting out and burning up due to the amount of leakage. Our aircraft were being regularly flown in icing conditions over the Sierras, and we often faced the Arctic weather while operating in Alaska.

Fuel leaks from the wing tanks were never allowed to be repaired correctly and according to Coast Guard and Air Force standards. Only temporarily stopping the fuel leak with an oilite stick was the common practice. An oilite stick is like dumdum or a sticky material like gum. I became even more alarmed when a section of the wing leading edge of the aircraft was removed because of a fuel leak. There was a two feet section on the bulkhead where the fuel was leaking from the rivets and the fuel was running down the bulkhead and under the wing and then dripping onto the deck. The leak was directly behind the wing de-icing duct that carried extremely hot air the length of the wing. Being inside an enclosed area and with extremely hot air, the fuel leak was a recipe for an explosion and certain death to all aboard.

I told the maintenance officer that the plane was grounded for unallowable fuel leaks behind the hot air duck in the leading edge. He came out to look and told the maintenance crew to dum-dum the rivet heads and put the leading edge back on the aircraft. He said that he was the only one that would ground one of his aircraft. I told him that what he was doing was deadly and illegal and that I would have to take the matter higher. He went to the engineering office and built up a story of how he was right and asked the engineering officer to have me removed from the hangar deck. I told the engineering officer and assistant engineering officer of all the unsafe maintenance practices being performed on our aircraft. The engineering officer sided with the maintenance officer and persuaded the captain to assign me to the Command Enlisted Advisor's position. The maintenance cover up didn't stop there; and since I was the senior enlisted man on the base, I continued to frequent the hangar deck and monitor the abusive maintenance practices. I also informed my commanding officer of problems still with our Engineering department.

I really felt we were going to lose a flight crew; and more disturbing, we were transporting Coast Guard dependant wives and children back and forth from Alaska while en-route to aid US Coast Guard Air Station Kodiak and flying throughout the Aleutian Islands and Bearing Sea Patrols.

One flight was all it took to convince our commanding officer of what I had been trying to expose. Upon landing at Kodiak Air Station in Alaska, the plane from our air station was grounded. The engineering officer at Kodiak, Commander Tom Gordon, grounded the C-130 and immediately sent a message to our air station. The message informed that the C-130 from Air Station Sacramento was plagued with fuel leaks; furthermore, the aircraft, after much needed safety fixes, would only be suitable for a one-time flight back to an overhaul facility. After temporary fuel leak repairs were completed on known areas of leak sites, sixteen more leaks were found during routine weekly inspection. All of these leaks needed to be temporarily repaired before Commander Gordon would release the aircraft back to the flight crew for a one-time flight back to our base. That should have been embarrassing enough but would not be enough to stop the arrogance by a few in engineering. What Coastie elevated in rank and having the authority would allow a plane in this condition to start an engine, much less fly.

Both of the engineering officers had recently converted from helicopter pilots to fixed wing C-130 pilots and this may be the reason that they were so vulnerable to the maintenance officer's unprofessional directions. After several discrepancies of the propeller fluctuating in flight by indication on the tachometer, one engineering pilot didn't know that the engine tachometer generator played a role in controlling the speed of the variable pitch propeller through the propeller synchrophaser. By not knowing this, a simple fix of changing the tachometer generator at a cost of ninety-eight dollars would result in changing the propeller and sending the propeller back through overhaul, costing the Coast Guard many thousands of dollars plus not correcting the discrepancy. On the other hand a fluctuating propeller out of limits requires the propeller to be feathered and the engine shut down in flight, therefore increasing flight risks. A simple action of switching the propeller synchrophaser switch to that engine to mechanical operation would identify whether the tachometer generator was faulty or the propeller was at fault. This would avoid the unnecessary engine shut down and allowed the aircraft to continue on its mission instead of having to abort the mission and declaring an emergency.

I made a special trip to the Quality Assurance Library and printed a copy of the Lockheed Service News that describes the tachometer generator operation on the C-130. I gave a copy to the pilot, and still he was unconvinced as he said that he had flown helicopters for numerous hours and that what I was trying to tell him was not possible. This kind of stubbornness was what I had to deal with in trying to change men's mindset that were in positions of leadership when it came to aircraft safety. (Or was the conspiracy planned before my arrival part of his thinking not to believe me?????) It became very challenging. In my position of responsibility, for the sake

325

of our crews and families, I would have to find a way to get through to some of our leaders.

I was no longer back at our base in Elizabeth City where this kind of attitude would not be tolerated. I was 3,000 miles away on the west coast. My previous engineering commanders Steinbacker, Koslovsky, Whitley, Krietmeyer, Ricks, Winchester, Rice, Gutridge, Reid, Gordon and Seimens would explode inside if they could only see what was going on at this base.

No matter what happened to me, I was not going to let our flight crews and dependants perish because of my not standing up against unsafe operations. Our whole crew, air station and Coast Guard would be blighted for years if one of our planes went down due to neglect. I had taken a stand for less important reasons, and I considered this at the top of the list. Changing an entire system loaded with negativity was every bit more than the challenge I thought it would be, proving to me that this type of behavior not only happens in commercial airlines but shockingly also in the military even with our stricter guidelines and code of conduct. It seemed every day I would get an adrenaline rush, not by aiding in a rescue, but in my battle to win this foolish but extremely necessary war against neglect.

During the fall of 1990, our unit would host the Bi-Centennial celebration for the Coast Guard's 200th birthday. Retired Captain Mohlenbrok's wife Gail asked if our Air Station would provide our hangar for the event. She also asked if we chiefs would handle the decorations. We chiefs put our heads together for what would be an extremely successful event. We planned and worked for nearly a month while also keeping tabs on our other responsibilities. The Sea Powers Association sponsored the event, and guests from all over the country would be invited. The Coast Guard commandant would be there to celebrate our 200th with us. We built a large model ship and C-130 aircraft to put on display. Everyone praised us for our efforts, and we even surprised ourselves with the outcome of the event.

Captain Jerry Mohlenbrok (Ret) and wife
Gail with Master Chief Tanner.

Sometimes a little break from our normal duties to be
involved with a project such as this would seem to bring
our group with a closer bonding and a reassurance that
we as a team can accomplish anything. Sometimes going
back to our normal responsibilities would bring out an
unpleasant reality of just what level our crews were
working.

The one new engine being built up in the engine shop would never be useful to our unit or the Coast Guard. Finally, the engine was readied for run-up test. The engine failed in the test stand from contamination, so another engine would have to be built from scratch. I wasn't there when the engine build-up work started; but when I arrived and saw the contaminated workspace, I made unpopular changes to clean up the site and change bad work habits, but a little too late. What a waste of time and money!

Being a part of this crew was becoming more embarrassing as I knew my past Coast Guard shipmates would not believe what shoddy maintenance was being performed at a unit that I was assigned to. The word spread around the other Coast Guard air stations as to the unsafe maintenance practices being performed at our unit.

Even after all the exposure of pitiful maintenance, we experienced one more near catastrophic failure. Our engines on our newer C-130s were salvaged from the old retired aircraft. The engines would mount just fine to the newer aircraft, but we were encountering an abrasion problem of our turbine inlet temperature wiring connected to our thermocouples in the turbine section or hot section. Each time we would go to takeoff power and begin our roll down the runway, our turbine temp indicators would indicate that we needed to pull back the throttles to correct for a possible turbine over-temp on takeoff. As power was applied, the engines would vibrate; and the brackets holding the over-temp detection bulbs would rub against the thermocouple wiring and short them out. This occurrence would send a false signal to the cockpit TIT indicators.

The maintenance officer would not let us ground the aircraft and shorten the brackets that were cutting into the wiring causing the problem. We continued to fly our aircraft in very hot conditions when maximum available power was often necessary to maintain safe flight. On one takeoff at Sacramento in very hot conditions, takeoff roll began and at lift off all four engines produced erroneous indications that the throttles needed to be retarded. The aircraft was at critical takeoff and climb speed. If the pilot retarded the throttles the aircraft would stall and crash.

That still wasn't enough for all in the engineering group to get the message. Come to find out, one of our crew had put in for a beneficial suggestion to change the brackets causing the problem; and the maintenance officer was going to let the suggestion go through before he would see that the problem would be corrected. This was just another case of blowing your horn with incompetence just to get notoriety and being allowed to do so by those in command.

After being embarrassed while in Kodiak by all of Coast Guard aviation for the showdown in our poor maintenance practices, the Engineering department assigned five of our best structural mechanics to begin repair of our aircraft wing fuel cells. All of our C-130s had been neglected for several years, and all required massive amounts of repair work. The men worked continuously month after month to catch up on years of neglect by our maintenance practices. When the five men's tours of duty were over and it was time for them to sign up for another tour, they all quit because of being subjected to nearly a year inside of a wing fuel cell. If repair had been done on a regularly required basis, we would still have five of the best. The Coast Guard lost super good Coasties because of what had happened, and some were trained as flight engineers. Stacy Appel was a young flight engineer and an up-and-coming asset in Coast Guard aviation. This is just one of the undesirable results that happen when inappropriate influence is allowed to be applied and flourish and good people are damaged. This is a good lesson for us all to be reminded of at times.

Thankfully, we were finally rid of the maintenance officer due to his duty rotation and then the engineering officers.

His failure to have safe and proper maintenance procedures performed on our aircraft, I found out, was to have the Coast Guard engineering record for the most hours of aircraft availability of any air station throughout the service.

Our station had the best record of aircraft availability, but it was so far out of the norm that it was unbelievable. Several years of this kind of conduct, all for the sake of aircraft availability record, and look at the severity of what might have happened to our crews and dependants.

Most of the men and women were good Coasties, but some rode the coattails of those not so great and followed their influence. I just hoped that they didn't retain any of their misguided practices and carry that to their next duty station.

I'll get back to the better part of my tour in Sacramento. We were flying to Alaska in support of the Coast Guard's efforts with the cleanup of the Valdez oil spill. Captain Mont Smith and his crew were totally engaged in the massive efforts to save the environment from such a huge disaster. At the same time we were assisting his air station at Kodiak with logistic flights to remote duty stations and patrols throughout the Alaskan islands chain. We would fly patrols to the end of the islands and US territorial border. Coast Guard Air Station Kodiak had just lost one of their C-130 aircraft trying to deliver supplies and personnel to the LORAN navigation station located on Attu Island. Attu LORAN Station is the furthermost Coast Guard station near the end on the Aleutian Island chain. While trying to land on the runway, the crew experienced bad weather; and during the approach, the aircraft struck the side of the mountain terrain. Unfortunately, we lost one Coastie and several sustained injuries. Also, aircraft completely burned after the crew was freed. But our crew was lucky this time since in most of our aircraft accidents flying in this environment, we usually lose our whole crew.

Coast Guard C-130 aircraft number 1600 crashed and burned on Attu Island in Alaska.

One of my duties was to attend the district level civil rights training in Long Beach, California. I regrettably was at one meeting that informed us that President Clinton authorized that homosexuals could serve in the military. Personally knowing what adverse affects we in the Coast Guard would encounter, I protested and disagreed with the speaker. I presented my thoughts on the subject. I told him that our ships are small and that we have many small remote units. I also pointed out that the military ranking system provides the perfect opportunity for a person only one rank higher to coerce a young vulnerable military person to do almost anything he wishes all due to the fear factor of that person's rank. I didn't get anywhere with my argument as many attending the meeting had California ties to the heavily homosexual population of the Bay area. I know of many homosexual people of good character, but I have experienced many encounters of those with lust for young military men that will become disastrous to our services in the not so distant future. We must protect all citizens but we must not create an epidemic to destroy our security. The Defense Equal Opportunity Management Institute definitely has ties to one political party that makes their program risky for the security of our military and country.

The people assigned to the civil rights programs in the military should be limited to direct civil rights conflicts and barred from expressing social promotion views. Most of the program should be disbanded, and putting these people back to a productive mission would save our country millions. All service persons attached to military civil rights programs or representing unit civil rights should be screened to ensure they are not members of or influenced by racial promotion groups; this includes Caucasians.

The next year a request was sent to all units requesting suggestions for topics for this years' training. I still had a dislike for the topics of last years' discussions, and I let it be known as I filled in the document. Before I sent the document to the Civil Rights Office in Long Beach, I called on the phone and discussed my entries with the officer responsible for the training. I told her that I was putting my concerns in the training topics, and I explained what the subjects were about. She said that the information was what the training group wanted and for me to send it in as quickly as possible. I sent my outline to the district office, and one of their civil rights workers didn't like what I had to say. He complained to the District Chief of Staff and wanted me removed from my duties as civil rights advisor and enlisted advisor of my unit. After cover-up of the previous year's discussion, the civil rights worker won the discussion; and my captain was forced to remove me from those job titles. My captain was man enough to stand up for me but was threatened with being removed if he didn't follow the Chief of Staff's directions. Instead of thoroughly investigating my information, it was typical protocol in the upper ranks to squeeze the junior ranks in order not to create a controversy that may conflict with their next promotion or high award. Civil rights workers had enough influence in Washington that if one complaint was noted in an officer's record, that officer just as well retire, his career was finished. This is just what happens when any politically engineered group is allowed too much power in the military.

My captain said we would let someone else handle those responsibilities as you have enough on your plate. We will just change your job description to Command Master Chief instead of Command Enlisted Advisor. After this change, all of the larger units in the Coast Guard now have a Command Master Chief.

Captain Vagts and wife Myra
A captain with integrity and caring for troops

After this controversy, I felt I did my duty in following the Uniform Code of Military Justice. That is what my responsibilities were.

Until that Code is changed or considered no longer in effect for military men and women, then it was my sworn duty to uphold its extremely vital importance within our ranks. I did just that!

Soon there were new Coasties reporting to the station, and I briefed the new chiefs and maintenance officer of our problems with aircraft maintenance.   These men had learned the safe way to perform maintenance, just as I did at all other units.   When the operation of our aircraft exposed near critical failures, things began to turn around at this station. I could breathe a sigh of relief since new blood had begun a turn-around in the maintenance failures that we were experiencing.   Even so, there were a few with negative attitudes about willingness to change their bad habits. I guess that's the norm in any operation comparable to our size.

Young Mr. Pat Posey (kneeling) with Fred, Wanda and Pat's wife Wanda.

Young Pat (son of retired Master Chief Patrick Posey) and other men brought some confidence back to our unit.

One chief named "Reggie" Vanderpool brought a little humor anywhere his presence was noted. He supervised the Public Works Department for a while. He worked with a few of the very young Coasties. His humor was noted as soon as you would enter his office.

Reggie's desk

Reggie's locker

Reggie's infectious likeability would become a vital part of the turn around in attitude of many of our young men and women who had been misled in the past few years. With attitudes being in the way of cleaning up our near-fatal maintenance policies, Reggie, by mere coincidence, was assigned the supervisor position in the Aircraft Quality Assurance office. I took the time to talk with Reggie and tell him just how important his job was in correcting the attitudes of some whose actions had nearly caused fatal accidents to our flight crews. We discussed the lack of technical compliance that was endangering our crews' safety and how it had to be corrected. We discussed the people involved in the evasion of proper maintenance practices. Reggie was a straight shooter when it came to aircraft safety. He worked with those assigned to his office and convinced them to only accept one hundred percent compliance in proper maintenance procedures. Things further improved soon after he had time to work his magic. Reggie was a tall Coastie, and not many would try and force their opinions on him. Even with his humor, his likeability and seriousness with aircraft safety influenced many young Coasties into the right attitude about aircraft safety. I always felt his devotion to duty was equally as instrumental in the magnificent turnaround at our unit as the fortunate arrival of several devoted new chiefs and a new maintenance officer.

Reggie was also involved with the morale of the troops at any time he could volunteer. He loved to clown around, and his clowning seemed to keep everyone smiling. While stationed in Savanna, Georgia, Reggie loved to play Santa at the children's Christmas party at the air station.

Reggie Claus arriving in Coast Guard helicopter

Chief Reggie Vanderpool

Reggie had served at many units with numerous types of missions. Once he had served as aircrew/flight mechanic on helicopters while breaking ice on an icebreaker in the Antarctic. While flying in the Antarctic, Reggie's helicopter had to make an emergency landing on an iced-over mountain after experiencing mechanical failure. The pilot, Reggie, and two civilian scientists were lost in the icy mountain terrain. Thankfully, Reggie's crew survived the emergency landing; but the unstable ice could not hold the helicopter upright, and the helicopter rolled over.

Reggie flew from the deck of the icebreaker *Staten Island*. He and his crew were rescued by other helicopter crews. The rescue helicopters were from both the icebreakers *Burton Island* and *Staten Island*.

Reggie and crew as spotted by Coast Guard helicopter search and rescue crew.

Reggie's helicopter, rolled over on the ice.

As the ice gave way with the pressure on the ice under the tires, the helicopter rolled over on its side. The crew had maintained a survivalable environment with the special gear carried aboard the helicopter. If search crews hadn't found Reggie, I'm sure he would be somewhere sharing humor with the Happy Feet Penguins. The Coast Guard helicopter will remain on the mountain as a marker and testament to a near-tragic ending. Fortunately for the crew, they would return home to their families after their mission was complete.

The write-up in the Mobile, Alabama, newspaper reported the story.

Antarctica Save Made by CG Craft
Choppers pick up four on slopes of mountain

A helicopter and two crewmen from the Mobile Coast Guard Air Station, missing in the Antarctica since ten o'clock last night, were sighted on the slopes of Mount Erebus this morning and rescued at eight fifty-one a.m. by two other choppers, also from Mobile.

Crewmen on the downed helicopter were identified as Lt. Jack L. Conerly, the pilot, and Reginald M. Vanderpool. Two civilians on the craft were listed as Charles Neider and Stuart E. Rawlinson.

All were taken to McMurdo Station where they were found to be in good health. Lt. F. J. Wright, of the Coast Guard Air Station here, identified the men and said the helicopter from the station had been assigned to the Coast Guard icebreaker, *Staten Island.*

He said that the Mobile air station is the center for all helicopters on icebreakers in the vicinity of the Arctic and Antarctic.
The helicopter left McMurdo Station in the Antarctica on a flight to a field camp at Cape Bird on Ross Island. Contact was lost last night.

No signal was received by radio station from the craft, which was carrying the two crewmen and others, described as scientists.

Lt. Wright advised today that the helicopter had landed, probably as the result of an emergency, at Mt. Erebus, which is about forty-five miles from McMurdo Station.

Pilots of the rescue helicopters were listed as Lcdr. N.A. Nicholson and Lcdr. L.M. Shilling, both stationed at Mobile and on special assignment aboard two Coast Guard icebreakers, *Staten Island* and *Burton Island.*

Reggie and the few good men made an impact on the safety of our unit, and I can directly relate this change to the saving of one if not more of our flight crews and possibly many military dependents.

Chiefs Ronnie Dye and Reggie Vanderpool

The bravery of Senior Chief Vern Erickson to speak out and expose a conspiracy eventually led to the recovery of a unit that didn't deserve to be operating as poorly as it was. Vern, Reggie and a few other good men made a difference and saved lives. The lives saved were not by our normal experiences of flying over the ocean and saving those in maritime distress but by standing up like real men and doing what was right. These are the real Coast Guardsmen that I appreciate standing beside in our daily duties. In order to be ready to save lives, we must first be sure our aircraft will keep us alive.

Yearly, I would travel to McCord Air Force Base in Washington to attend C-130 flight simulator refresher training. Two pilots and two engineers would spend a week practicing normal and emergency procedures while flying the simulator. On one trip, I was able to drive and take Wanda with me. After our training was over we made a vacation of the following week. We visited a lot of her friends in Port Angeles where the girls were born. I also had the opportunity to check out possible prospecting sites along the northern California, Oregon and Washington highways and rivers.

Fred, flight simulator training at McCord Air Force Base.

Chapter Eighteen

Things were even more relaxing at home. We lived in Air Force's Capehart housing located a short distance from McClellan Air Force Base. Most of the time we had great neighbors. Some of the Air Force men and women would deploy to Southeast Asia sometimes as long as a year and had to leave their family there in housing. We were invited to socialize with the Air Force chiefs' group and help with their fundraisers for the total Air Force family. Chief Ken Neilson and Birdie were the last family that I was stationed with where Ken was the top chief on the Air Force base. Chief George Moses was the oldest retired, proudest and always a friend.

Chief Master Sergeant Ken Neilson and Birdie.

We made friends with several of my close neighbors.
Sergeant Willie Keys lived in the next unit. He and his
wife Denise became good friends and still send Christmas
cards today.

Senior Master Sergeant Willie Keys with
Wife Denise and children.

Willie had an easygoing, southern Louisiana personality
about him, and he and Denise were kind-hearted people.
When we traveled to North Carolina, Willie would keep our
house keys and take care of our house.

My wife also enjoyed having good neighbors as I was often
deployed. Wilma Burroughs' husband Jerry was deployed
to Asia, and Wanda tried to give her comfort when long
months became sometimes emotional. Also Barbara Kaya,
another Air Force neighbor, found comfort from Wanda's
friendship.

I often wondered why there was no Prisoner of War (POW)
flag flown at any site on the base. I brought up the
question at our CPO meeting, and my fellow chiefs decided
to purchase a flag and hoist it along side our Coast Guard
pennants. When we hoisted our POW Flag, Air Force
units around the base began to display the flag.

Master Chief Tanner and Chief Angeles hoisting first POW flag to be flown at McClellan AFB.

As Master Chief of my base, I worked with the men and women in advancing their careers. The troops that demonstrated a positive attitude towards our mission were my main target. With others, I tried my best to encourage them to give their best to the Coast Guard and their country. I had had this spirit of loyalty to my country ever since I was influenced, as an orphan, by great role models both in and out of the orphanage. It is a special feeling that I have never regretted.

I also worked with the families to assist them at times with difficult stressful relationships. Occasionally, these stresses came from financial difficulty or hardship issues from home. Some unfortunately came from drugs and alcohol abuse within the home. I managed the drug and alcohol program as part of my job. This was not a pleasant part of my duties watching a few Coasties destroy themselves and their families. Handling discipline was another difficult task. Often, it transcended into the homes of families. Responding to accidents in the emergency room or dealing with families brought a lot of humility and sometimes sadness to my duty, but those experiences were humbling.

Fortunately, my wife Wanda volunteered to be Co-Ombudsmen with Sandi Morton; and when Commander Hal Morton was transferred, Wanda assumed full duties as the Sacramento Air Station Ombudsman. She helped many families with sensitive issues. She even sent her own money to an incoming family broken down in the desert on their way to this new unit, and she had never met them. She helped many young wives who often would be away from home for the first time and beginning their own family without their parents nearby to give assistance. She kept in constant touch with the mother of a deceased young Coastie, Jim Frost, from our unit. We named our little recreational park in memory of young Jim. He would have made it to the top if not struck down in his youth. He was a very smart and polite young Coastie.

Wanda standing, getting assistance with Ombudsman project from Captain Vagts' wife Myra and Roxanne Delikat.

During this time we were flying a lot, but flying was what we enjoyed. During the Kuwait invasion by Iraq, we took over much of the Air Force missions on the west coast. We gathered groups of servicemen and women from many different locations in the west and transported them to the larger bases in Delaware and New Jersey. There the Air Force would assemble many groups to fill their gigantic transport planes headed to war in the Mid East. We flew more than sixty missions from Sacramento Coast Guard Air Station in support of the war. Our efforts saved the Air Force costs and gave them a boost in timely deliveries. Our planes on the east coast would transport support equipment and provide oil pollution response when Iraqi troops ignited the Kuwaiti oil fields. Our surveillance capabilities on our Coast Guard aircraft greatly expedited control of the massive environmental damage created by Sadam Hussein's forces.

Along with the war effort, we were still supporting our brothers in Alaska with their massive responsibilities. We just happened to be on the island of Shemya as the last C-130 aircraft from Sacramento while the base was still named Shemya Air Force Base. The name would be changed to Richardson Air Force Site. The photo taken before the name change was of Radioman/Navigator Lou Gurnon and Flight Engineer Fred Tanner.

Lou and Fred

Each year on our Coast Guard birthday, August 4, our station would join together with our wives and children at one of the recreation parks on the American River in Sacramento and celebrate with a gigantic picnic. The different shops would build a floating craft and then race them down the river. We had plenty of food and drink and games for the children. The retired old timers would join us and tell old salty tales from the past.

Old timers Bob, Bob, Jerry, Fred, Jim and Reggie at Vern and Claudette's house.

Fred, "Blue" and Al.

Vern, Bertha and Fred.

When there was a good man like Senior Chief Paul Herman aboard to fill my billet, I would try to take a break. Like me, Paul also grew up in an orphanage in Pennsylvania. (Hershey Orphanage)

Our daughter Amy was in Pharmacy School at UNC Chapel Hill. On her summer breaks she would stay with us in California. She would work for a local food chain in the pharmacy department. I would take my wife Wanda and her on trips when she could have time off from her work. One trip was to Hawaii. The girls had a fabulous time. When leaving on our trip to Hawaii, Reggie volunteered to take us to the airport and pick us up when we returned. He kept my Blazer while we were gone. When we arrived at the airport on our return, Reggie was there waiting and what a surprise was in store for us. He knew of my dislike for the hippie generation so he had decorated every one of the windows on the Blazer with colorful flowers. It was the flashiest attention-getting vehicle in the entire airport area. We laughed all the way home. Reggie even wanted me to dress up with a wig and beads so that he could take a picture of me.

Master Chief Fred's Blazer decorated with flowers by Reggie.

Reggie welcoming Amy and Wanda home from Hawaii.

Then we traveled to southern California and visited Disneyland, Sea World and Hollywood. Our good friends and supporters of the military, Anhauser Busch, gave the military special military passes to those events in appreciation for their military service.

On many occasions we would drive to Lake Tahoe or Reno, Nevada for entertainment. The drive was only a few hours, so we would drive over the mountains and visit with Wanda's cousin Joe. Yosemite National Park was only four or five hours away and San Francisco only two hours. Being stationed at Sacramento had its benefits in being close to many attractions. We drove to the Humboldt Redwoods and the Shasta Mountains and Caverns. When we had visitors like Terry and Lynette Meads or Wanda's cousin Jean and her husband Willard Williams from back home in Elizabeth City, North Carolina, we wore them out with the many places to visit. It was a great joy to have friends and family visit while we were stationed away from home. There was nothing we would not do to see that they had a memorable time during their visit.

On weekends we would travel above Auburn to the American River where I would attempt to pan for a little gold. I always had a desire to pan for real gold ever since I had watched western movies as a child. I stopped by Pioneering Mining supplies store in Auburn and bought a gold pan and sluice box from old story-telling Jim. He had very large yarns to tell and gold samples for sale. Jim tended the store for the owner named Frank who was busy managing his other store in Sacramento. We would drive over the ridge on Hwy 49 and down to where two branches of the American river joined. I would shovel into my sluice box while the girls would lie sunning on the gravel bar. I would shovel for a while and take a break for lunch. While on lunch break, I would clean my sluice box and pan out my concentrates. Hot doggity! My first gold nuggets--and boy, were they pretty! I really didn't have this gold panning art perfected, but I did have nuggets. I showed the girls my treasure, and they seemed a little confused about what they were looking for. Well, I went on shoveling more gravel into my sluice box until it was time to go. I panned out my final concentrates, and there were some more nuggets. I showed the girls my collection, and they were still confused about my excitement. I had picked up a little glass vial at the gold store and put my collection into the vial filled with water. I held the vial up to the sun, and there were the prettiest nuggets that I had ever seen! Still the girls were not impressed. They kept asking, "Where is the gold?" I said, "Look real closely and you can see it glitter in the sun." I took my gold home and proudly displayed it. My wife said she could not see it; but I knew it was there, even though not large enough for her to see.

I would go back on another weekend, but I went alone this time. I parked my Blazer and walked down the steep path on the other side of the river from where I had begun my gold rush. There I saw an elderly black man was camping overnight under the bridge. I spoke to the man and asked if he were there to pan for gold. The black man said that he has been coming to the river for many, many years and loved to pan for gold. I introduced myself and told him that I was stationed at the nearby airbase. He told me his name, but said, "They call me Gold Digger." He told me that he lived in Sacramento, and a friend would drive him to the river to stay for a few days at a time and then return for him. I told him that I thought that I found some nuggets the week before, and he just grinned when I showed him my treasure. I shared my sandwiches and drinks with him, and he offered to show me how to pan for gold. He showed me where the likely spots in the river were that gold would collect. He then began panning a shovel full of gravel. I paid close attention to how he was panning the gravel. There was definitely a proper way to pan with out losing all of your gold. I practiced for a while, and he would assist me now and then. I began picking up more of those nuggets like I had found before, and my panning was becoming more efficient. Finally, I found a piece that was sure to impress my wife. I mean this nugget was the size of a half of a pinhead. I was surely going to get rich. That day ended, and I said good-by to the old prospector, Gold Digger. On future visits to the river, I never saw Gold Digger again; but I never forgot meeting another good person like him in my life.

Getting away to the river always seemed to clear my head before my next weeks' challenges. When Amy was home from college, she liked going to the river and hanging out with me while I searched for my gold. The scenery was pretty to enjoy, and the water holes were refreshing to cool off in. The more time I spent at the river, the more people I would meet while in their quest for that elusive yellow nugget. I would meet my now long time friend, Jim Eakin, after I shoveled gravel all day in the river.

Big Jim Eakin
"Little Paul Bunyan"

Jim had come from the mountains and had been hunting for gold nuggets with a metal detector. He asked me why didn't I try a metal detector and gave me his friend, "Little Jim" Williams's phone number. Little Jim sold detectors. I bought a couple of different metal detectors used for different purposes. One was for hunting relics and the other used for hunting nuggets. Little Jim showed me how to use the machines, but it would be some time before I was half good at finding anything. Before long I had met up with my friend Big Jim, and we were looking for nuggets from time to time. I would go all day sometimes and find only a small piece of gold, but I was beginning to learn more about my machine. One day I was searching over a well-worked area, and I heard a faint signal. I dug a small hole and tried again. The signal became louder! That sometimes meant that there was a gold nugget in the hole; but with my luck, it would probably be only a rusty nail. I dug a little further, and the sound really got loud. I swung one more time with my miner's pick and pulled the dirt back. I looked in the hole, and there stuck in the red dirt was a pretty shinny piece of yellow gold. What a thrill to see a piece that I could pick up in my hand. I tossed it to Big Jim and asked him, "Is this what we were looking for?"

Big Jim said, "That is what we were looking for." Soon Little Jim arrived where we were hunting, and I showed Little Jim the nugget. Little Jim fell to his knees and shouted, "By golly that's a real nugget!" Little Jim ran to his vehicle and brought back a weigh scale. He put the nugget on the scale, and the nugget weighed in at nearly one half pound. I was tickled, and Little Jim had me follow him to show his friends at the local watering hole. I only had in mind to hurry home and show my wife, as she hadn't seen much progress in my gold hunting efforts. She said that she began to wonder if I might have a lady friend in "them thar hills." As time went on, I would meet many of Big and Little Jim's hunting buddies.

Ted, Mike, Little Jim, Big Jim

Big Jim and I seemed to have the same abilities of climbing the steep mountains in search of the elusive shinny nugget except that with his younger years, he could carry a backpack weighing one hundred pounds or more. We seemed to be on the same energy level and have the same desire in dedication of hunting.

I took a week off and invited my friends Little Jim and Fred Asmos on a fishing venture to Kodiak, Alaska. Our planes regularly flew missions to Kodiak in support of our Coast Guard Air Station there. Our flight crews' responsibilities were tremendous, especially during the open fishing and crabbing season. Our crews would share their Bearing Sea patrols and assist them in logistics and search and rescue flights. I enjoyed every moment helping our station in Kodiak. Only this time Jim, Fred, and I would be flying in a space available category. We were riding along to go fishing. Jim and Fred were retired Air Force sergeants and had authorization to fly with us. They both served in Viet Nam while in the Air Force, and I was proud to be in the company of a couple of more veterans that had served their country. When we arrived in Alaska, we were lucky to find space in the transit quarters not being used by incoming families. I met up with my friend and former student from Elizabeth City, Floyd Brickhouse and his wife Pam. Floyd offered us the use of his van and offered to take us out in one of the recreational boats. We caught fish and toured the island. We stayed busy every minute we were there. We brought back halibut and salmon that would last for quite a few meals.

Little Jim, Fred and Fred touring.

Fred, Floyd Jr., Little Jim catching halibut.

My wife Wanda had never flown on a Coast Guard aircraft before, and I decided to take her on one of our missions to Kodiak, Alaska. I signed out on leave, and we boarded our C-130 bound for Alaska. She was invited to the cockpit for a tour and a look at how it was when I spent many hundreds of hours flying.

Wanda in flight engineer's seat with Lt. Rick Savage piloting and Greg Buxa co-piloting.

She experienced how the men and women in our military were transported and saw the difference between the comforts of an airline. Floyd and Pam made our visit memorable as we visited one end of the island's accessible roads to the other. I took Wanda fishing for silver salmon. We immediately began hooking up with the large fish. I helped Wanda as we were standing on the riverbank next to the water. She hooked into a large fish that almost yanked her into the river. I set the drag on her reel so that the line would slip a little more. She fought that fish for quite a while and finally pulled it close enough to shore for me to drag it in. She had fished before back in the mainland but had just gotten her first experience at fishing in Alaska. What a surprise for her to catch that large fish! She had to rest a minute before throwing her bait back into the water.

Wanda with large silver salmon on hook.

Fred with friend Stew Austin, going for the big ones!

Our four C-130 aircraft were kept busy as we covered the entire west coast. We often flew into Mexico to recover a US citizen needing emergency medical attention or a boat off shore needing help. We spent much time flying out of Kodiak, Alaska. Our flight crew happened to be on patrol and found a Chinese fishing boat illegally driftnet fishing 900 miles south of Attu Island, Alaska. The Coast Guard cutter Sherman responded and found three miles of driftnet on the ship's deck. The Sherman had previously sent home another Chinese ship that one of our aircraft had found illegally fishing a few days before. Now our job would be to conduct surveillance on the two ships until they reached their territorial waters. We would fly all day and into the night, land at the nearest refueling base, and begin our chase all over the next day. We took a great deal of pressure off of our brothers in Kodiak, as they were responsible for monitoring the Bearing Sea fishing operations and providing safety to the fishing fleet and crews. We provided as much help as our aircraft availability would allow.

No matter how late we would fly, we would always try to get to a river before we turned in at night and catch a salmon. There is always plenty of light to see to fish in Alaska in the summer months, but "Beware." The bears seem to know this.

When we returned to our base in Sacramento, California, we usually brought back halibut, salmon and king crab. Getting back to the other half of our job, our desk job was always busy but not nearly as exciting as flying and having time to catch a fish.

My last flight as a flight engineer in the US Coast Guard would be a somber one. One of our helicopter crews from Air Station Humboldt, California, had perished in a rescue attempt on the Pacific Ocean coastline. None of our Coasties survived. After the recovery of the helicopter, we loaded it into the C-130 and flew it back to the Coast Guard Aircraft Repair Facility in Elizabeth City. Nothing on the helicopter was salvageable, but Coast Guard aviation engineering always made every attempt to search for any beneficial evidence that might increase our flight crews' chances of survival.

I couldn't wait for the chance to go back to the Sierra Mountains and search for gold nuggets. One Saturday I had been panning for gold in the hills above Nevada City. On my way out of the hills, I decided to stop by the gold supply store in Nevada City. I walked in and started looking at what items they had for sale. A gentleman, looking at my Coast Guard vehicle identification decal on my truck asked me if I was in the Coast Guard. I told him that I was, and he asked me if I had been stationed in Elizabeth City, North Carolina. I said, "Yes," and then he asked if I had ever heard of Earl Bundy. I said, "Yes," and then told him that I knew Earl and that Earl was my friend. He told me that Earl was his dad. I told him that I knew his mother and his Aunt Elizabeth who is married to James Gaskins. I told him that my wife's dad and James Gaskins are first cousins. He was totally surprised to meet someone from North Carolina that knew his family. He said, "Horace is my name, but everyone out hear calls me Hoss."

Hoss has a gold supplies store called Action Mining Supplies on Hwy 20 in Smartville, California. Hoss enjoys living on his little ranch with his wife Janie. Hoss ended up in California after serving his country during the Viet Nam War. Hoss is a proud patriot, and I liked being around that kind of person. He would tell me about his experiences during the war. He told me that he was nearly shot from a light pole by a communist sniper one day. He usually climbed the light pole to replace the security light bulb. As he was reaching for the light bulb, a bullet hit the bulb; and the bulb burst. He said that he quickly came down from that pole and waited until the darkness of night to replace the bulb.

Horace "Hoss" Bundy
"Where is Viet Nam?"

Outpost where "Hoss" stood his duty. Another mortar round had just hit roof of building. Security light pole near center right.

I enjoyed meeting Hoss that day, and we still keep in touch. Each year when I go prospecting in California, I spend some time hunting or dredging with Hoss.

Hoss dredging on his gold claim.

Even after my retirement and returning to North Carolina, I would come back to California and hunt with my friends.

Little Jim and some of his friends have crossed the bar, but I keep in touch with Jim's family on visits every summer.

Each summer Big Jim and his friend Wes invite me to climb the hills while hunting for that hard-to-find nugget. We see lots of wildlife in our journey. We see bobcats, cougars, bears and their cubs, eagles, fish and on occasions, rattle snakes.

When it came close to the time for me to retire, I had to make a decision to time my retirement with the timing of my house back in North Carolina becoming vacant. The renters of our house had received their orders to be assigned to another base. I decided to retire, so I put in my request. At the time, I was so disappointed with the actions of President Bill Clinton that I made note on my retirement request that President Clinton not sign my retirement orders--not knowing at the time that the only "Thank you for your honorable service" from the President came from a stack of mimeographed certificates in a yeoman's (secretary) drawer file.

I would retire after serving nearly four years in the Army Reserve and thirty years and one month in the Coast Guard.

I knew that I would miss my Coast Guard, but I didn't realize just how much I would miss the mission and being with the many great people with whom I had shared many close calls, friendships, partnerships, hardships and loyalties. I would miss flying night and day, watching the C-130's instruments telling me how the planes powerful engines were performing. I would miss the long hours looking out the cockpit window for a troubled mariner or a criminal carrying out his deeds in the ocean waters, both near our shores and abroad.

I would miss working with the Air Force's First Sergeants' Group and the Air Force's Chiefs' Group. What a great group of professional military men and women. All of their social events and meeting their spouses and the base commanders were impressive.

Ruth Plyer Thomas and husband Chief Master Sergeant Ed

Ruth grew up at the same orphanage as I, and I was fortunate to get to see her and Ed while stationed on their base. I attended the Air Force chiefs' meetings with Ed and social events with Ed and Ruth.

Wanda with General Phillips at Air Force military social.

General Phillips was the last base commander at McClellan AFB while we were stationed Coast Guard Air Station Sacramento. He even took the time to attend my retirement.

My Friends from the Air Force Chiefs' and First Sergeants' Groups reciting the "Airman's Last Parade." What an appreciative farewell!

Fred and Wanda being saluted upon retirement, US Coast Guard Air Station, McClellan Air Force Base, Sacramento, California.

Wanda with cousins Joe Sawyer and Delores "Sis" Tillett Whitley.

Wanda's cousins came to my retirement. Joe came from Reno, Nevada; and "Sis" traveled from Franklin, Virginia.

As my time serving my country in the military was coming to an end, I would have in mind of how I could continue. I had the feeling that I could still make a difference in caring for my country, but I just didn't know what that might be.

We had a great drive across country even though I would miss all of my friends that I had made while serving in California.

After returning home, it was great to be near the children and grandchildren. We decided to build our retirement home on the water. We finally found a place on the Perquimans River in Perquimans County overlooking the town of Hertford just across the river. The land was on high ground, and cypress trees laced with Spanish moss dotted the waterfront. The sunsets glittered across the water every evening, and the waterfowl entertain us with their constant frolicking in the water.

We built a house with open views of the river. The openness would always allow a light and airy feeling and a view of the Carolina moon glimmering across the water.

We would continue to be volunteers and serve where we could. Wanda would continue to volunteer with school projects. She would also get to see her grandchildren at the schools she picked. She would make crafts for each child in the classes that she read to. She would make the crafts to pertain to the different holidays. The children loved it, and she is still continuing her work today.

Wanda and Fred
Still Serving

Our Coast Guard troops continue with the pride and devotion to duty. As news reports are issued through our local newspaper and television, continuously we hear and see the great job our troops are doing. I get a feeling of wanting to be present at the scene of each rescue when lives continue to be saved by our young Coasties. To hear of the newer flying machines and their capabilities and the heroic efforts of the crew makes me awfully proud to have been a part of this great mission. As I hear of the pride still evident by all reports, I remember the adrenaline rushes that I experienced. Now when I see a military person in uniform, I want to express my gratitude for their contribution to our nation and to helping the many in need of our assistance around the world.

I had the privilege to see the news report on the rescue of a cruise ship that was sinking, and I thought right then that the younger Coast Guard really had control of the "watch."

Many rescues happen daily throughout the Coast Guard. One days' rescue involved a C-130 and three of our helicopters saving 34 lives from a sinking ship in a storm-tossed sea 200 miles off the Virginia Capes. The C-130 #1504 Piloted by Cdr. Holman and Lt. Storch launched to cover the rescue of the 600' cruise ship *Ocean Breeze I.* The C-130's flight engineer was AMT2 Welch with Navigator/Radioman Fuller and Acuna. Searching and loadmaster/dropmaster duties were performed by Benson and Vickrey. The C-130 crew located the troubled cruise ship and provided direction, weather advisories, and safety coverage for the helicopters while they were attempting their rescue. The rescue crews would have to penetrate two weather fronts before arriving to the rescue sight. Once on scene for the rescue, the rescue crew was in marginal weather conditions while attempting to perform an amazing rescue. One HH60 helicopter #6031, piloted by Lt. Dan Molthen and copiloted by Ltjg. Craig Neubecker rescued 26 survivors on one attempt. Rescue Swimmer Darren Reeves was lowered to the ship's deck by Flight Mechanic AMT2 Loren Green. They hoisted as many survivors as possible onboard the helicopter. The winds on scene were 50 knots and gusting up to 70 knots. The seas were 25 feet with swells to 35 feet. Lt. Molthen gave the order to continue to pick up survivors as he thought his helicopter was the only aircraft available to save this desperate crew of the cruise ship as the ship was going under at a rapid pace. As the pilots made every attempt to keep their helicopter in the air during terrible weather and being greatly overloaded, the crew was able to get 26 survivors and two aircrew back onboard (28 an historical record) as they received a message that another Coast Guard helicopter was quickly approaching to try and recover the remaining crew from a certain death. The second rescue flight crew arrived, and they were able to save eight more of the ship's crew. The HH60 Seahawk Helicopter #6001 was piloted by Lcdr. Randy Watson and

Ens. Steve Bonn. Air Rescue Flight Mechanic AVT2 Sam Pulliam and Air Rescue Swimmer Bob Florisi facilitated the hoisting of the survivors. After the remaining eight were hoisted into the helicopter, the ship slipped under the water. As the helicopter grossly overloaded with survivors hastily returned towards the coast, another HH60 helicopter #6026 was launched to provide safety escort coverage for the helicopter #6001 until it safely made it back to shore. All of the ship's crew was saved, and both rescue teams arrived safely at home base. No better feeling of goodness could be experienced after accomplishing such a dangerous task and everyone is safely home.

Coast Guard rescue swimmer was the last one hoisted from the ship's deck after rescue as cruise ship *Ocean Breeze I* slipped under the ocean's surface.

Lieutenant Dan Molthen, Rescue Swimmer Darren Reeves and Flight Mechanic Loren Green

Along with very successful rescues as demonstrated here, our men and women still face the odds of other missions not being so successful or forgiving. Although, the saving of many lives everyday is our business, we face the tragic consequences of losing some of our crews in training and attempts to perform such rescues. If you have been in the business of rescue long enough, the list of these brave crewmen becomes lengthy in our memories. Even though my memory of the hundreds of men and women that I served with begins to fade, those memories of some fellow Coast Guard crews that perished seem to linger. God bless them for their great sacrifice to America and humanity.

I know for sure that the Coast Guard I grew too old to serve is in capable hands as demonstrated by the brave men and women I hear about daily. I hope my name is still cast about the flight lines and in the cockpits as the rescue crews try to be at their best. I hope the flight crews can have piece of mind that in the middle of the night above a storm tossed sea they can say, "Our crews have protected me by providing me with the safest aircraft possible."

I would continue to volunteer in community activities and my Coast Guard chiefs' organization with fund-raisers to help those in our community.

Our country was attacked by a group of radical Muslims, trained and commanded by Osama Bin Laden. President Bush made a promise that our country would make every effort to rid this earth of the likes of such evil and to build up our security as to not allow this to happen again. Our troops were off to war in Afghanistan and Iraq. Guantanamo Naval Base in Cuba was selected to build a confinement area for the enemies involved in terrorism against our nation.

My wife's cousin Jill had been called up from her Coast Guard Reserve Port Security Unit #305 to provide assistance in the New York City disaster when the twin towers were attacked. She had served in the Gulf War. She served in Spain and now had been ordered to Guantanamo Bay, Cuba.

When their unit arrived in Cuba, there was very little transportation for the troops to travel the long distances between where they were living and where they ate their meals and where they performed their duties. My good friend Lee Gutman and I wanted to help after hearing of the Coasties being called up again and experiencing the hardships of minimal transportation. I attended a city council meeting in Elizabeth City and requested that I be allowed to have all of the police impound bicycles that were just wasting away. The City Council allowed me to have the bikes after they found my intentions were to repair them and send them to our troops.

I received support for some local businesses to help in our efforts with parts for the bikes in much need of repair. Elizabeth City's Cycle World's owner, Mark Turner, donated many spare parts for the bikes. The Chiefs' Association donated the helmets and Margaret at Wal-Mart allowed us a discount so that we could stretch our chiefs' dollars a bit further.

Lee and I worked on the bikes for several months. As we finished our first batch, I contacted my friends at the local Coast Guard Air Station in Elizabeth City to coordinate the shipment to Cuba on one of their scheduled patrols. After that shipment was cleared from my garage, we began a maximum effort to ready more bikes for the troops. When we finished repairing what was fixable we ended up with forty-two bikes. Well, we thought the troops could use more bikes than we had repaired, so Lee volunteered to buy ten more brand new bikes for the Coast Guard troops.

Lee delivering new bikes to Coast Guard Air Station Elizabeth City destined for Security Forces in Guantanamo Bay, Cuba.

Lee had served in the US Army; and as a proud veteran, he had the Coast Guard troops' best interest in mind. He would do anything he could to assist our troops. Lee's wife Marion had been a Coast Guard dependant while growing up so she was very excited with what efforts her husband Lee was doing. Marian's dad, Lee's father in law, Andy "Andock" Burnette, was a chief on the Coast Guard lightship *Chesapeake*. During the Ash Wednesday Storm of the early sixties, the ship was on station protecting mariners sailing the entrance of the Chesapeake Bay. The storm was so intense that the ship's anchor chain broke, and the ship was set adrift in the midst of the storm. The ship suffered structural damage by the fierceness of the storm. Another Coast Guard ship was sent to rescue the lightship and tow it back into port in Norfolk, Virginia.

I know that across our homeland there are thousands of Americans volunteering their time and money to support our troops. What a difference it makes in the morale of these courageous young men and women when they see the caring from back home. I wished there were millions more doing the same.

Fred and Lee repairing bikes.

Jill and helpers unloading new transportation.

Jill with one of Coast Guard Air Station
Elizabeth City's flight crews proud to help.

Jill sent us a report that the bikes made a huge morale
influence. I forgot to mention that we specially prepared a
very small child's bike for the old man (Captain). We
found a squeeze horn and a bell to mount to the handle
bar. We thought a little Coast Guard humor was needed
at a time like this.

After Jill's tour of providing security at Gitmo she would serve on our Gulf Coast in New Orleans after Hurricane Katrina completely wiped out the Coast Guard rescue station. She and the rest of the crew operated out of trailers for the year she was there. She is now serving in Connecticut awaiting orders to a high endurance cutter.

The men and women of the United States Coast Guard have affection to duty. Our desire to perform our duty anytime anywhere is exemplified by actors Kevin Costner and Ashton Kutcher in the movie, *The Guardian.*

Personal pride and devotion to country grew deep into our souls from the many years of performing our duty. After retirement, many felt the desire to wear their pride in many ways. Retirees continually volunteer to support their communities through service organizations and personal efforts.

Master Chief James Matthews loved to remember his Coast Guard by completely rebuilding old WWII Jeeps and mastering the identity of the military Jeeps as they were during the war.

James and wife in Christmas parade in Bath, North Carolina.

I wish I could look over the shoulder of every air crewman and give him or her my encouragement and enlightenment with what I experienced during my tours of duty. I hope they never have to experience some of what I faced, when just remaining faithful to our country and doing things correctly will eliminate all the unnecessary risky operations and the strife amongst crewmen.

With what I hear and see, our Coasties are working harder than ever at saving lives and keeping our country safe. May God protect you! Coasties will always be my family.
I wish to thank all of the Coasties that I served with for their patriotism and friendship and for their part in helping keep me alive.

Please, be thoughtful of all American men and women that volunteer to don the uniform and give their lives for the liberties to which we have become so accustomed. Each of us can make a difference in showing our appreciation in some way.

Semper Paratus

(Always Ready)

The End

Manufactured By: RR Donnelley
Breinigsville, PA USA
August, 2010